George Boleyn:
Tudor Poet,
Courtier & Diplomat

George Boleyn: Tudor Poet, Courtier & Diplomat

Copyright © 2014
MadeGlobal Publishing

ISBN-13: 978-84-937464-5-2

M

MadeGlobal Publishing

For more information on
MadeGlobal Publishing, visit our website:
www.madeglobal.com

Dedications

For David, for putting up with me and my George Boleyn obsession. George has definitely been the other man in my life.

Clare Cherry

For Tim, Christian, Verity and Joel, for their ongoing love and support, and their acceptance of the Boleyns in our daily life.

Claire Ridgway

Now cease my lewte! This is the last
Labour that thow and I shall waste,
And endid is that we begunne;
Now is this songe both sunge and past,
My lewte be still, for I have done!

(attributed to George Boleyn, Lord Rochford)

Contents

Introduction

There has never been a detailed biography of George Boleyn, Lord Rochford. The closest we have to a biographical record of his life was written by Edmond Bapst; entitled *Deux Gentilshommes-Poètes de la Cour de Henry VIII* (Two Gentlemen Poets of the Court of Henry VIII), it was written in 1891, but also includes the life of Henry Howard, Earl of Surrey. The absence of a record of George's life is primarily because he is so closely affiliated with his sister Anne. Their stories are so integrated that any study of the Boleyns naturally focuses on Anne, whose name will always be remembered thanks to her status as one of the wives Henry VIII had beheaded.

In 1536, a concerted effort was made to effectively wipe the Boleyns from history. In the case of Anne, this was halted upon the accession to the throne of her daughter Elizabeth I in 1558. The same did not happen to George Boleyn, who to a large extent was lost to history. There are no known portraits of him, and, if there ever were any, they were either destroyed in 1536 following his execution, or were simply lost over time. As we have no idea what he looked like, it may be possible that there is a portrait of him somewhere that has not been identified as such. It may also be possible that there is a portrait of him in a private collection, but as time goes by, this seems more and more unlikely.

Likewise, although he was an official court poet, none of his poetry is known to have survived (although it has been argued of various pieces that they might be attributed to him). Although George Boleyn's poetry was supposed to rival that of Thomas Wyatt the Elder and Thomas Howard, Earl of Surrey, it is they who are lauded for their talent because their poetry can be identified. Similarly, although he was a gifted politician and diplomat, as a result of dying so young, little credit is given to George, who at the time of his death had only been prominent in those spheres for six years.

Due to Henry VIII's love for her and her position as queen, Anne was able to achieve significant influence in politics and religion. Her brother, who was equally evangelical and dedicated to reform of the church, was a huge influence in his sister's life and worked tirelessly in support of not only her cause but also his own religious convictions. He was a looming presence at court and in Anne's life, yet his role has, to a large extent, been overlooked just as his famous sister overshadows him.

There is of course substantially more contemporaneous information regarding Anne Boleyn than is available for her brother. This makes her life story much easier to tell. Source material relating to George Boleyn is not so easy to come by and is nowhere near as voluminous. However, in gathering information for the purpose of this book, a surprising amount of source material relating to him emerged. By piecing together the information from various sources, including foreign, it is possible to assemble a biographical record for a young man who was unjustly executed.

What is more difficult to ascertain is what George Boleyn was like as a man - his personality and character. As with Anne, this is often contradictory, as much of what has come down to us through history derives from the Boleyns' enemies and rivals for power. The general consensus is that like his sister, he was proud and arrogant, but also that he was intelligent, witty and charming. On the one hand, he was a talented poet and interpreter, a highly intelligent and respected courtier and diplomat, and a man who was capable, loyal and earnest in his genuine religious convictions. On the other hand, he enjoyed a range of frivolous pastimes, and had a reputation as a charming womaniser with a mocking, disrespectful sense of humour bordering on the reckless. A possible reason for his multi-faceted personality was that he was a very young man raised early into high offices of responsibility, and his natural exuberance could only be kept in check for so long. Yet ultimately, how he was viewed was correlated with the political and religious attitudes of the beholder. Catholics loathed him while Reformers adored him. From the contents of Henry VIII's Privy Purse expenses, in which George Boleyn figures prominently, we can see that he lived life to the full, whether for good or bad. The difficulty in pin-pointing his personality is that his character appears to have been as complex as his sister's.

This account tries to adhere strictly to the actual evidence available as much as possible. Unfortunately, there are gaps in George's life, particularly with regards to his childhood, adolescence and personal life. For instance, despite age-old debate, there is no contemporaneous documentation relating to the state of his marriage. To try and establish what his day-to-day personal relationship with his wife was like is impossible. Over time, various assumptions have been made in order to fill the gap. Such assumptions are based on the fact that his wife allegedly provided evidence at the trials of the Boleyns, but in reality it is extremely difficult to assess precisely what evidence, if any, Jane Boleyn, Lady Rochford, provided at her husband's trial. The sources are vague and contradictory. The available evidence regarding her involvement is set out in Chapter 22, and although she clearly provided the prosecution with a damning statement, her involvement with respect to the incest charge is inconclusive. Weighing the available evidence, it seems appropriate to give her the benefit of the doubt.

However, the exact truth of the matter, like many other instances in the lives of people so long dead, will probably never be established unless a previously undiscovered treasure trove of source material comes to light.

Lack of knowledge of George Boleyn as a person has led to an interesting, but unfounded, theory as to his sexuality. A 1989 biography of Anne Boleyn suggested that the men who were executed as her alleged lovers and co-conspirators were "libertines", men who "were expected to move in a progression from adultery and fornication to buggery and bestiality".[1] These men included, of course, Anne's brother. This theory is not based on fact, and there is no evidence whatsoever to prove it. The suggestion has, however, been perpetuated in works of fiction, and as there are some people who learn their history solely from works of fiction, the theory is rapidly gaining momentum. Proponents of this viewpoint argue the impossibility of knowing for sure what the sexual preferences of these men were. Of course the same can be said of any dead person, particularly when they have been dead for nearly 500 years. Yet relying on this argument ignores the actual evidence, which suggests the total reverse of these theories. It may be argued that because these people have been dead for so long, why would they care what we write about them and likewise, why should we care? That is not the point. If we take the trouble to write about real people from history, we have a responsibility to write about them as accurately as we can, taking into account the actual evidence available. We cannot look at sixteenth century historical personalities and give to them our twenty-first century morality. Homosexuality in the sixteenth century was not only illegal, it was also considered an offence against God. George Boleyn, a deeply religious young man, would have been horrified and appalled at any suggestion of homosexuality or bisexuality, and to suggest that this does not matter is a sad indictment on us.

George, like every other successful person in the sixteenth century, was no saint. He shared his family's corrosive and ultimately dangerous ambitions, and just like them he was selfish and ruthless when necessary for the furtherance of those ambitions. Anne and George Boleyn's joint commitment to religious reform triggered the deaths of many people. Although there is nothing to say they supported those deaths or delighted in them, likewise they made no stance against them, turning a blind eye just as a blind eye was turned to their own deaths in 1536. Yet none of this means that they were bad people. Much of the hatred directed at them was due not only to their evangelism, but also to their closeness to the throne. This gave them unprecedented power and influence, and in turn created envy and malice in those who aspired to greatness. The siblings, like their father, were people of their time, and whether they were loved or hated largely depended on factors that seem alien to the vast majority of us today.

It is difficult to think of people who lived so long ago as real personalities - hence the cavalier attitude to the way they are often portrayed. But these people *were* real, with the same feelings and emotions that guide our own actions. The Boleyn siblings were capable of genuine affection and loyalty, particularly towards each other. Their very human responses to the situation of their lives were the very things that could be used against them so effectively. They proved themselves to be spirited and courageous in the face of adversity, but while Anne has always been admired for this in the majority of biographies written about her, little recognition has been given to George.

George and Anne Boleyn were, in the words of historian James Carley, "an immensely attractive pair, intellectually and physically, and after their fall the court became a much less glamorous place without them."[2]

Part 1 - Beginnings

1 Family Background

The origins of the Boleyn family have caused debate and controversy for centuries, and there still does not seem to be complete agreement over them. Some historians and authors see the Boleyns as social upstarts or *nouveaux riches*, while others regard them as an ancient French family, even descending from the Norman Counts of Boulogne. The general consensus in ancestry groups concerned with the Boleyn family is that Simon de Boleyne, who held lands in Norfolk around 1252, descended through an illegitimate line from Count Eustace II of Boulogne. Rev. Canon Parsons, Rector of Salle, used primary sources, such as contemporary wills and the Court Rolls of the manors of Salle and Stinton, to build up a family tree for the Boleyn family, and was able to link Queen Anne Boleyn back to Simon de Boleyne.[1]

Whatever the truth about their ancient origins, the family into which Anne and George were born was one of the most respected in the English aristocracy. George and his sisters were the children of Thomas and Elizabeth Boleyn, both of whom were from an aristocratic background.[23] Their paternal great grandfather was Geoffrey Boleyn, the son of a tenant farmer. It was Geoffrey who made the Boleyn family fortune as a mercer. He married into the aristocracy by taking as a wife Anne Hoo, the daughter of Thomas Hoo, 1st Baron Hoo and Hastings. Helped by the respectability his marriage brought, and through his own achievements, Geoffrey worked his way up to become Lord Mayor of London in 1457. Geoffrey and Anne had a number of children, including William, the grandfather of Anne and George Boleyn. When Geoffrey died in around 1462, William received a substantial inheritance, including numerous estates and manors accumulated by his father.

William Boleyn was born around 1451. He married Margaret Butler, second daughter and co-heiress of Thomas Butler, 7th Earl of Ormond, an Anglo-Irish peer owning substantial land in England. The Butlers were a wealthy family in Ireland, and Margaret was descended from men who had been magnates, landowners and justiciars of Ireland. She could trace her roots back to Edward I, and ultimately to Eleanor of Aquitaine and Henry II. Through his marriage to Margaret, William brought further wealth and social standing to the Boleyn dynasty. William and Margaret had a total of ten children, four daughters and six sons. The eldest son was Thomas Boleyn, Anne and George's father.

William Boleyn died on 10 October 1505, leaving the majority of his estate to Thomas. William's estates were substantial; the scale can be seen from the provisions of his will, which states, "I will that my son Thomas Boleyn, according to the will of Geoffrey Boleyn, my father, have the manors of Blickling, Calthorp, Wykmore and Mikelbarton, to him and his male heirs... my manors of Hoo, Offley, Cokenhoo, Fylby, West Lexham, Stiffleby and Betingham in Norfolk, and my manors of Heber [Hever] and Seale in Kent".[4]

Thomas Boleyn was born around 1476/7 and became a very wealthy man upon his father's death. Furthermore, his mother had no brothers, and as the eldest of only two daughters of the Earl of Ormond, was heiress to the Ormond estates. Upon the Earl's death in 1515, Margaret's eldest son Thomas therefore received a further substantial inheritance through his mother. Although the title of Earl of Ormond was not settled on him until 1529, in 1515 Thomas Boleyn inherited various estates from his grandfather, including the Palace of Beaulieu, which had been granted to the Earl of Ormond in 1491. It was also in 1515 that Boleyn inherited the honour of Rochford and acquired the estate of Rochford Hall in Essex.

Through the connections of his extended family, and through his own diligence, hard work, ambition, gift for languages and intelligence, Thomas Boleyn became one of Henry VIII's leading diplomats. In 1512, he was appointed ambassador to the Low Countries, at the court of Margaret of Austria, and acted as ambassador to France between 1519 and 1521. Thomas was closely involved in arrangements for the historic Field of Cloth of Gold meeting between Henry and the French king, Francis I, in 1520. He was sent on many diplomatic missions abroad, including those relating to the King's desire for an annulment of his marriage with Catherine of Aragon, which would enable him to marry Thomas's daughter, Anne Boleyn. Thomas was created Lord Rochford in 1525 and Earl of Wiltshire on 8 December 1529. It was also in 1529 that the title Earl of Ormond was finally settled on him.

Thomas Boleyn's wife Elizabeth was born sometime between 1476 and 1480, and was one of the many daughters of Thomas Howard, Earl of Surrey (and later Duke of Norfolk), and his first wife Elizabeth Tylney. Elizabeth Boleyn's brother was Thomas Howard, 3rd Duke of Norfolk, the man who presided over the trials of his niece and nephew in 1536. The Howards were one of the premier families in England, coming from ancient stock and having a long history of service to the monarch. Elizabeth's father had been attainted and stripped of his titles and lands after the Battle of Bosworth in 1485 because he had fought on Richard III's side, but he managed to work his way back into favour with Henry VII, and by 1497 had been restored as Earl of Surrey. In 1514, he was finally restored to the title of Duke of Norfolk. Traditionally, it is said that Elizabeth joined the royal court as a young girl, serving as lady-in-waiting to Queens Elizabeth of York and Catherine of Aragon, but evidence is lacking. She met and married Thomas Boleyn around 1498-9, and it is likely that the couple met at court. Rumours circulated that for a time Elizabeth Boleyn was the mistress of the young King Henry. The King always denied this, and it is more likely that the rumour began by confusing her with Henry's mistress Elizabeth Blount (who bore him an illegitimate son), or simply through the desire to vilify the Boleyns following their rise to power. Indeed, all of the sources for the alleged affair are hostile.[5]

Like all courtiers, Thomas's purpose in life was to obtain wealth and power, which meant getting as close to the throne as possible. His children were brought up accordingly, and certainly Anne and George shared many of their father's motivations, including his ambition. Thomas Boleyn was very much a man of the age he lived in, a self-serving survivor. Looking at his actions in 1536, this would seem a compassionate assessment of a man prepared to sacrifice his children in order to save himself. Likewise, Elizabeth Boleyn appears to have made no attempt to save her children or even to send a comforting word to them while they were awaiting trial, and later sentence of death. Compassion in the sixteenth century was an unaffordable commodity. No plea for clemency has ever been discovered, and it appears that both mother and father accepted that their children were beyond help, and were able to cut them off, irrespective of what their personal feelings may have been. To survive court life, families had to pick themselves up, dust themselves off and move on. Their priority was to serve the King loyally so that they could rise and benefit once more.

2 Birth and Childhood

In the early years of her marriage, Elizabeth Boleyn gave birth on an annual basis.[1] It is not known how many children the Boleyns had in total, but there is clear evidence for five: Mary, Anne, Thomas, Henry and George. Thomas and Henry, named after their father and the King respectively, died in childhood, and their graves in the parish churches of Penshurst and Hever are marked with simple brass memorial crosses. Only one Boleyn son survived childhood: George.

George and his two sisters were probably born at the family home of Blickling Hall in Norfolk. The property had been in the Boleyn family since its purchase by Geoffrey Boleyn in 1452, and it passed to Thomas Boleyn when he married. Thomas formally inherited the property upon his father's death in 1505. He and Elizabeth lived there from the date of their marriage in around 1498-9 and remained there with their three children until 1505-6, when they moved to Hever Castle in Kent. The Blickling Hall the Boleyns knew no longer exists; the current property, which occupies the grounds of the original, was built during the reign of James I.

There is a long-standing dispute as to the ages of the three surviving Boleyn children and their order of birth. Anne's date of birth is often given as either 1501 or 1507. However, Anne went to the court of Margaret of Austria in Mechelen in the spring of 1513 as a maid of honour, a position usually only open to a girl of 12 or 13 years of age. A letter written by Anne to her father shortly after she left England is clearly in the neat and precise handwriting of a child of at least ten and not that of a child of six or seven.[2] The letter is written in French, and although there are spelling mistakes, this is hardly convincing evidence to suggest she was a small child when it was written, particularly bearing in mind that French was Anne's second language and that she was in the process of learning it. Also, to suggest that Anne was only six years old when she was sent as maid of honour to Mechelen and that she was only seven years old when she was appointed to serve Mary Tudor, Queen of France, stretches credibility to an unbelievable degree. Anne must surely, therefore, have been born around 1501.

The next question is whether Anne's siblings were older or younger. Mary's birth has been given as any time between 1499 and 1508. Mary was alleged to have been the mistress of King Francis I of France, and the relationship is supposed to have taken place from around 1517 to 1519. This would have made her between 9 and 11 years of age if she had been born in 1508, and 12 when she married William Carey in February 1520. Although girls could legally marry at the age of 12, this would still have been unusual even in the sixteenth century. That she actually had a relationship with Francis is inconclusive, but her reputation whilst in France, whether deserved or not, must mean that she was older than 11 when she was sent to France. What is known for certain is that Mary was later the mistress of Henry VIII, although even this is only known because Henry VIII applied to the Pope for a dispensation in 1527 to allow him to marry "one with whom he had already contracted affinity in the first degree through illicit intercourse".[3] It cannot be established precisely when Mary's relationship with Henry started or when it ended, or indeed how long it lasted. All that is known for certain is that the couple slept together sometime between 1519 and 1525. As the affair was never publicised, it may be that it was a brief fling that ended with Mary's marriage in 1520; this seems the most likely conclusion. Whatever the truth of the matter, her background must surely lead to the conclusion that a birth date of 1508 cannot be correct for Mary.

If we accept that Anne's date of birth was around 1501, the question still remains whether she was older or younger than Mary and George. Anne travelled abroad before her sister, which would suggest she was the eldest. Yet Anne was also Mary's intellectual superior; it is perfectly possible that Thomas Boleyn would send his bright, articulate and ambitious youngest daughter abroad before Mary, irrespective of seniority, if she showed more promise. What should clinch the issue is that in 1597 Mary's grandson, George Carey, 2nd Baron Hunsdon, petitioned for the Boleyn earldom of Ormond on the basis that his grandmother was the eldest of the Boleyn sisters. If Anne had been the eldest, the title would have belonged to Queen Elizabeth I, Anne's daughter. In the circumstances, Lord Hunsdon would have needed to be very confident of his facts to have risked presenting such a petition. If we accept Mary as the elder sister, this would put her birth at around 1500.

What about George? Thomas and Elizabeth Boleyn were married in around 1498-9; if we accept that Mary was born around 1500 and Anne around 1501, then unless George bordered on being illegitimate, he must surely be accepted as the youngest of the three. It was traditional for sons to be named after the king or their father, so the fact that his brothers were named Thomas and Henry suggests that they were older than George. George did not receive his first royal grant in his sole name until 1524[4] (the offices granted to him in 1522 were in joint names with his father), suggesting that he had only just attained an age deemed

old enough to enjoy royal grants. A letter written by Jean du
Bellay, Bishop of Paris and one of Francis I's ambassadors, has been
used as evidence that George was rather young to be appointed as
an ambassador by Henry VIII in 1529, but this letter is open to
interpretation. Although du Bellay refers to George as Thomas
Boleyn's "petit prince" (little prince), this comes across more as
du Bellay seeing George as the apple of his father's eye, following
instructions from Thomas to make sure that the ambassadors in
France treated his son well and "often dined with him", rather
than him seeing George as being too young for such an office.[5] A
poem by George Cavendish, Cardinal Wolsey's gentleman usher,
in his *Metrical Visions*,[6] has George saying that he gained a place in
the Privy Chamber at the age of about 27. Although George had
served the King as page for a number of years, he lost his post in
the Eltham Ordinances of January 1526.[7] He was restored to full
adult status in the Privy Chamber, as a Gentleman of the Privy
Chamber, in 1529, and it must be this to which Cavendish was
referring. Cavendish, in order to make his laboured verses more
rhythmic, gives the age of 27 (thrice nine) as a maximum age,
and thus a birthdate of 1502 or 1503; Eric Ives, however, points
out that Cavendish may not be reliable because he was writing 30
years later and "since the dictates of the verse made the next lowest
number 'years thrice eight', he may have been trying to say no
more than 'about twenty-five'".[8] This suggests a birthdate of about
1504. This is even more persuasive when taking into account a
letter written by Thomas Boleyn to Thomas Cromwell following
the deaths of Anne and George. In it, Thomas confirms that upon
his marriage his wife gave him a child every year, and as we know,
at least two children did not survive to adulthood. The evidence
suggest Mary was born in 1499-1500, Anne in 1501, Thomas
and Henry between 1502 and 1504, and George 1504-5, making
George approximately 31 at the date of his death.

   Although the Boleyn children were probably born in Norfolk,
they were primarily brought up at Hever Castle in Kent. Hever
was built in the thirteenth century and was bought by Geoffrey

Boleyn in 1462, shortly before his death. He built a comfortable home within the existing structure of the original walled bailey, meaning the home the Boleyn children were brought up in was more akin to a manor house than a castle. Thomas Boleyn made significant improvements to the property after inheriting it and moved his family from Norfolk to Hever around 1505-6. Depending on whether he was born in 1504 or 1505, it is possible that George was the only Boleyn child to be born at Hever, although it is more likely the family moved there when he was a baby. After Thomas Boleyn's death in 1539, Hever Castle passed to the Crown, and in 1540 Henry VIII bestowed it on Anne of Cleves as part of her divorce settlement. The property is extremely attractive, surrounded by a moat and set in extensive grounds with a large lake about 200 feet from the property. In the heart of the Kent countryside, yet only about 25 miles from London and the court, it was the ideal location for the Boleyn family. It was also an ideal setting for three small children to be raised.

In the depths of the Kent countryside, there would have been few other children of a suitable social standing with whom the Boleyn siblings could socialise. This obviously helped to create an enduring closeness and bond between George and Anne, although seemingly less so with their sister Mary. As their parents were often at court as favoured courtiers of the royal couple, the children would only have had each other to rely on, besides the bevy of servants and tutors paid to take care of them (and especially of the Boleyns' most valuable asset - young George). As a son, particularly as the only surviving son, he would have been the favoured child. That Anne would capture the King's heart and eventually become queen could never have been envisioned. She, like Mary, was a mere girl, and her primary relevance to the family was in marrying well. From 1527 onwards, for the first time in his life, George's significance in the family became secondary to Anne's. It would have been easy for him to feel resentment, but it is a testament to both his character and his affection towards his sister that he exhibited nothing but love and loyalty.

It is well documented that both Anne and Mary spent some of their formative years in France, but little is known of George's childhood or early adulthood. There is no record of him travelling abroad for his education, and it would appear that he remained in England. He did, however, speak fluent French at least as well as his sister Anne, who lived in France for seven or eight years. Thomas Boleyn became ambassador to France in January 1519, and it is possible that George spent some time in France as a child with his father when Thomas was on embassy. This is certainly a theory advanced by Edmond Bapst, George's earliest biographer, who proposes this as an explanation as to how George spoke such perfect French from a young age.[9] The possibility that George spent significant time in France during the late 1510s would also help explain how he and Anne remained so close throughout their lives. As Anne left England in the spring of 1513 and returned at the end of 1521, the siblings may have been separated for over eight and a half years - a very long time for young children. Yet the bond between Anne and George never appears to have broken, making the possibility of them spending time together in France more likely. It could also provide another reason why George was sent to France as ambassador in 1529 at the tender age of about 25. If he had already met the King of France as a youth, this could have been perceived as an advantage. Although this is speculative, and it is just as likely that George simply received an excellent grounding in French while remaining in England (helped by his father, who spoke fluent French and was said to be the best French speaker at Henry VIII's court), it is certainly a possibility.

Anne and George were both quick-witted and blessed with natural charm. Their father recognised the potential not only of his son but also of his youngest daughter from early on in their lives, and, as is clear from her being sent abroad at such a young age, took pains to ensure that Anne as well as George had the best education available. It is possible that prior to her leaving England Anne was educated side by side with her younger brother through personal tutors, but again this is pure speculation.

As we have seen, Anne left England for Mechelen in the spring of 1513 to become a companion to Archduchess Margaret of Austria. It was through Margaret that Anne got her first taste of the new religious ideology, which she, like her brother, came to embrace in adulthood. When Anne left for the Low Countries, George would have only been about 8 or 9 years old. The tradition for the sons of particularly wealthy Tudor families was to have private tutors up to the age of 14, and then to attend university from the age of 14 to approximately 18. What is known from the success of his later career is that George received an excellent education, speaking French, Latin and some Italian. Despite speaking Latin and Italian, he did make an honest confession in a letter of February 1530, "I do not direct my other letters to the bishop of Worcester nor Sir Gregorio, because I can neither write Latin nor Italian well".[10] This was a failing which he rectified in his later career. In addition to languages, he was also accomplished in courtly skills, literature and verse, had a keen interest in theology, and was a talented poet and translator. He is said to have attended Oxford University. Anthony Wood, editor of *Athenae Oxonienses*, listed George as a former Oxford student and described him as a man who "was educated in all kinds of polite learning among the Oxonians".[11] The lack of any record to confirm his attendance at Oxford, however, makes it impossible to say for definite whether he was actually educated there. Whatever the case, like his sister Anne, he developed an interest in religious and political theory, no doubt influenced by his father. As Dr David Starkey points out, he had "many of Anne's talents and all of her pride".[12] From the way his court career took off in late 1529, one could go further and say he had all of Anne's talents. She merely had more scope for exhibiting hers due to her relationship with the King and her influence. Many of the positions of responsibility awarded to George may have been acquired through his sister's influence, but they were maintained due to his own talent and intelligence. In addition to this, he had a more amicable disposition than his tempestuous sister. Though they were equally single-minded and determined, Anne had an acknowledged fiery temper, compared to her brother's more amiable approach. In 1534, when Anne threatened to put the Princess Mary to death if the King ever left her as Regent, her brother sensibly, if somewhat nervously, advised her that this would insult the King.[13] Throughout her tempestuous life, her brother was the one consistent, trustworthy person. He was also the voice of reason in Anne's more flamboyant moments. The affection that bound them meant she was far more likely to listen to, and take advice from, her brother than any other person.

George's sister Mary was around the age of 14 when she was sent abroad in 1514. Her father secured her a place as maid of honour to Henry VIII's sister, Mary Tudor, who was moving to Paris to marry King Louis XII of France. Anne left Mechelen and joined her sister in France in the winter of 1514 to continue her education in the French court. Anne was only in France a matter of months before Louis died in January 1515. Mary Tudor left France shortly after her husband's death having already married Charles Brandon, Duke of Suffolk. Brandon was a close companion to Henry VIII and a trusted courtier. However, his marriage to the King's sister took place without the couple obtaining the prior permission of her brother. This caused a major rift between brother and sister and nearly cost Brandon his head. Despite Mary Tudor returning to England with her disapproved-of new husband, Anne remained in the court of the new king and queen, Francis I and Claude of France. It is not known what happened to Mary Boleyn at this point but traditionally she is thought to have stayed on in France, becoming Francis I's mistress. The French king cruelly called Mary his "English Mare", and later in his life described her as "a great whore, the most infamous of them all".[14] After her relationship with Francis ended, Mary is alleged to have embarked on a number of affairs with a variety of different men, and her promiscuous behaviour led to her eventual expulsion from France in 1519. There is little hard evidence to support the allegations of her promiscuity, save for the King of

France's comments, which could have been made out of malice, particularly as they were made following the fall of Anne and George in 1536. As Mary was married in February 1520 it may well have been that she returned to England purely in readiness for her forthcoming marriage.

The Boleyns were a highly ambitious family, and there could be little merit in having a daughter considered to be a whore by the majority of Europe (if the rumours relating to Mary were true). Her promiscuity would only have caused shame and embarrassment to a family keen on creating excellent marriage matches for their children. Mary's exploits would have meant she was "spoiled goods", which in turn meant her hopes for an advantageous marriage were damaged. Yet despite Mary's apparent disgrace, upon her return to England her father secured a marriage between his eldest daughter and an ambitious, up-and-coming young courtier - a marriage that was also attended by the King. It therefore has to be questioned whether Mary did in fact behave as she is alleged to have done whilst in France.

Mary married William Carey on 4 February 1520. It has been suggested that by Boleyn standards the marriage was not particularly advantageous, but William Carey was a respected and popular nobleman at court, and was a Gentleman of the Privy Chamber. It is not known whether Mary became Henry VIII's mistress before her marriage or during it. In all likelihood the affair began in 1519 when the King's previous mistress Elizabeth Blount gave birth to his illegitimate son, Henry Fitzroy, and may well have ended upon Mary's marriage. Mary gave birth to a daughter, Catherine, in around 1524 and a son, Henry, in March 1526. Although the royal affair may well have been over long before these children were conceived, it was rumoured that one, if not both, had been fathered by the King. Neither child was acknowledged by Henry VIII. As she was a girl, even if Catherine Carey had been his daughter, Henry might have chosen to ignore her. After all, he already had one useless *legitimate* daughter, so why boast about an illegitimate one? However, if Henry Carey had been his son it would have been surprising for the King not to have recognised him as such. He readily acknowledged Henry Fitzroy as his illegitimate son, and had enormous pride and affection for the boy, making him Duke of Richmond and Somerset at the age of 6. By 1526, Fitzroy was Henry's only living son; it is far more likely the King would have proclaimed his acknowledgement of Henry Carey to the rafters, as confirmation he could father sons, validating his argument that Catherine's failure to produce a son was proof that the marriage was cursed. To suggest that Henry did not acknowledge Henry Carey because he was in a relationship with the boy's aunt, Anne Boleyn, is disingenuous. By March 1526, Henry's intentions with regards to Anne were as a potential mistress, not as a potential wife.

George would have been somewhere between 15 and 21 years of age when Mary was Henry's mistress. Although he had been appointed one of Henry VIII's pages in around 1516,[15] [16] it would still be many years before he would play a prominent role at court. In 1520 he was still continuing with his education, and despite being Henry's page, both he and his father would have wanted him to continue receiving the best education available. For George Boleyn to have achieved the prominence at court that he did, and to have maintained that prominence for as long as he did, required not only a first-class education but also a grounding in courtly skills. Hence George's own introduction to the English court at a very young age. When George finally came to court permanently, it was his intelligence and scholarly conversation as much as his humour and gaiety which fascinated Henry and kept the King entertained, in much the same way that Anne was able to fascinate the King with her own blend of Boleyn charm. It was also his courtly skills that earned George the less commendable reputation as a womaniser.

While George was making his own way at court in England, Anne became a favoured and respected lady-in-waiting to Queen Claude of France, and also received an excellent education. She remained in France until the end of 1521, by which time she spoke fluent French and had acquired an interest in French culture, fashion and etiquette. She also developed a fascination with religious philosophy, with which she had come into contact through her father and, during her time in Mechelen, through the influence of Archduchess Margaret. It was a fascination that she was later to share with her brother, and which would ultimately change the religious persuasions of a nation.

The whole basis of the Boleyn children's upbringing was focused towards each of them entering into royal service. Thomas Boleyn was determined that his children follow in his footsteps. Just as he had introduced his daughters to the dazzling French court, so Thomas set about introducing George to the English court at an early age. The first record of George Boleyn attending the royal court of Henry VIII is as a child during the Christmas festivities of 1514-15.[17] The season included a fancy dress dance and an indoor "mêlée", which he attended with his father. There was a mummery (a traditional English folk play) which featured George and his father, together with a number of other courtiers and their children, including Charles Brandon, Nicholas Carew and Elizabeth Blount. It is chilling to see the names of Brandon and Carew. They met the little Boleyn boy when he was just 9 or 10 years old and in another 21 years' time, Brandon would be one of the members of the jury that would find George and his sister guilty of treason, while Carew would help coach Jane Seymour on how to win the King's heart.

That Christmas was probably the first time a Boleyn child was introduced to the King of England. Though George was very young, Thomas clearly felt he had the intelligence and maturity to be brought to Henry's attention. That Thomas took the trouble to take his young son to the festivities demonstrates his pride in the boy, and perhaps his affection for him. Clearly Thomas's confidence was well founded. Even at such an early age, George obviously made a good initial impression on Henry because, as we have seen, it was shortly after this that George became one of the King's pages. Bapst suggests that an introduction to the scandalous court of Henry VIII at such a young age had a corrupting effect on young George, hence his later reputation as a prolific womaniser.[18] It would certainly have been difficult for any young person to be brought up in the brutal world of Henry VIII's court and emerge completely unscathed.

It could be considered surprising that Anne and Mary were sent abroad to be educated whilst a boy, the only son, remained at home. However, George Boleyn's designated future was to follow in his father's footsteps, to be a servant to the King of England and enter the world of politics and diplomacy. He did not necessarily need the same level of sophisticated courtly skills that his sisters required in order for them to ensure a good marriage, and which Thomas Boleyn obviously felt were best learned at the European courts. George's education was directed towards becoming an accomplished courtier, politician and diplomat, and those skills were best learned in the cauldron of Henry's court. That George Boleyn did acquire sophisticated courtly skills in addition to his other attributes, to the degree that they were commented on in poetry, and that Anne did acquire skills as an accomplished politician in addition to her courtly skills, is a testament to their extraordinary capabilities as people.

It is not known for certain whether George and Anne Boleyn had any direct contact with each other after she went abroad, but it is probable that George attended the Field of Cloth of Gold meeting between the French and English Kings in June 1520 with his parents and sisters. Anne and her father were already in France and were joined by Lady Boleyn and Mary.[19] Although George is not mentioned, it is unlikely that he would have been left behind on such a momentous occasion. George would have been about 15 or 16 at the time and he was probably among his father's allocation of 11 attendants or one of the 3 gentlemen allowed for his mother.[20] It is possible that this was the first time he had met his sister Anne since she had left for the Continent in the spring of 1513.

They would next meet when Anne returned to England in

late 1521. Shortly afterwards, Anne became lady-in-waiting to the queen and George would quickly become a prominent member of Henry's inner circle of favoured courtiers.

3 Court Poet

From early on in his court career, George Boleyn was recognised as a talented court poet, musician and translator. During his lifetime, he received praise and respect for his accomplishments, and was considered by his contemporaries to be as talented as the renowned poets of the age, Thomas Wyatt the Elder and Henry Howard, Earl of Surrey. Unfortunately, we only know of George's talent for poetry from contemporary writings and comments. The court chronicler Raphael Holinshed confirms of him, "He wrote divers songs and sonnets",[1] and Anthony Wood wrote of how it was during his time at Oxford University that "his natural inclinations to poetry were discovered and admired by his contemporaries".[2] George Cavendish, gentleman usher of Cardinal Wolsey, praised his skills in verse:

> Dame eloquence also taught me the art,
> In meter and verse to make pleasant ditties.[3]

Sixteenth century dramatist and historian John Bale wrote of his "*rhythmos elegantissimos*"[4]. Whilst imprisoned in the Tower of London, Anne Boleyn wanted to know whether the other prisoners had anyone to make their beds for them. When told that they had to make their own, she suggested that they make their pallets (beds) as they make ballets (ballads), but said only her Lord Rochford had the skill to do so. She had to be reminded that Thomas Wyatt was equally skilled at verse.[5]

Although George Boleyn devoted less energy to poetry and more to his diplomatic role as he got older, a passage of verse, written by Richard Smith in 1575 and prefixed to a selection of poems written by George Gascoigne, confirms George's verse skills by including him amongst such worthies as Chaucer, Surrey and Wyatt:

> Chaucer by writing purchast fame,
> And Gower got a worthy name:
> Sweet Surrey suckt Parnassus springs,
> And Wiat wrote of wondrous things:
> Olde Rochford clambe the statelie throne
> Which Muses hold in Helicone
> Then thither let good Gascoigne go,
> For sure his verse deserveth so.[6]

The reason we can only determine George Boleyn's talent from the writings of his contemporaries is because, within a few years of his death, his poetry was lost, and none can now be definitively assigned to him. It is possible that some of his work has survived. *Tottel's Miscellany* (1557-1587) is an anthology of selected popular poetry of the sixteenth century. Contained in it are a number of poems by "uncertain authors". It is probable that these poems are a mixture of those by Francis Bryan, George Boleyn and Lord Vaux, all of who were talented lyricists. It is possible that some of George's poems have survived by being included in the category of uncertain authors, although it is impossible to say which poem belongs to whom. All of the works are of similar form, and of a style popular in the sixteenth century. *Tottel's Miscellany* also contains the poems of Thomas Wyatt and Henry Howard, Earl of

Surrey, renowned poets of the age. Surrey was the son of George Boleyn's uncle, Thomas Howard, 3rd Duke of Norfolk, and was therefore George's cousin. Henry VIII executed Surrey in January 1547 at the age of 30, just days before the King's own death. Thomas Wyatt was caught up in the tragedy of 1536 and was lucky to escape with his life.

One particular poem in the *Miscellany*, "The Lover Complaineth the Unkindness of his Love",[7] has been subsequently assigned to George Boleyn. "Extolled for its simplicity, harmony, and elegance" by Horace Walpole, 3rd Earl of Orford,[8] this poem appears, attributed to George, in the manuscripts of Sir John Harington, an author of literature in the sixteenth century.[9] Bale's *Scriptorum Illustrium* makes use of Harington's manuscripts when assigning the piece to George, and likewise Walpole used Harington when writing his *Catalogue of Royal and Noble Authors of England, Scotland and Ireland*, published in 1806. A letter of Walpole states:

> I have had a piece of luck within these two days. I have long lamented our having no certain piece by Anne Boleyn's brother, Lord Rochford. I have found a very pretty copy of verse by him in the new published volume of the Nugae Antiquae, though by mistake he is called Earl of, instead of Viscount, Rochford. They are taken from a MS. dated twenty-eight years after the author's death, and are much in the manor of Lord Surrey's and Sir T. Wyatt's poems... A little modernized and softened in cadence, they would be very pretty.[10]

Tottel's Miscellany assigns the poem to Thomas Wyatt. Harington, however, was scrupulous in correctly attributing other compositions to the correct authors; it is therefore entirely possible that the poem, "The Lover Complaineth...", is that of George Boleyn. Another poem, known as "O death rock me asleep", has at times been attributed to George and at others to Anne Boleyn.

Some have suggested that they worked on the poem together while imprisoned in the Tower of London; this is unlikely, though, as the siblings were not allowed to see each other after their arrests. Both poems can be found in Appendix A. Edmond Bapst believes that *A Myrour for Magistrates* (published in 1559) is another anthology which "must contain some of Lord Rochford's poetry", but misattributed.[11]

The poems contained in *Tottel's Miscellany* display the calibre of the poetry written in the court of Henry VIII. Edmond Bapst in *Deux gentilshommes-poetes de la cour de Henry VIII* attempts to show that the gentlemen poets of Henry's court effectively kick-started the English Renaissance with the elegance, brilliance and beauty of their poetry. He suggests that such high quality of verse is remarkable bearing in mind the baseness of the court and the dominant tyranny of Henry VIII. Bapst promotes George Boleyn, in addition to the Earl of Surrey, to being the harbingers of the English Renaissance, the cultural and artistic movement which dated from the early sixteenth century through to the seventeenth century.[12] Whether George Boleyn deserves such high acclaim is debatable. As his poems cannot accurately be identified, and are now unlikely ever to be, it is sadly impossible to assess the accuracy of this theory.

George Boleyn, Thomas Wyatt and Henry Howard were acknowledged to be the three most talented poets of Henry VIII's court. The poetry of Wyatt and Howard survived, while George's did not. Thomas Wyatt died a natural death in 1543, and although Howard was executed in January 1547, the King died a matter of days later. The answer to George's "lost" poetry seems obvious. Either his poetry was deliberately destroyed after his death and never spoken of again, or other poets took the credit for it. If a young man had been executed on charges of incest and treason, would the King realistically have wanted that young man's poetry to continue to be proclaimed around court, particularly when the young man in question seems to have been a far more talented lyricist than the King himself?

What can be said with certainty is that by the late 1520s the court was a completely different place to that which George Boleyn had first came into contact in 1514. Anne Boleyn had brought French fashion and French sophistication back with her to England. Her brother, together with the likes of Francis Bryan and Thomas Wyatt, gave the court a gaiety and frivolity that had not been evident in the early years of Henry's reign, and especially so following their own trips to France as ambassadors. Everywhere, throughout the late 1520s and early 1530s, the old was replaced with the new. The courtiers who had been around in the days of Henry's father, Henry VII, were pushed into the background as a new batch of dynamic, witty, talented young men dominated the court. Their poetry was admired throughout London, and their songs and sonnets were heard everywhere. They were the beloved courtiers of the King, and were adored wherever they went. It was a new, fashionable, light-hearted court, and the young men of their generation shone as never before. As we know, many of these young men would have their lights extinguished far too soon, but for a period of about ten years they dominated the rarefied world of power and glory; whilst they pleased him, the King looked on with pleasure at their talent, wit and exuberance. And the leading lights in this very different court were the two Boleyn siblings.

4 Personal Attributes

George Boleyn has a reputation as an attractive, high-living womaniser who used his charm and celebrity to great personal effect. The question is how this reputation came about, and whether it is fair and accurate.

George is described in his entry in *Athenae Oxonienses* as a man who "was much adored there [at court], especially by the female sex, for his admirable discourse and symmetry of body". He is also attributed popularity, particularly with the ladies, by George Cavendish, who would have seen George at court. Cavendish's *Metrical Visions* were written in 1557 and are a set of verses relating to certain individuals executed during the reign of Henry VIII. They are written as from the mouths of those facing death. Cavendish had served Cardinal Wolsey as his gentleman usher, and was a staunch Catholic. Cavendish was prepared to accept as fact the charges brought against the Boleyn siblings, who he would have considered to be almost heretics and blamed for the downfall of his master. Despite his antagonism towards the Boleyns, he cannot prevent himself from singing the personal virtues of George Boleyn, who he portrays as being graceful, elegant, attractive and highly intelligent. He starts by having George say:

> God gave me grace, dame Nature did hir part,
> Endewed me with gyfts of natural qualities:
> Dame Eloquence also taughte me the arte
> In meter and verse to make pleasant dities,
> And fortune preferred me to high dignyties
> In such abondance, that combred was my witt,
> To render God thanks that gave me eche whitt.[1]

Cavendish, who would have known George from when he was a young man, portrays him as being blessed with a high degree of natural and physical advantages, as well as eloquence and elegance. It was a sign of wealth and status to dress well, and there were few at court that could compete in this area, either physically or financially, with George Boleyn. Top-quality clothing and tailoring was an expensive business even in the sixteenth century, and it was not unheard of for a gentleman to spend as much as £1500, in today's money, on a single cape. George Boleyn's particular style may partly explain the debts he had at the date of his death.

In addition to George's looks, Cavendish's verse praises the quality of his poetry and his wit (intelligence), and mentions the positions of trust to which he was exalted at an unusually young age:

> A rare thing saw or seldom ever heard
> So young a man so highly to be preferred.

For Cavendish - a staunch enemy of the Boleyns and all they stood for - to have felt the need to write such glowing praise, George's physical and mental attributes must have been well above and beyond those of the normal courtier. But despite the gushing attributes, *Metrical Visions* were not written with the intention of complimenting George's virtues – indeed, quite the reverse. Cavendish goes on to have George say:

> In this my welthe I had God clean forgot,
> And my sensuall apetyte I did always ensewe,
> Esteming in my self the thyng that I had not,
> Sufficient grace this chaunce for to eschewe,
> The contrary, I perceyve, causithe me now to rewe;
> My folly was such that vertue I set asyde,
> And forsoke God that should have been my gwyde.
>
> My lyfe not chaste, my lyvyng bestyall;
> I forced wydowes, maydens I did deflower.
> All was oon to me. I spared none at all,
> My appetite was all women to devoure,
> My study was both day and hower,
> My onleafull lechery how I might it fulfill,
> Sparyng no woman to have on hyr my wyll.

Cavendish is obviously biased, but he is clearly suggesting that George's fine talent was especially employed in satisfying his sensual appetites as a womaniser of renown, and that he lusted after all women, both widows and maidens. Cavendish goes even further, providing in the suggestion "all was one to me" an indication that George may have seen his sister Anne as no different to any other woman. Likewise, Edmond Bapst suggests that George had so much success in the art of seduction as to leave an indelible stain on his character, although he does not accept the incest charge with the same naivety as does Cavendish.[2] Cavendish goes on to imply that George acknowledged on the scaffold that his death was deserved due to his lewd behaviour. The rest of the poem is Cavendish's interpretation of George's statement in his scaffold speech that he was a great sinner deserving of death. He finishes by having George say:

Alas! To declare my life in every effect,
Shame restraynyth me the playnes to confess,
Least the abhomynation would all the world enfect:
Yt is so vile, so detestable in words to expresse,
For which by the lawe, condempned I am doughtlesse,
And for my desert, justly juged to be deade;
Behold here my body, but I have lost my hed.

If Cavendish is to be believed, there can be little doubt that George Boleyn used his own personal attractions as well as his social position to flirt outrageously as much as his sister did. As we have already seen, in addition to his personal attributes, he was a talented linguist, poet and musician, whose gallant and witty conversation was used by Cavendish to support the notion that he did more than merely verbally delight the ladies of the court. His charm and courtly skills were as lauded as his sister's, and from the harshness of Cavendish's criticism, it seems his gallantry probably went above and beyond that of the average courtier. However, there was never any major scandal surrounding him, and no other Boleyn enemy felt that his behaviour was base enough to comment on. It is therefore questionable whether his behaviour went beyond flirtatious banter in the guise of courtly love, or at least not to the degree Cavendish suggests.

Court chivalry tended to be a defence against the boredom of having little meaningful employment within the court set-up. A man could be married and have a wife at home, but still woo a "mistress" at court "with poems, songs and gifts" and wear her favour at jousts.[3] Such wooing was not necessarily sexual; it served as a sign of chivalry and was expected to be platonic. George was highly gifted, yet up until the end of 1529 his main employment was in keeping the King busy. The enigmatic young man's flirting could merely have been in pursuit of fun rather than a serious expression of love, or indeed pursuit of sex. It has to be borne in mind that George's womanising reputation, whether fully deserved or not, stems solely from Cavendish's verses, and that these verses have also been used to accuse George of rape and domestic abuse. There is, however, no evidence – not even hearsay - that George raped anyone, or that he was cruel to his wife.

George's worst characteristics appear to have been his pride and arrogance. He was good-looking and clever, and he was well aware of that. How much of the criticism levelled against him was based on envy we will probably never know, but certainly these more negative elements were an aspect of his character. At the time of George's death, Thomas Wyatt, who is supposed to have been a friend of George Boleyn, wrote of his pride:

> Some say, 'Rochford haddest thou not been so proud
> For thou great wit each man would thee bemoan,
> Since it is so, many cry aloud
> It is a great loss that thou art dead and gone.'

One of the reasons for his pride, in addition to the natural Boleyn pride, could be the position in which he had been put from an early age. His sister Mary had been mistress to the King at some point between 1519 and 1525, and then in around 1526 the King began lusting after George's second sister. Every grant made to George Boleyn throughout his life, and every honour, every position of trust and power he received, would have been questioned. Was it through his own merit, or through the King's relationship with one or other of his sisters? From his late teens, he was not just another courtier, he was the brother of the King's mistress or wife. George was a proud, intelligent, competent young man and although it is always assumed he would have derived pleasure from his good fortune, there must have been an element of frustration that whatever he did, and however hard he worked, he would merely be considered lucky. He would have known the court gossip. He would also have been well aware that by usurping the popular Queen Catherine, Anne and the rest of her family were viewed with malice and loathing by large numbers at court. In addition to this, by 1528, at the age of just 24, both

George and his sister had come to embrace the new religious ideas. This alone made them unpopular with large numbers of people who held true to the Catholic faith. It is not difficult to see how a young man, already prone to pride and cockiness, could easily take on an additional air of arrogance as protection against his enemies. Or how in times of crisis, that air of arrogance could become even more pronounced merely as a defence mechanism.

There is much emphasis placed on George's pride and arrogance, and Wyatt's poem is often used to suggest that he was personally disliked, even hated, by large numbers at court. Yet his pride was not so pronounced that Eustace Chapuys, the imperial ambassador, felt it appropriate to comment on - save for saying that George was proud of his evangelical views – this despite Chapuys actively seeking faults in order to demonise the Boleyns. Neither does Chapuys make any mention of George's supposed sexual promiscuity. In fact, his criticisms of George are mild compared to his reports relating to Anne and the siblings' father. As far as Chapuys is concerned, George gets off quite lightly. Likewise, although Cavendish lambasts George for his womanising, he makes no mention of him being particularly arrogant; again, Cavendish was looking for faults. So let us take Wyatt's verse at face value; "some" said if George had not been so proud then he would be more bemoaned. It would be difficult to argue that George did not have character flaws; no doubt there were those who personally disliked him because of his pride, but "some" is a long way from suggesting a majority. Wyatt goes on to say that despite George's cockiness, "many" said that his death was a great loss. Because extant records that give an insight into the characters of people living so long ago are rare, when we do read something tangible relating to them we tend to seize on it eagerly. George may well have been a womaniser, and without doubt pride was an aspect of his personality, but to what extent? Certainly his charm, which must have been substantial, appears to have compensated to a large extent for his supposed arrogance. Although open mourning for the May 1536 victims was a dangerous pastime, Wyatt's poem clearly exhibits the admiration and respect in which George was held; "many" still risked declaring that his death was a great loss.

Yet setting aside the root cause of his arrogance, and its extent, it did exist and was obviously a less attractive part of his personality. Add this to his dogmatism regarding his religious views, and his lack of tolerance for anyone who did not share his Reformist vision, his exuberance then his alleged womanising and, despite his many merits, George appears to have been a young man to whom it might not have been desirable to be married.

5 Social Pursuits

There is very little source material showing characters from the Tudor era as human beings, rather than two-dimensional caricatures or merely names on a page. As far as Anne and George are concerned, this problem is exacerbated by the fact that the people who actually cared about them mostly kept their feelings to themselves out of self-preservation following the Boleyns' executions. What we are left with are comments made by Boleyn enemies, who made the most of the siblings' fall from grace. Unfortunately, this gives a very unbalanced view of what they were really like. It is only by seeing the Tudors at their leisure that you can get a glimpse of the real people, and it is only by thinking of them as human beings rather than names on a page that you are able to empathise with them, particularly when you read of their words on the scaffold minutes before they died.

Up until the end of 1529, George Boleyn's main role was keeping the King entertained, and it appears to have been one in which he was highly accomplished. Henry VIII and his court enjoyed a wide range of entertainments, including archery, hunting, card games, shovel board, dice, bowls, tennis and jousting. In addition to his acknowledged intellectual prowess, George was particularly adept at archery, bowls and shovelboard, winning large sums of money from the King on numerous occasions.[1] He was also very much the sportsman, enjoying tennis and jousting. But his particular delight appears to have been hunting with either dogs or hawks.

Falconry was a particularly expensive form of entertainment in the sixteenth century and was enjoyed almost exclusively by the nobility. The sport involved the capturing of quarry using trained birds of prey.

On 17 October 1533, George wrote to Lord Lisle, who had been appointed Lord Deputy of Calais in March of that year. He began his letter with the formal courtesies of the age, "My very good Lord, as heartily as I can I commend me unto your Lordship", and goes on to request safe passage for his servant to enable him to purchase various hawks for his master:

> This my letter shall be to desire you to be good
> lord unto this bearer my servant, William Atkins,
> insuring him your favour to pass in Flanders with
> such small baggage as he shall bring with him:
> which when he hath sold it at the most, with the
> same money buy for me certain hawks; praying
> your lordship also that at his return from thence
> that he may have passage with the first that shall
> come over.

Lord Lisle received a number of similar letters, mainly from wealthy people of importance, promising to do similar favours for him at another time. George Boleyn's letter therefore ends, "and if there be any pleasure or service that I may do for you in these parts, I pray you write unto me and I shall not fail to do you any pleasure that in me is."[2]

The nobility would hire professionals to train the birds for them, or spend large sums on already-trained birds, often purchased from abroad, rather than training them themselves. It was not unusual for gentlemen either to travel themselves or to send their servants abroad in order to purchase the best birds. Such purchases were an important show of wealth and respectability; when your brother-in-law was the King of England, such a show was essential, a matter of keeping up appearances as well as of the enjoyment of the sport, an important symbol of respect and friendship between nobles.

George's determination to flaunt his wealth and social position resulted in him writing to the Searchers of Dover and Calais two months after his letter to Lisle. On 11 December he wrote again in pursuit of the best hawks, calling the searchers, his "well beloved friends":[3]

> I desire and heartily pray you to permit and suffer my servant this bearer to pass by you into the parts of beyond the sea with the sum of twenty marks in gold or silver or under the coin of this Realm of England or of any outward parts, to make provision for me in the said parts of beyond the sea of certain hawks. And I shall see you discharged in this behalf and besides that do unto you the pleasure that lieth in me...

It was not just hawks that the young Boleyn hankered after. It was also a symbol of status to be seen riding the best horses. On 4 June 1534 he again wrote to Lord Lisle, thanking Lisle and his wife for a gift given to his sister, for which George, as was often the case, had been the intermediary. However, the main purpose of the letter was to enquire as to the purchase of a horse:

> My Lord, I understand by your servant that the horse which was Highfield's is sold, wherein I do desire your Lordship to do me some pleasure, and if possible (to find him) that hath bought him, paying for him as he paid... And if you can get him

at a reasonable price, then to let him be sent unto
me, and I will not only pay for his charges that
shall bring him but also I will be glad to do you or
any of yours such pleasures as in me lieth.[4]

There was a style to George Boleyn's letter-writing, which,
although following the general style of the age, is particular to
him. This probably owed much to the manner of his upbringing
and education. With Lisle, and others of whom he asked a favour,
he always promised "not to fail to do them any pleasure that lay
in [him]". Although this was usual, and was a civility taught to
him from the cradle, it was a lesson he always followed diligently,
never once deviating from the courtesy. Even in brief, hastily-
written letters, he includes these civilities, because it was the
honourable thing to do. George Boleyn need hardly promise to
"do unto you the pleasure that in me lieth"; this was the queen's
brother, and brother-in-law to the King of England, after all. No
doubt Lisle and the Seekers of Dover and Calais were falling over
themselves to assist him, but George had been brought up to be
the perfect courtly gentleman, and old habits die hard. Similarly,
he always ended his letters with such phrases as "and so I make
an end", or "and to make an end", and it is a particular style
that sets his letters apart from others of the day. Yet despite the
politeness of the sentiments, status and pride were also evident in
his correspondence. All three Boleyn children had been brought
up to consider themselves superior to the majority of the nation.
It was an early lesson that George and Anne took very much to
heart. All the letters discussed here specifically state that they are
being written from Hampton Court Palace, the royal palace where
George was obviously residing at the time. This was a statement of
fact as well as a subtle reminder that he was very much part of the
King's limited circle of intimates, enjoying close personal contact
with Henry himself.

Henry VIII's Privy Purse Expenses from November 1529
to December 1532 show that when George was not on embassy

abroad, he was the King's constant companion. One of the King's favoured few, the high regard in which he was held is obvious from these entries. The first occasion upon which George (by then Lord Rochford) is mentioned is on 28 March 1530, when he was shown to have received "xx Angells" (an Angel being 7s. 6d.), denoted as a reward.[5] Although there is no indication as to why he received the reward, George had just returned from embassy in France, and it would seem highly likely that the money was paid for services rendered to the Crown in this regard.

On 5 April 1530, George received money "for the use of Master Weston for 4 games which he won of the King's Grace at tennis at 4 Angells a game".[6] Although it is supposed that Henry VIII hated losing, and that his courtiers took pains to deliberately lose when playing him, the Privy Purse Expenses show this was not the case. The King regularly lost at all kinds of games, and he lost huge sums of money to George Boleyn at a variety of different pursuits. Payments were made to George in August and September of that year for the hunt, and for archery at Hunsdon on 15 September, when he was awarded £5. On 8 July 1531, George received £58 from the Privy Purse "for shooting [archery] with the Kings Grace at Hampton Court", and in August he received £6 in Ryalles (a Ryalle being 11s 3d), again for shooting.

1532 continued to show George regularly receiving money for beating the King at a variety of games. In January and February, he won nearly £60 for playing the King at shovelboard, and on 17 April he, his father, Francis Bryan and Edward Baynton won £36 from the King at the same game. Shovelboard is a game in which coins or discs are slid by hand across a board toward a mark; clearly George was highly accurate while his heavy-handed monarch was not. Shovelboard was an indoor sport, and the fact that it was still being played in early April suggests the weather was not particularly good that year. However, by 20 April the weather had obviously improved, since on the 20th and 22nd of that month, George is shown beating the King at bowls. On 20 April, he played the King in a one-on-one match, while on 22

April he and his father played the King and Edward Baynton, winning £30. On 28 June, George won £18 for beating the King "at the Pricks [archery] and by betting at the same", and on 12 July payment is again shown for hunting in Sussex. George appears to have excelled at any game which required accurate hand-to-eye co-ordination. Bearing in mind we are talking about the sixteenth century, the amounts being wagered on frivolous pastimes were vast. George's entire yearly income as a courtier only amounted to £100 (considered a high income for the age he lived in), and in just one day he could win over six months' salary. However, the sums won must be qualified by the inevitable losses, and it is probably likely that these too were substantial.

The King prided himself at being excellent at all sports, but by the amount of money his future brother-in-law won from him, George was clearly a match for him. Of course by the early 1530s, Henry had reached his forties and was beginning to put on weight, whereas George Boleyn was in his late twenties and in the prime of life.

The final entry relating to George Boleyn for the period available is dated 6 October 1532, for playing and beating the King at the new card game primero, and for winning a wager of the King "with a brace of greyhounds". Primero was a popular gambling card game of the day and is believed to be the direct ancestor of poker. George was clearly unafraid of beating the King and was more than happy to take his money on a variety of bets. Obviously these sports and games would have continued into 1533 and beyond, but the Privy Purse Expenses are only available up to December 1532. There is no reason to suppose that George Boleyn did not continue to be the King's companion and confidante almost to the last.[7]

The Privy Purse Expenses put to rest the notion that George enjoyed royal favour purely because of his sisters' relationships with the King. Henry was a selfish, self-centred man with little patience. He would never have suffered the continued presence of a courtier whom he did not personally like, or one from whose company he did not derive pleasure. Yet George was a regular companion to the King for at least 12 years, and favour continued to be bestowed upon him until a month before his death. Henry bet high stakes with his favourite courtiers, and of course what the Privy Purse Expenses show are his losses, and not his winnings. They demonstrate the extent to which men had to spend in order to remain within the royal presence. As much as George, his father, Suffolk and other favourites won, it is likely they lost just as much if not more. Courtiers' debts to the King were often covered by either selling land or borrowing from others. This could also go far to explaining the level of George's debts at the date of his death. He was flamboyant, carefree and seemingly financially irresponsible.

In addition to the leisure activities scheduled in the Privy Purse Expenses, there was also the ever-present joust, a sport particularly dear to the King's heart. Thomas Boleyn had been an adept jouster in his day; since any gentleman who excelled in this area immediately won Henry's approval, Thomas ensured that his son was also well-equipped in the tiltyard. George was certainly competent at the sport, serving as one of the principal jousters in the May Day joust of 1536, along with the equally ill-fated Henry Norris.

Jousting is first recorded in 1066 and enjoyed widespread popularity during the thirteenth century. It remained popular until the late sixteenth century, when it went out of fashion. The sport was particularly dangerous, and one at which Henry had excelled in his youth. Thomas Boleyn himself had jousted with the King before Henry was forced to give up the sport following a nasty fall in January 1536. Participation in the sport took courage and recklessness, of which Henry would have approved, together with grim determination and a competitive spirit. The only record we have of George Boleyn in the joust is the May Day tournament of 1536, but to have been considered as a principal competitor, it must have been a sport in which he had previously indulged frequently. The thought of him jousting contrasts sharply with the view of him as a poet and intellect, but any courtier who wished to remain in the intimate royal circle had to have all-round abilities in order to keep the King amused and entertained. Similarly, the constant jockeying for position and status must have been exhausting - or exhilarating, depending on your point of view. To be constantly employed in keeping the King amused must also have been debilitating, as well as nerve-wracking. It would be rather like keeping a small child entertained, only one who was particularly egotistical and dangerous. Thomas More phrased it best when he wrote in his collection of Latin poems:

> You often boast to me that you have the king's ear
> and often have fun with him, freely and according
> to your whims. This is like having fun with tamed
> lions, often it is harmless, but just as often there is
> fear of harm. Often he roars in rage for no known
> reason, and suddenly the fun becomes fatal.[8]

In addition to sporting pursuits, both George and his sister Anne were keen readers. Most of the books that we know belonged to them are religious, but George Boleyn's collection also contains volumes that were read purely for pleasure and amusement. Two books survive that were provably in his possession at some stage. The first is a manuscript containing a translation in French by Jean Le Fèvre of Mathieu of Boulogne's thirteenth century poem *Liber lamentationum Matheoluli* (The Lamentations of Matheolus), a satire on marriage, followed Le Fèvre's *Le Livre de Leesce* (The Book of Joy/Gladness), which appears to be a refutation of Matheolus's work.[9] There is controversy over *Le Livre de Leesce*, with some scholars taking it at face value as a pro-feminist defence of women and a rebuttal of Matheolus' misogynistic arguments,[10] while others see it as playful and tongue-in-cheek, with "a heavy dose of make irony" to amuse male readers.[11] Karen Pratt has gone so far as to say that, rather than it praising marriage, *Le Livre* actually praises "the joys of marital sex", something which Henry VIII's courtiers may well have found amusing.[12] George certainly owned the manuscript because it is inscribed "thys boke ys myn George Boleyn 1526" (**See Figure 2**); it has been suggested that Thomas Wyatt the Elder may have given it to George as a wedding present because it bears Wyatt's signature at the end, along with two teasing verses in Italian and French. Historian Susan Brigden points out that 1526 was "the time of Wyatt's own marital catastrophe" so his inscriptions "can be read in the light of his experience".[13] However, George was married in 1525, probably early in the year, so it is more likely that George purchased the book or was given it some time after his marriage.

At some point George gave or loaned the book to the court's young musician, Mark Smeaton, because it also bears the inscription "A moi M. Marc S." The fact, that the book was, at some point, in the possession of both George and Mark Smeaton has been used by one historian as the sole piece of evidence to support a theory that George was having a homosexual relationship with the musician.[14] Such an assertion, ignoring Thomas Wyatt's endorsement, seems to be a matter of turning a small, inconsequential fact into so-called "evidence", in a poor attempt to prove a pre-conceived theory. The satire on marriage was widely circulated amongst scholars in Europe and clearly did the rounds of courtiers, many of whom, like Wyatt, were trapped in loveless matches and could appreciate its irony. While Smeaton may have seen the acquisition of the book as a mark of his acceptance into the society of men like Boleyn and Wyatt, the sad truth was that to the Boleyns and their circle he was as important as a grain of sand is to a desert. Wyatt's scribbling of a French proverb mocking a social upstart may well reflect the group's views on Smeaton. To suggest that either of the proud Boleyn siblings would have chosen the lowly commoner as a lover is not credible.

The second book in George's collection is a copy of Ramon Lull's *Libre del Orde de cavalleria*, reworked in French by Symphorien Champier as *Lordre de Chevalerie* (the Book of the Order of Chivalry). The book describes the progress of a young squire's meeting with an old knight who has become a hermit. The hermit instructs the squire in what is expected of a knight and the ways of chivalry. Interestingly, the book says that on entering the order of chivalry, a knight must confess his sins against God, and that if he is cleansed of sin he ought to receive his saviour. George's scaffold speech demonstrates that this was a lesson he took very much to heart. Charles Brandon, Duke of Suffolk, may have given the book to George, after 8 December 1529 (when George became Viscount Rochford) since George proudly and endearingly entered on the title page, "Thys booke is myn George Rocheford".[15][16] If the gift was indeed Suffolk's (something which may never be established conclusively), he was obviously better disposed towards George than he was to George's sister Anne, whose relationship with Suffolk and his wife, Mary Tudor, was always strained. It would also indicate that Suffolk had taken it upon himself to take the newly-knighted George under his wing, perhaps out of respect and affection for the young man, perhaps as a way of ingratiating himself with the by then powerful Boleyn family. George went on to have the book translated into English by Thomas Wall, Windsor Herald, as a gift for the King in 1533.[17] Julia Fox notes that Wall's manuscript has various underlinings and corrections, which she believes were made by George because his knowledge of French was "more up to date than Wall's".[18]

George Boleyn certainly lived life to the full in all respects, and it is a tragedy that his life was cut so short. His love of sports, gambling and outdoor pursuits such as hunting gave him even more in common with his future brother-in-law, the King, than merely his intellectual prowess. He was not only a young man after whose sister the King lusted, he was also someone whom the King personally liked. Before their deaths, George Boleyn, Henry Norris, and to a lesser extent Francis Weston, were all intimates of the King, and had been for many years. It makes the tragedy of 1536 even more poignant, since these men were not strangers who meant nothing to the King - they were the people with whom he chose to spend his leisure time, and his friends.

6 Religion

To the medieval mind, religion was not a matter of choice. God's existence was a fact, not a question of personal belief or faith. Failure to accept this amounted to heresy and could result in a fiery death at the stake. Belief in demons, omens, vengeful spirits and witchcraft was equally strong. Science was in its infancy, and to an ignorant people any unexplained phenomenon was caused either by the forces of evil or the wrath of God. The only way to defend yourself was through total adherence to the church. Fear and devotion could be exploited through greed and corruption, resulting in the church acquiring vast wealth, land and power. In the early 1500s, the church meant the Catholic church and its inherent rituals. There was no other permitted faith, and adherence to any other religious format was considered heresy. Religion shaped and formed an integral part of the lives of the Tudors. Everything worked around the church calendar, and the laws of the land were based on the church's doctrines. However, there were those who actively pursued religious reform, often at great personal risk. It is impossible to write about George Boleyn's life without writing extensively about his religious beliefs, which were staunchly Reformist and evangelical, and an essential part of his life. They helped to shape his character, and ultimately helped to destroy him.

Until Henry VIII broke with the Church of Rome following the annulment of his marriage to Catherine of Aragon, England was a devoutly Roman Catholic country. Henry himself was fervently Catholic and, until his desire for the annulment led him to break with Rome, he actively persecuted religious Reformers. Henry's defence of the Catholic church, in his pamphlet *Assertio septem sacramentorum adversus Martinum Lutherum* (Declaration of the Seven Sacraments Against Martin Luther), led to the Pope granting him the title "Defender of the Faith", a title of which he was immensely proud. The man against whom Henry VIII was defending the church was Martin Luther (1483-1546), a German monk, theologian and church reformer. He is to this day considered to be the founder of Protestantism and the main catalyst of the Reformation.

Luther's writings, which included *The Ninety-five Theses, To the Christian Nobility of the German Nation, On the Babylonian Captivity of the Church, On the Freedom of a Christian* and *On the Bondage of the Will*, were circulated widely around Europe and had a major impact. His theology challenged the papacy by holding that the Bible was the sole source of religious authority, and that salvation and redemption were attainable only through faith in Christ and God's grace, unmediated by the rights and rituals of the church. Luther translated the Bible into German, making it more accessible to ordinary German people. He rejected the idea of the priesthood mediating between God and man through the miracle of the mass, and attacked the sale of indulgences by the church, complaining that Christians were being led to believe that this practice would give them absolution when salvation was actually available free through Christ.

In short, Luther preached faith rather than ritual, thereby directly challenging the basis of Catholicism. Luther's writings, along with those of his followers, were widely banned throughout Europe. Luther was excommunicated in January 1521, and Charles V, Holy Roman Emperor, declared him an outlaw and heretic in May 1521.

Despite Henry's active persecution of those who failed to conform to the orthodox Catholic faith, Thomas Boleyn favoured religious reform, as did his youngest two children. Both Anne and George were drawn to reform of the Catholic church, no doubt initially through their father's influence. Some historians see Thomas Boleyn as a conservative Catholic;[1] however, his links to French Reformers suggest otherwise, as does his use of his godson Thomas Tebold as an agent on the Continent, reporting back on the current state of religious persecution in France, and spreading the word that Thomas Boleyn was "a promising patron of works - theological and other". Tebold also sent Thomas Boleyn a religious work by French Reformer Clément Marot, an action which would only make sense if Thomas was sympathetic to the cause of Reform. Another man linked to Thomas Boleyn is Reyner Wolf, a bookseller who used his travels abroad to work as an agent for the English government, carrying messages between Reformers such as Heinrich Bullinger and Thomas Cranmer. It is hard to believe that a conservative Catholic would have such links.

The Boleyns' religious idealism bred in zealous Catholics a hatred of the family, a hatred that continued long after their deaths, and which spawned many of the rumours, innuendos and slanders against them that persist to this day. When the Boleyn siblings first entered court life, the aristocracy were mainly staunch Catholics, appalled at the thought of any reform to the church, let alone the drastic approach of Reformers such as Luther. The Boleyns' faith and evangelism resulted in them acquiring many powerful enemies, who made the most of the family's later fall from grace.

Although religion was an enormously important part of sixteenth century life, at the time the Bible was only available in Latin, and only the highly educated were able to read it. The common people had to rely on parish priests to interpret the Bible for them and to teach them the doctrines of Christianity. There was a significant movement in England that supported reform of the Catholic church - for the rites of the faith to be reformed, and for the word of God to be accessible to the masses. George and Anne Boleyn were not merely devotees of this group; in time they came to embody it. Their desire for reform came from their natural and genuine religious tendencies. With a traditionalist Catholic English King on the throne, this reform seemed an unlikely prospect. In time, as we obviously know, Henry VIII also came to accept reform, but his motives for instigating the Reformation were very different to those of the Boleyn siblings: he wanted a break with Rome because this fulfilled his desires. Eventually, he also came to believe that he should have supremacy over the Church of England. The Boleyns were Reformers, and the fact that the eventual break achieved Henry's annulment and facilitated his marriage to Anne was a marvellous bonus.

Henry's views hardened towards Rome between late 1532 and 1535, but in the late 1520s and into the 1530s, Reformist literature was still banned in England. George Boleyn's regular trips abroad in the early 1530s enabled him to obtain religious literature that was banned in England and across most of Europe. We know of George's trips to France as ambassador because these are referred to in the state papers. There may also, however, have been private trips that he made abroad that would not have been documented, some of which could have taken place prior to his first diplomatic mission. Any literature he brought back was read with interest not only by George but also by his sister Anne. When Anne and George's goods were confiscated after their deaths, they were found to include a number of evangelical books written in French.

The religious manuscripts owned by Anne and George Boleyn were acquired either by George himself or through other intermediaries. George turned two religious works into magnificent presentation manuscripts for Anne. These manuscripts were based on works by Jacques Lefèvre d'Étaples: *Les*

Epistres et Evangiles des cinquante et deux sepmaines de l'an (The Epistles and Gospels for the Fifty-two Weeks of the Year) and *The Ecclesiaste*. The manuscripts were based on cheap printed books that would have been hard to obtain in England in the early 1530s (unless you happened to be the King's future brother-in-law). *Les Epistres* consisted of the dates of the liturgical calendar followed by the Epistle or Gospel in French rather than the usual Latin, and then an exhortation, or homily, by Lefèvre. Anne's copy of *The Ecclesiaste* consisted of the book of Ecclesiastes translated into French by Lefèvre, with an English translation of German theologian and Reformer Johannes Brenz's commentary. Both books were written with the aim of making the Bible accessible to the masses; Brenz's commentary stressed the need for a living faith in Christ rather than a reliance on the rituals and practices of the orthodox Catholic Church, which was precisely the ideology of Martin Luther. Brenz called for reform, and exhorted priests to serve the laity by following the pattern of Christ's Great Commission laid out in Matthew 28 – that is, "preaching and baptising in a positive evangelical service" rather than "controlling salvation through the dispensing of the sacraments".[2] Interestingly, while Martin Luther's *Notes on Ecclesiastes* was aimed at monks and clerics, Brenz's commentary focused on rulers and those who are ruled. Brenz saw King Solomon as a preacher and "the chief spiritual watchman and spokesman for his people", a man who had religious responsibility as well as that of a ruler.[3]

Jacques Lefèvre d'Étaples, the original author of *Les Epistres* and *The Ecclesiaste*, was a French theologian, humanist and Bible translator. In his biography of Lefèvre, Philip Edgcumbe Hughes writes of how "Lefèvre blazed the trail that led from Renaissance to Reformation", and he is seen by many as the precursor of the Protestant movement in France. Although his name is not as famous as that of Martin Luther, Eric Ives refers to Lefèvre as the "herald of the Protestant Reformation";[4] he was promoting the doctrine of justification of faith as early as 1509, well before Luther's *Ninety-five Theses* (1517). In fact, all three foundations of the reformed theology, which became the hallmarks of figures such as Luther, Zwingli and Calvin, were propounded first by Lefèvre. First, *sola gratia* (by grace alone): the idea that Christians were saved by the mercy and grace of God; secondly, *sola fide* (by faith alone): the doctrine of justification by faith, that Christians gain God's pardon for their sins, and eternal life, through faith alone and not human works; and finally, *soli Deo gloria* (to God alone be the glory): the idea that Christians should live their lives to glorify God and not themselves or others.

Putting these doctrines together, Lefèvre believed that sinners were justified and pardoned by faith alone, through the divine grace of God and Christ's sacrifice on the cross, and that all the glory should go to God for his mercy and grace. Lefèvre also saw scripture as the highest authority, being the Word of God.[5]

Les Epistres was printed in 1525, and was condemned by the Sorbonne later that year. The doctrines implicated in that condemnation included: justification by faith alone and the idea that good works did not contribute to a believer's salvation; salvation by the grace and goodness of God alone; Jesus Christ as the sole mediator between God and man; and the idea that only the Word of God should be preached and taught by the church.

Yet all these beliefs were derived from the New Testament.

Lefèvre writes in his exhortations that sins will be forgiven if we simply have faith in Christ, because He has paid the price of our sin.[6] This is a recurrent theme in his exhortations, and this doctrine of justification by faith was obviously taken on board by George and Anne. These two volumes were not the only books by Lefèvre that Anne owned; she also owned a copy of his French Bible, and clearly valued his work.

Lefèvre never left the Catholic church, and was not a schismatic. He sought to reform and renew the church by going back to scripture and making scripture accessible to everyone, so that all could receive God's grace and learn about God's message. Theologian Guy Bedouelle views Lefèvre "neither as a Catholic with a bad conscience nor as a crypto-Protestant, but rather as an evangelical who firmly believed that the truth when positively proclaimed would triumph over error."[7] [8] This description of Lefèvre could also fit the Boleyn siblings. Although Chapuys described the Boleyns as "Lutheran", their influence was French, and like Lefèvre, they appear to have been evangelical Catholics looking to reform the church from within, and to bring renewal to their country through the dissemination of the Bible in the native language.

When translating *Les Epistres* and *The Ecclesiaste* for Anne, George left the scriptural texts in their original French, a language in which the Boleyn siblings were fluent, but translated the commentaries into English. *Les Epistres*, which can be found in the British Library, is badly damaged, particularly by water. It is prefixed with a dedication, which until recently had led scholars to believe the translation was the work of Henry Parker, Lord Morley, who was George's father-in-law (**See Figure 4**). This erroneously led scholars to suppose that Morley enjoyed a close relationship with Anne. Recently, however, a passage prefacing the dedication, "moost lovyng and frynddely brother", was discovered by means of ultraviolet light. This led historian James Carley to the inevitable conclusion that the author of the translation was actually George Boleyn himself. This is supported by the presence on one of the pages of a cipher that was probably designed by Holbein, and is clearly one of George and Boleyn.[9] (**See Figure 1**)

The dedicatory letter to his sister which George prefaced to *Les Epistres* reads as follows:

> To the right honourable lady, the Lady Marchioness of Pembroke, her most loving and friendly brother sendeth greetings.

> Our friendly dealings, with so divers and sundry benefits, besides the perpetual bond of blood, have so often bound me, Madam, inwardly to love you, that in every of them I must perforce become

your debtor for want of power, but nothing of my good will. And were it not that by experience your gentleness is daily proved, your meek fashion often times put into use, I might well despair in myself, studying to acquit your deserts towards me, or embolden myself with so poor a thing to present to you. But, knowing these perfectly to reign in you with more, I have been so bold to send unto you, not jewels or gold, whereof you have plenty, not pearl or rich stones, whereof you have enough, but a rude translation of a well-willer, a goodly matter meanly handled, most humbly desiring you with favour to weigh the weakness of my dull wit, and patiently to pardon where any fault is, always considering that by your commandment I have adventured to do this, without the which it had not been in me to have performed it. But that hath had power to make me pass my wit, which like as in this I have been ready to fulfil, so in all other things at all times I shall be ready to obey, praying him on whom this book treats, to grant you many years to his pleasure and shortly to increase in heart's ease with honour.[10] [11]

The above dedication from George to his sister, in addition to exemplifying the strength of the Boleyns' shared religious beliefs, demonstrates the depth of affection between Anne and George. It was written between September 1532 and January 1533, prior to Anne's marriage. It refers to her as the Marchioness of Pembroke, which was a title she did not receive until 1 September 1532, and it may well be that George translated the manuscript as a gift for her upon her being granted the honour, or as a New Year gift in January 1533. It covertly refers to a possible forthcoming marriage, "shortly to increase in heart's ease with honour", and Anne married Henry VIII on 25 January 1533. In the dedication,

George sets out beautifully expressed compliments to his obviously much-loved sister. This highly intelligent young man incorporates in the dedication the type of self-deprecation that only the very clever would risk, knowing that it would be received by a recipient who could fully appreciates the false modesty. Be that as it may, George clearly demonstrates an anxiety as to whether his translation will please his sister. He does, however, include the proviso that if there are faults, she is to remember that it was she who asked him for the translation in the first place. The dedication refers to Anne's, "meek fashion", for which she was not particularly renowned, and claims that George is not giving her jewels and so on, since she has enough of them. It is possible to read this as a dedication by a younger brother to his sister which is not only caring and affectionate, but also written with a little jovial cheekiness. This dedication is the closest we come to a glimpse of the actual relationship between the two of them.

We even have the actual text that George used for his translation. Although there are three surviving copies of the B text of *Les Epistres*, which was used for Anne's manuscript, James Carley points out that the copy held by the British Library (BL 1016.a.9) shows evidence of use.[12] In a number of margins someone has inserted a picture of a pointing finger. There is also an error in the text that has been amended in the margin. However, in George Boleyn's translation this amendment forms part of the text, suggesting that George used this copy. George would then have sent the original manuscript together with his translation to the scribe. The transcribed manuscript is beautifully presented. The salutation to his sister is in blue ink, with a gold initial in a red frame. Alternate colours and patterns indicate textural divisions which are obviously carefully designed and highly individualised. It would have been magnificent when it was new.

The translation of *The Ecclesiaste* does not contain a dedicatory letter. It is probable that one did originally exist, and has been either lost or deliberately removed. The lack of a dedication makes it hard to determine who translated it. However, it shares the individualised characteristics of the *Les Epistres* translation, although it is even grander and more elaborate. It still has the original binding, and has complex illustrations. The colouring of the initial letter for each verse follows the characteristics of *Les Epistres*. Because of the individualised style and the strong similarities in technique, Carley attributes *The Ecclesiaste* to the same scribe who executed *Les Epistres*. As he points out, both books represent a quality of manuscript normally commissioned by royalty or the highest level of aristocracy.[13] Only George Boleyn or someone of his calibre would have been able to afford to employ the same competent scribe and first-class artists on two separate occasions.

Although George Boleyn was known and admired as a scholar even during his own lifetime, these are the only two translations that can definitely be attributed to him. However, in his scaffold speech he refers to being "a setter forth of the word of God", which suggests there were others which are now lost or which, like his poetry, are attributed to other people. Certainly Henry Parker, Lord Morley, was a prodigious translator for the King. It is highly probable that if he had lived, George would have become at least as well known for his translations as his father-in-law. The translations for which we know George was responsible prove that when it came to issues of religion, he was equally as active as Anne. When George went on embassy to France in 1534, Thomas Cromwell wrote in one of his remembrances that George was instructed by Henry VIII to deliver "a Book of Instruction" in French to Francis I.[14] This may have been similar in content to those manuscripts that were owned by either Anne or her brother.

Carley demonstrates that in various aspects of Anne Boleyn's life - the pious follower of religious reform, the gay frivolous courtier, the queen whose household was the centre of "elegant artifice" - the presence of her brother loomed large.[15] He demonstrates this by proving beyond doubt that George was the translator of *Les Epistres* and *The Ecclesiaste*, and by the nature of George's dedicatory letter to his sister, which is full of courtly gallantry. Certainly, the influence of Anne's brother on her religious views and opinions is undeniable. The two surviving manuscripts show that George was much more than simply a reader of novelty religious literature. His evangelism was not a newfound trend that he discovered shortly before his death, or something that he used for political gain. He was an active participant from a much earlier point, and from his youth identified himself as well as Anne with the new theological idealism. In matters of religion they were a team, and they read cutting-edge texts by the forerunners of the Reformation.

George's translation of Lefèvre's accompanying annotation reads:

> For faith which giveth the true fear of God, is it that doth prepare us for to keep the commandments well, and maketh us good workmen, for to make good works; and maketh us good trees for to bear good fruit, Then if we be not first well prepared, made good workmen, and made good trees we may not look to do the least of the commandments, Therefore Moses giving the commandments for the beginning said: 'Hearken Israel, thy God is one god', which is as much as to say as, believe, have faith, for without faith God doth not profit us, nor can we accomplish nothing: but the faith in God and in our Lord Jesuchist is it which chiefly doth relieve us from the transgressions that be passed of the sentence of the law, and yieldeth us innocents, and in such manner that none can demand of us anything, for because that faith hath gotten us Jesuchrist, and maketh him our own, he having accomplished the law, and satisfied unto all transgressions, Then faith having reconciled us unto the Father, doth get us also the Holy Ghost, Which yieldeth

witness in our hearts that we be the sons of God. Whereby engendereth in us true childerly fear, and putteth away all servile and hired fear. And then it sheddeth in our hearts the fire of love and dilection, by the means whereof we be well prepared for to keep the word of God, which is but love: and without the which it is aswell possible for us to keep the said commandments, as unto the ice to abide warming and burning in the fire. For our hearts (without this fire of the Holy Ghost) be over hard frozen and cooled, and overmuch founded and rooted in the love of ourselves.[16]

The quote emphasises the Reformist doctrine of justification by faith, of salvation being found only by faith in Jesus Christ. For Anne to have asked George for the translation of *Les Epistres*, and for George to have personally undertaken this monumental task, confirms their level of commitment to religious reform. It has been suggested that their interest was on a superficial level, more to do with being drawn to a trendy new idealism than genuine religious fervour, but their commitment is proved to be far greater than mere fashion. George spoke at length on the scaffold regarding his religious views and is unlikely to have spent the last minutes of his life doing so had he not been fully committed. The fact that George is responsible for these translations authenticates a passage in his scaffold speech uniquely recorded by a Calais soldier named Elis Gruffudd. Gruffudd was attached to Sir Robert Wingfield's household, and was in the Calais garrison in 1536. His source is unknown, but may have come directly from the executioner. Gruffudd's original account of the speech is in Welsh, but the translation reads:

Truly so that the Word should be among the people of the realm I took upon myself great labour to urge the King to permit the printing of the Scriptures to go unimpeded among the commons of the realm in their own language. And truly to God I was one of those who did most to procure the matter to place the Word of God among the people because of the love and affection which I bare for the Gospel and the truth in Christ's words.[17]

There can be little doubt that the Boleyns used their positions at court, and the protection that derived from the favour of the King, to promote their religious ideals. Sometime during 1528 Simon Fish, a religious controversialist, sent an evangelical and revolutionary 16-page pamphlet he had written to Anne Boleyn entitled *A Supplication for the Beggars*. It was a piece of religious propaganda promoting the abolition of the monasteries by emphasising the abuses of the ecclesiastics, and accusing the church of holding half of England's wealth. The pamphlet was a religious rant, including phrases such as:

And what do all these greedy sort of sturdy, idle, holy thieves with these yearly exactions that they take of the people? Truly nothing but exempt themselves from the obedience of your Grace. Nothing but translate all rule, power, lordship, authority, obedience and dignity from your Grace unto them.

George either noticed the pamphlet or was given it by Anne. According to Fish's wife, "this book her brother seeing in her hand, took and read, and gave it to her again, willing her earnestly to give it to the king, which thing she did".[18] When George read it he obviously recognised its potential as a document that would be easily understood by the King, and one which would appeal to his mercenary nature and egotism. As George well knew, as early as 1528 this document amounted to heresy, and only Anne could have brought it to Henry's attention with a guarantee of impunity.

As George foresaw, Henry was impressed with the pamphlet and had a personal meeting with Fish some two years later, during 1530.

George's influence in the religious changes which swept the country in the mid-1530s has been largely overlooked. But his translations for Anne and the incident with *A Supplication* clearly demonstrate his influence over his sister and, through her, the King, when it came to reform. These elements also further authenticate his scaffold claim to be "a setter forth of the word of God". Anne may have been the mouth-piece due to her influence over the love-struck Henry, but her brother was alongside her throughout. Henry was by no means a natural Reformer, but if it suited his purpose, he allowed himself to be easily influenced. The King's lust for Anne meant that he was ripe for conversion, provided Reform meant getting what he wanted; the evangelical Boleyns had the intelligence to exploit their King's shallowness, for the greater good.

We know that Anne used her positions as queen-in-waiting and queen to provide patronage to Reformers. It appears that she, George and their father financially supported Nicholas Heath, who became one of Thomas Cranmer's evangelical circle, at Cambridge University.[19] Heath became the rector of St Peter's Church, Hever, the Boleyn family church, in 1531.[20] Heath was later involved in embassies to the Lutheran Princes of Germany, and he worked closely with Archbishop Cranmer and Cuthbert Tunstall, Bishop of Durham, in overseeing the Bible translations which became the 1539 Great Bible. Heath later distanced himself from evangelicals, becoming Archbishop of York during Mary I's Catholic reign, but he seems to have been a keen evangelical in the 1530s, during which he was known and patronized by the Boleyns.

From his first introduction to court as an adult, George was particularly open in his support of religious reform. This, together with his intelligence, charm and linguistic skills, had the effect of distinguishing him from the run-of-the-mill young courtier, but it also turned many against him who continued to support the orthodox Catholic religion. It is easy to look back with hindsight and see that George Boleyn set himself up for a fall at a very early age. The imperial ambassador, Eustace Chapuys, complained that Rochford insisted on entering into religious debate whenever he was being entertained by him,[21] [22] and George spoke passionately of his religious beliefs on the scaffold:

> I was a great reader and a mighty debater of the Word of God, and one of those who most favoured the Gospel of Jesus Christ. Wherefore, lest the Word of God should be slandered on my account, I now tell you all Sirs, that if I had, in very deed, kept his holy Word, even as I read and reasoned about it with all the strength of my wit, certain am I that I should not be in the piteous condition wherein I now stand. Truly and diligently did I read the Gospel of Jesus Christ, but I turned not to profit that which I did read; the which had I done, of a surety I had not fallen into such great errors. Wherefore I do beseech you all, for the love of our Lord God, that ye do at all seasons, hold by the truth, and speak it, and embrace it; for beyond all peradventure, better profiteth he who readeth not and yet doeth well, than he who readeth much and yet liveth in sin.[23]

Irrespective of the piety of the sentiments, many honourable people lost their lives as a result of Anne and George Boleyn's joint commitment to religious reform. It is unlikely either of them would have contemplated the deaths resulting from their commitment. Whilst neither of them can be proved to have actively supported the atrocities, they passively condoned them by making no stand against them. On the scaffold George Boleyn admitted being a wretched sinner deserving of death, but did not recount his many sins. Perhaps one of them was his determination to accept the deaths of innocent people as collateral damage in order to achieve the religious aims of himself and his sister.

7 Court Life

Anne Boleyn was recalled from France in late 1521 due to negotiations taking place for her to marry James Butler, one of her Irish relations. The date on which she arrived in England is not known, but she was certainly at court by the beginning of 1522 since she attended a court pageant on Shrove Tuesday of that year, 1 March, at which she put her acquired French sophistication to use. Her sister Mary and her future sister-in-law Jane Parker both joined Anne in playing parts in the elaborate "Château Vert" pageant. Prophetically, Anne played Perseverance and Mary played Kindness, while Jane played Constancy.[1]

Jane Parker was lady-in-waiting to Queen Catherine of Aragon, and according to George Cavendish had been brought up in the court since childhood. It is likely, therefore, that she had already come into contact with her future husband; the fact that they were both in close attendance on the royal couple would suggest they knew each other fairly well.[2] They were both good-looking, wealthy and well-placed, and there is no evidence to suggest that there was no attraction between them. In 1522, both George and Jane were about 17 or 18 years old. Whether or not issues of religion and politics caused later friction in their marriage, most teenagers do not allow such trivialities to get in the way.

By 1522, Mary Boleyn had been at court nearly three years, but this was Anne Boleyn's first introduction to the English court. The Boleyn girls obviously knew their future sister-in-law for some time before she married their brother thanks to their pageant appearance and time at court. Were the young women friends? Jane, like everybody else, was aware that Mary had had, or was having, an affair with the King. That alone might have put a strain on their friendship, particularly as Jane's loyalties appear to have always remained with the Queen. But whatever Jane's views may have been, once she married into the Boleyn dynasty her loyalties as a woman would be expected to lie with her husband and his family.

Prior to Anne's return to England, it is unlikely that the three Boleyn siblings had even been together since the Field of Cloth of Gold meeting in June 1520. By the time Anne came to England, Mary was well-known to the King, having probably already slept with him, and George was one of the King's favourite pages; Anne had some catching up to do. It is impossible to assess the dynamics of the relationship between the sisters, but whether or not they remained close, 1522 was the first time in nine years that all three Boleyn children were in a position to spend any significant time together.

George probably took a permanent position at court in around 1522 or 1523, at the age of about 18, around the same time as Anne's return (or shortly afterwards). There is no record of a precise date for the commencement of this position. The earliest extant record of George as an adult is in 1522. On 29 April, he and his father received a joint grant of various offices at Tonbridge, Brasted and Penshurst that had belonged to the executed Duke of Buckingham.[3] This supports the earlier date of 1522 as the year George was permanently at court. There is no record of him attending the Château Vert pageant, but the only people specified were those who were actually starring in it. As George would only have been about 17 at the time, he would not have featured as one of the gallants who rescued the ladies. Instead, if he had been there, the precocious Boleyn boy would have had to sit on the sidelines and watch his sisters and future wife take starring roles.

Shortly after Anne first attended court, she began a romance with Henry Percy, the son of the Earl of Northumberland and a member of Cardinal Wolsey's household. They fell in love and were apparently intending to marry when Wolsey and the King put a stop to their relationship. Cavendish claims that the King ordered Wolsey to stop the marriage because of his "secret affection" for Anne, but there is no other evidence that the King was attracted to Anne at this time. It is more likely that the intervention was down to marriage negotiations designed to marry Anne to James Butler and Percy to Mary Talbot. Anne and Percy were separated; Percy was quickly matched to Mary Talbot, while Anne appears to have been sent home, where she remained until the beginning of 1525. Little is recorded of the Boleyns during the mid 1520s, though, and it is impossible to be certain of their movements. If Anne was indeed banished while her brother and sister remained at court, one can only imagine her frustration at being trapped alone in the depths of the countryside. Rural Hever was a far cry from the pleasures of the French and English courts.

By the middle of 1525, Anne shone as the most fashionable woman at court and acquired many admirers, including the poet Thomas Wyatt. It is clear from his poetry that he was in love with her, and there has been much speculation as to whether there was a sexual relationship between them. Thomas Wyatt's family were neighbours of the Boleyns in Kent, and Wyatt may well have known the Boleyn siblings since childhood. George was one or two years younger than Thomas and it is possible that they were playmates as children. As with George Boleyn, Thomas Wyatt was adept at the game of courtly love, and like George he had an arranged marriage at an early age. Many courtiers had mistresses at court and wives at home, seeing court life and home life as completely separate. This in itself would have caused difficulties for George Boleyn whose future wife was at court alongside him as lady-in-waiting to the Queen. Any dalliance by George would have immediately come to his wife's attention. Thomas Wyatt on the other hand, was separated from his wife, and he became an acknowledged courtly suitor of Anne Boleyn. From the contents of Wyatt's poetry, there can be little doubt that his love was unrequited. As Wyatt was married, the most Anne could have expected was to be his mistress, and it is clear from her subsequent response to the King's advances that this was something for which she would not have been prepared to settle.

More importantly, it was at some point during 1525 or early 1526 that Anne Boleyn first caught the King's eye. The marriage negotiations with the Butlers had fizzled out, and by the spring of 1526 Henry was infatuated with Anne. By the autumn of the same year, he was bombarding her with love letters in an attempt to make her his mistress. Anne's refusal to be his "maîtresse-en-titre", or official mistress, changed history and the religious persuasions of a nation, as Henry set about annulling his marriage to Catherine of Aragon in order to marry Anne.

Henry's decision was not based solely on his fascination with Anne Boleyn; it was also to do with his conscience. Henry appears to have stopped having sexual relations with Catherine in 1524, and in June 1525 his illegitimate son Henry Fitzroy was created Duke of Richmond and Somerset, at the age of 6. The boy was given precedence over every other noble at court, and there was speculation that the King would make him his legitimate heir. Henry was, therefore, probably considering divorce as early as June 1525, long before his relationship with Anne became serious. Catherine had been the wife of Henry's brother Arthur, Prince of Wales, who had died at the age of 15, and the Book of Leviticus states in chapter 20, "If a man shall take his brother's wife, it is an unclean thing:; he has uncovered his brother's nakedness. They shall be childless". This worried Henry VIII and although the Book of Deuteronomy appears to go against that law, advising in chapter 20 that a man should marry his dead brother's widow ("When brothers live together, and one of them dies without children the wife of the deceased shall not marry to another: but his brother shall take her, and raise up seed for his brother"), Catholic canon law gave Leviticus precedence over Deuteronomy.[4] A dispensation for the marriage of Henry and Catherine had been granted in 1503, but Henry felt that he had proof that his marriage was contrary to God's law: all his sons by Catherine had died. Catherine maintained to the end of her life that her marriage to Arthur was never consummated. Historians Patrick Williams and J.J. Scarisbrick point out that the dispensation was therefore defective, in that the lack of consummation already freed Henry and Catherine from the impediment of affinity (which only existed if Catherine had consummated her marriage to Arthur).[5] [6] Henry may well have missed a trick by not arguing that point in his quest for an annulment.

In April 1527, after 18 years of marriage, Henry VIII began consulting advisers, and in May instructed his chancellor Thomas Wolsey to obtain an annulment. Thomas Wolsey was born in the early 1470s in Suffolk. He was a cardinal of the Roman Catholic Church as well as a statesman. He became Lord Chancellor in 1515 under Henry VIII, and was one of Henry's closest friends and confidantes. Wolsey loved wealth and power, and lived in splendour at his palace at Hampton Court. He survived the inconsistencies of Henry's policies and character by adapting his morality to meet the King's requirements. Though Wolsey was anti-war, in 1511 he supported the King's wish to invade France, and made persuasive speeches in favour of war. This pragmatism - or hypocrisy - won him much favour with Henry and greatly assisted his acceleration of power. Likewise, despite his loyalties to the papacy, Wolsey was first and foremost Henry's servant. He was bitterly opposed to the Boleyns and their Reformist associates, but his power relied solely on maintaining good relations with Henry, which meant doing everything in his power to make Anne Boleyn queen consort. When he failed to obtain an annulment for Henry, his influence waned. In 1526, however, Wolsey was Henry VIII's most trusted aide, and he ruled the Privy Chamber with a rod of iron. Although George Boleyn had been serving Henry VIII as a page for a number of years, he lost his position in January 1526 following Wolsey's Eltham Ordinances, so called because they had been devised at Eltham Palace. These were intended to reform the royal household, but Wolsey used the opportunity to gain full control of the Privy Chamber, and secured the expulsion of those he believed to be troublemakers - including, for a £20-a-year consideration, George Boleyn.[7] The real reasons for the expulsion of George and his associates were their popularity and influence with the King. Many of those expelled also supported religious reform, and were hence perceived by Wolsey to be a threat to his position. Wolsey's view that it was necessary to remove George Boleyn, who would only have been about 21 at the time, demonstrates the influence that George was exerting, even at a very young age. The Eltham Ordinances provided for 6 gentlemen of the Privy Chamber where there had previously been 12, plus 2 gentlemen ushers, 4 grooms, 1 barber and 1 page. By reducing the number of men so dramatically, Wolsey was able to exert more authority and maintain more control over the Privy Chamber, at least for a while. However, he also acquired a number of enemies, who when they came back into positions of power would not forget his actions.

In the early days of Henry's reign, his courtiers were all men of the old world, who had come down from his father's court – men such as Thomas Boleyn, William Compton and Charles Brandon, all of whom were in their late twenties or thirties at their King's accession at the age of 17. Despite the age gap, these men were not only Henry's sporting and drinking companions, but also the men to whom Henry looked for advice and guidance in the early days of his reign. But by the 1520s this landscape was changing, as new blood and new ideas came to the fore. The first of a new band of courtiers included men like Francis Bryan, Nicholas Carew and Henry Norris, who were of a similar age to the King. These names were later followed by Thomas Wyatt and George Boleyn, who were both considerably younger than their royal master, but who had great presence, intelligence and talent. They also had a youthful exuberance and passion for life. The King adored them for their ability to keep him entertained, and his royal favour gave them influence. This did not suit Wolsey, particularly as some of the new ideas espoused by a number of these precocious new favourites involved religious reform. George Boleyn made little attempt to hide his evangelical leanings, using his position and favouritism as armour against a possible charge of heresy.

The original intention of the Eltham Ordinances, prior to Wolsey's abuse of it, had been a good one. The court was a huge undisciplined society, involving hundreds of people. These included courtiers and their own servants, below-stairs servants and hangers-on. Wherever the King was, a huge entourage of raucous, over-ambitious, backstabbing people would follow. Some routine and discipline was urgently needed. After the demise of Wolsey, Thomas Cromwell continued to try and introduce a modicum of order into the court. In addition to limiting the numbers in the Privy Chamber, rules were introduced that the King's councillors, the Lord Chamberlain, captain of the guard, master of the horse and six gentlemen of the Privy Chamber were only allowed to keep one page each. Other lower-ranked courtiers were not entitled to bring their servants to court on pain of risking a fine and possible expulsion. The proud young Boleyn must have been incredibly displeased at his loss of status.

The world in which these courtiers lived was complex, and ultimately dominated by the King. The closer you were to the King, the closer you were to all power in the land. The court was a huge social structure with the King at the top, followed by his councillors, gentlemen of the Privy Chamber and so on, down to the lowest kitchen servant. Where you were in the structure dictated the privileges to which you were entitled, even how many horses you were allowed to keep at court and how many beds you were allowed. In the glamorous world of the court, there was a constant struggle for power and profit, and a constant jockeying for position. Those outside viewed those in favour with malice and jealousy. In an attempt to protect their positions, courtiers formed factions, through which they could attempt to collectively climb the slippery pole of success. It was not an environment for the faint-hearted or anyone lacking a ruthless streak. Alliances changed quickly and a friend could swiftly become a deadly enemy, as the Boleyn siblings later found to their cost. This was particularly the case when an issue of self-preservation was at stake. George Boleyn had been thrown into this maelstrom of vicious backstabbing and malice as a boy, and it says a lot about him that he was able not only to survive, but also to thrive in such an atmosphere.

The royal household was divided into two. The household below stairs was concerned with mundane duties, such as food preparation, and was supervised by the Lord Steward. He would insist that members of the court ate at the prescribed times, and would allocate daily food and drink rations to each gentleman, lady and upper-class servant according to their rank. This was no mean feat considering the sheer number of people to feed, and vast amounts of food were consumed daily. Each of the king's gentlemen and the queen's ladies were entitled to room and dining facilities, all at the expense of the Crown. Foreign visitors would often comment on the prodigious amounts of food presented at Henry's court. George and his future wife, as courtiers to the king and queen, would both have been entitled to be housed and fed by the Crown at the Crown's expense.

The household above stairs was supervised by the Lord Chamberlain and catered to the personal needs of the King. This was divided into the Privy Chamber, Outer Chamber and Great Hall. The Privy Chamber was the most influential of the three as it housed the king's private lodgings. In the Tudor court, the royal servants were chosen by the king from the men closest to him. The court itself was the seat of government in England, and a position in the Privy Chamber was to be in close proximity to the seat of all power in the country. At the age of 21, George Boleyn, as a member of the Privy Chamber, was in a privileged position, and his expulsion in January 1526 would have been a bitter blow.

Irrespective of his temporary expulsion from the Privy Chamber, George remained in the King's intimate circle. Henry liked to be entertained, and those close to him had to be able to do so, irrespective of their connections. Be that as it may, the King's lust for Anne Boleyn did have the effect of advancing her entire family during the late 1520s and early 1530s. But to believe that it was merely his sister's influence that advanced George Boleyn to such great heights toward the end of 1529 and into the mid 1530s would be to do him a great disservice. He was particularly intelligent, and as we have seen, his "great wit" was later commented on by Thomas Wyatt in his poetry. Wit in the sixteenth century was a generic term meaning not only intelligence and quickness of thought, but also that he was amusing and good company.

Many of those expelled from the Privy Chamber by Wolsey in 1526 eventually made their way back, largely with the patronage of Anne Boleyn, and by late 1528 the Privy Chamber had more or less reformed. To consolidate positions, various factions emerged. One revolved around Wolsey and his supporters, and one revolved around George Boleyn, which used its influence in support of Anne and religious reform. George became a leading member of this group through his own merits and his natural leadership, popular in his own right and also popular with the King himself. A third grouping supported Catherine and her daughter Mary, and was opposed to reform of the church. It was this latter faction that would later collude in the Boleyns' downfall.

Despite George and his sister's own merits, the evangelical Boleyns and their supporters could only retain their hold provided Anne remained in the King's favour. For George, it was not just a matter of loyalty and a natural brotherly desire to ensure his sister's happiness; he also worked tirelessly towards the religious reforms about which he was so passionate. The best way of achieving his objectives was for Anne to become queen.

8 Marriage

In 1524, George received the first grant made to him in his own right; the manor of Grimston in Norfolk.[1] It is supposed that this was an early wedding present from the King to a young man who was rapidly coming into favour. George married Jane Parker sometime in late 1524 or early 1525. The Public Record Office contains a document in Wolsey's handwriting assigned to January 1526, when the Eltham Ordinances were implemented (although Wolsey was known to have been working on the Ordinances in autumn 1525). It is entitled "prouysyon for such as shuldbe dyscharged out of the kynges preue chambre" and includes the instruction "Young Boleyn to have £20 yearly above the eighty pounds he hath gotten to him and his wife to live thereupon; and to admit him to be one of the cupbearers when the King dines out".[2] [3] This appears to have been intended as compensation for the loss of his position in the King's Privy Chamber, although it is unlikely George would have seen it as sufficient compensation. On top of this annual salary of £100, he and Jane, as courtiers, were housed and fed at the King's expense.[4]

Jane Parker was the daughter of Henry Parker, 10th Baron Morley, and Alice St John, both of whom were from old English families. Morley had been brought up in the household of Lady Margaret Beaufort, Henry VIII's grandmother, and he had acted as cupbearer at Henry VIII's coronation.[5] Jane was born in Norfolk around 1504-5, making her more or less the same age as George. She was lady-in-waiting to the Queen and would become lady-in-waiting to her sister-in-law in due course. Although the marriage was an arranged one, it was a good social match for both parties, and more particularly for their parents, merging two powerful and influential families.

George was as ambitious as his father, and would have recognised the advantages of a good marriage, but he was no pawn. His strength of character is evident throughout his court career. He was about 20 when he was married, and he had known Jane for a number of years within the claustrophobic confines of the court. It is difficult to believe that a young man as dynamic as him would have allowed himself to be married off to a woman he did not like, or that his father would have obliged his much-loved son to do so. Contrary to popular opinion, a couple was only supposed to become betrothed, and then married, if they liked each other. This "like" was then supposed to turn into love as they got to know each other better. It is highly unlikely that the match would have been one of dislike or hatred, as is so often portrayed in the realms of fiction. Although both George and Jane had been brought up in a world in which duty came first, there is no reason to think that either of them was disappointed with the match. Jane was an attractive young woman from an influential family;[6] George was a handsome, up-and-coming courtier who was popular with the King, and had ten years' experience in the cut-throat atmosphere of Henry's court. If he had had any serious objection to the marriage, there were other equally eligible young women to whom he could have been joined.

The wedding itself is not documented, and therefore no specific date or place for the ceremony is known, but the King himself provided part of Jane's dowry.[7] Set by Thomas Boleyn, that dowry amounted to 2000 marks (£1300), a substantial amount of money, which Jane's father was obviously unable to pay in full. The fact that the King made up the difference shows the extent of Boleyn favour at that time. A document of jointure was also drawn up, setting out exactly those things to which Jane should be entitled in the event that George should predecease her. The document itself is no longer in existence, but the act in which it was passed is still available, complete with the King's signature. Jane Boleyn's jointure ensured that in return for the dowry of 2000 marks, Thomas Boleyn guaranteed to convey to her the rents of certain manors, namely Aylesbury and Bierton in Buckinghamshire and others in Norfolk, or alternatively a specified yearly amount of 100 marks, for the rest of her life should George predecease her.[8] The jointure was drawn up and signed on 4 October 1524, and Wolsey mentions George having a wife in a document he was working on in autumn 1525, so the marriage must have taken place in late 1524 or early 1525. Couples were not allowed to marry during Lent, Rogationtide and Trinity, or during Advent unless they had a special licence,[9] and there is no record of a special licence being applied for. It seems probable, therefore, that George and Jane married before the onset of Advent in 1524, or before Lent commenced at the beginning of March 1525. Jane's family lived in Great Hallingbury, near Bishop's Stortford in Essex, so Great Hallingbury's Church of St Giles would have been the obvious choice of venue. The church is a beautiful building which dates back to the eleventh century and whose chancel arch is made of Roman brick.[10]

It has been suggested that George and Jane had a child, also named George, who became Dean of Lichfield and who died childless in 1603. It is more likely, however, that the Dean was simply a cousin of the Boleyns. There is no extant record of George fathering a child by Jane. If there had been children from their union, it would be very strange for the birth to have taken place without being commented on; George was close to his sister, and any child of his would have been Anne's niece or nephew (and later the King's also). Jane Boleyn's begging letter to Cromwell following George's death also makes no mention of any child for whom she had financial responsibility. Such a child would surely have been mentioned in her letter if it had existed. Appendix E discusses the legend that George had an illegitimate son.

It appears, therefore, that George and Jane Boleyn were childless, or that Jane suffered from miscarriages or stillbirths. As we have seen with Henry VIII's matrimonial problems, childlessness was considered the fault of the woman, and there is no indication that George Boleyn was any more enlightened than any other man of the age. The lack of a son was insufficient reason for the King to obtain an annulment, let alone George and Jane Boleyn, and obviously the marriage could not be nullified on the grounds of non-consummation. It has always been assumed that the marriage was an unhappy one, partly due to George's reputation as a womaniser, but mainly because Jane later gave evidence in May 1536 that implicated George, stating that Anne had told her the King was impotent. Jane provided this statement in the sure knowledge that it would be of assistance to the prosecution (although she could not have foreseen the brutal consequences). The natural conclusion to be drawn is that either Jane then passed this information to George, who was subsequently accused of spreading the rumour, or alternatively, that Henry's supposed impotency provided the motive for Anne taking lovers, specifically her brother. Either way, to suggest that Anne and George openly discussed the King's sexuality was enough to damn the siblings in his eyes, irrespective of the eventual incest charge, and Jane must have been aware of that. But rather than this being a deliberate attack on her husband and sister-in-law, her evidence was more likely a simple matter of telling the truth and of self-preservation.

George and Jane would certainly have spent a great deal of their married life apart. Being royal cupbearer during the early years of their marriage meant that George was present at every state occasion to serve the King. George was also regularly sent on diplomatic missions abroad, and when in England he was kept busy in Parliament and as a trusted courtier and confidante to the King. In addition to this, he would regularly have been in Dover from June 1534 onwards as Lord Warden of the Cinque Ports. As we have seen, he was the King's constant companion during periods of relaxation, and so it is difficult to assess just how much time George and Jane Boleyn spent together during their 11-year marriage. Although George's name regularly appears in the state papers, correspondence and foreign reports, extant records are virtually silent with regards to his wife. George was the Queen's brother, and his every move was scrutinised, particularly by enemies with the very intention of demonising him. Had marital problems been in the public arena, there can be little doubt that the imperial ambassador, Eustace Chapuys, would have commented on them. It was common knowledge that Thomas Wyatt was desperately unhappy in his marriage, yet nothing was said of George and Jane.

The married couple certainly enjoyed a life of wealth and comfort. An entry in the Privy Purse Expenses on 17 April 1531 states, "Paid to Richard Breme for the rent of a house in Greenwich wherein my Lord of Rochford lythe for two years behind and unpaid at Easter last past".[11] From this, it can be seen that for at least two years, George and his wife had rented a house away from court, and that the Crown had met the unpaid rent of £20, i.e. £10 a year. It is possible that this property had been rented by George since 1526 when he had first received the additional income of £20 per year, and that he had maintained the rent until 1529. The arrears could have accrued due to an oversight or because by then the Rochfords were living beyond their means. The property at Greenwich was in addition to the rooms that had been specifically appointed to them at court. The fact that the King paid the rent arrears shows his affection for George, but the very existence of arrears is an indication that George was not managing his finances.

Both George and Jane Boleyn were proud, ambitious people who would have wished to have been seen to be achieving an enviable lifestyle, even if they could not actually afford it. In addition to this, George was a poet and an intellect, and such people do not necessarily make the best accountants. As we have seen, he certainly gambled heavily with the King, and although he regularly won huge amounts of money, the probability is that he lost equally huge sums. Certainly the debts he had at the time of his death were large enough to cause him great concern for those to whom he owed money. Nonetheless, George merrily spent £50 on a cup of gold, and squandered a fortune on clothes, hawks, horses and other symbols of wealth and status. A later inventory of his wife's assets shows a large amount of expensive jewellery, at least some of which was presumably bought for her by her husband during their marriage. It is difficult to see how his income could cover such extravagance - and perhaps the simple answer is that it could not.

Keeping up with the King did have its advantages, however, and throughout the late 1520s, George's royal favour continued. In addition to becoming royal cupbearer in January 1526, he was appointed Esquire to the Body on 26 September 1528, for which he received an annuity of 50 marks payable "by the chief butler of England out of the issue of the prizes of wine", and a salary of £65 6s 8d per annum.[12] This position required attendance upon the King's person, and it exemplifies the extent of royal favour shown to George at that time. That same year he also became the first Master of the Privy Pack, later known as Master of the Buckhounds, thereby heading the list of Masters. This appointment was held purely at the King's pleasure and was a position George held until his death. It was a highly preferential appointment, as hunting with dogs was a pursuit particularly dear to the King's heart. George no doubt undertook this employment gladly. He was regularly provided with large sums of money to enable him to purchase meat to feed the animals, and needless to say, his expenses relating to the performance of his duties were met in their entirety.

Grants continued to be made to George Boleyn throughout his short life. In addition to the grant he received jointly with his father of manors previously owned by the executed Duke of Buckingham, George and his father also jointly received a grant with respect to the honour of Rayleigh in July 1531, together with other benefits relating to this property and the manors of Thunderley, Estwodesbury and Lonedon.[13] The Boleyns were not unique in this; the state papers clearly show the generosity with which Henry treated his favourites. Grants were made each month to a variety of favoured courtiers. Henry Norris and Francis Bryan feature heavily, and the Privy Purse Expenses show that the King paid for the musician Mark Smeaton to be clothed with "shert" and "hosen".[14] Compared to Norris and men like William Brereton, George's income was relatively small for such a prominent courtier - hence the question-mark over how he could afford his enviable lifestyle. At the date of his death, the only land he held in his sole name rather than jointly with his father was Grimston, which had been granted to him in 1524. All other properties in which he had an interest were of reversionary title, and would have naturally been returned to the Crown on his death.

George Boleyn mainly benefited from the offices and positions of trust and responsibility to which he was appointed and his wife's social position increased vicariously. She revolved in circles that would never have been open to her without the advantage of her marriage to a highly successful courtier. In addition to this, through that marriage, she was about to become sister-in-law to the King of England. Whether she was happy with this last honour is debatable.

Jane Boleyn's court career blossomed following her husband's execution. She was prepared to continue in her role of lady-in-waiting to Henry's next wife, Jane Seymour, and she seems to have had a good relationship with the Princess Mary. Her ability to separate herself emotionally from her husband's death, and more importantly from the circumstances of her husband's death, may suggest that by 1536 the couple were not particularly close; or it could simply be Jane's survival instinct. Just as Thomas Boleyn climbed his way back into the King's favour after the executions of his children, Jane knew she had to dust herself off and move on.

Jane's family were staunch Catholics, and supporters of Catherine of Aragon and the Princess Mary. There were many staunch Catholics in the country, and at court, who had been appalled at the religious changes being wrought on the country due to the King's infatuation with Anne Boleyn. Jane would have been doubly mortified due to her own husband's heavy involvement in the changes sweeping the country. She may have forgiven him for any infidelities; she may have forgiven him for his long absences; perhaps, however, she found his commitment to religious reform too much and it soured the marriage. However, there is no irrefutable evidence to confirm that it was the troubled marriage of fiction. George and Jane were not twenty-first century sentimentalists; they were people of their time.

9 Sweating Sickness

In 1528, as the Boleyn family fortunes flourished, an epidemic of the disease known as "sweating sickness" or "the English Sweat" swept through the country. The first outbreak of the disease was in 1485, when it killed several thousand people. Further outbreaks occurred in 1507, 1517 and 1528. The last major incidence was in 1551; the disease disappeared completely in England after 1578. Its primary cause remains unknown, but it was obviously contracted by contact with an infected person, and it was extremely virulent. It spread quickly around the country, to the horror of the King, who had an obsessive fear of sickness and death. The symptoms included redness of the face and body, headaches, thirst, stomach and joint pains, vomiting, breathlessness and severe sweating. It could kill within four or five hours of the first symptoms showing, but sufferers who survived to 24 hours usually made a full recovery.[1] The 1528 outbreak was particularly severe, first showing itself at the end of May and sweeping throughout Europe, killing many thousands of people.

London was especially badly hit, probably due to the sheer

number of people living in such close proximity. In a letter dated
30 June 1528, Jean du Bellay, the French ambassador, wrote of
40,000 people in London being infected by the disease and 2000
of them dying.[2] The London Charterhouse was badly affected,
and the Archbishop of Canterbury's household lost 18 servants to
the disease in just four hours.[3] One of Anne Boleyn's maids fell
ill, resulting in Anne's return to Hever Castle with her father in
June. In the meantime, George remained with the court. As royal
cupbearer, George travelled with the King and Queen Catherine
to Waltham Abbey, where he was taken dangerously ill shortly
after arrival. There was no effective remedy for the condition, save
to wrap the afflicted person in blankets and hope for the best.

In a letter to Anne, Henry VIII wrote, "For when we were
at Walton, two ushers, two valets de chambre, and your brother,
master-treasurer [William Fitzwilliam] fell ill, but are now quite
well."[4] It appears from this that neither Anne nor her parents were
aware of George's condition while he was fighting for his life,
but were only informed once he was out of danger. In the same
letter, before advising Anne of her brother's illness and subsequent
recovery, Henry asks after Anne's health: "The uneasiness my
doubts about your health gave me, disturbed and alarmed me
exceedingly...but now, since you have as yet felt nothing, I hope,
and am assured that it will spare you, as I hope it is doing with
us". We only know of George's illness from the content of Henry's
love letters written to Anne. Unfortunately none of the letters are
dated. It is clear, however, that Anne was taken ill shortly after
receiving confirmation of George's recovery, because a further
letter from Henry states, "There came to me suddenly in the night
the most afflicting news that could have arrived."[5] Anne and
Thomas Boleyn had also been taken ill while at Hever, and in an
age in which a high percentage of afflicted people died, Anne and
her father were lucky to recover. The siblings and their father had
caught the disease at more or less the same time. It is remarkable
that brother, sister and father all contracted the disease at virtually
the same time in two different places, and that all three survived.[6]

Both of the letters referred to would have been written in June, when the disease was at its height. Upon his own recovery, George would have immediately been faced with the news that his father and sister were seriously ill. When fit enough to travel, he would have wanted to be at home with them. Whether he was fit enough to do so, and whether he was released from his duties to enable him to return to Hever, is not known. A later letter of Henry's asks after Anne's health and asks her for news.[7] More often than not it was George who was the messenger for Henry's letters to his sister, but it is not known whether George was at Hever at the time that this was written, or whether he was still with the court.

The immediate Boleyn family survived the outbreak of sweating sickness, but George's brother-in-law, Mary Boleyn's husband William Carey, was not so lucky. William's death put great financial pressure on Mary and her two children, and it was her sister Anne who provided her with much-needed financial support. Anne initially wrote to Henry requesting he help her sister. Although none of Anne's letters to Henry survive, we know she wrote to him thanks to a letter of his dating from the end of June or beginning of July 1528. In it, he advises her that he will write to her father: "It cannot to stand with his honour, but that he must needs take her, his natural daughter, now in her extreme necessity." The onus is put squarely on Thomas Boleyn.[8]

The fact that the King had to write to Thomas Boleyn to shame him into helping Mary suggests that the elder Boleyns had distanced themselves from their eldest daughter. Despite the King's letter, Thomas Boleyn obviously did little to assist Mary, since Henry VIII later granted Anne the wardship of Mary's son Henry. This was a role that Anne took very seriously, ensuring that Henry had the best possible education, for which she paid personally. Anne also ensured that her sister received an annual pension of £100.[9] The fact that Henry offered no direct financial support to his former mistress is an indication firstly of his indifference towards those who no longer contributed to his pleasure, and secondly of his refusal to accept parental responsibility for either of Mary's children. As for Henry Carey becoming Anne's ward, it was not unusual in the sixteenth century for impoverished or bereaved families to have one or more of their children made wards of wealthier friends or relatives. In April 1533, George Boleyn (by then Lord Rochford) was granted the wardship of Edmund Sheffield, son of Sir Robert Sheffield who had been knighted by Henry VII after his performance at the Battle of Stoke Field (fighting the rebel John de la Pole, Earl of Lincoln). When Sir Robert died in 1531, his son Edmund was only ten years old. To be given the wardship of a child by the King was a great honour, and confirmation of royal favour, and George would have benefited by controlling Edmund's property until the child came of age, giving George and his wife extra income during that period.

The circumstances surrounding the sweating sickness of 1528 exemplify the difficulty we have in establishing a picture of George's marriage. We know about Anne, George and their father, but the documentation we have is completely silent with regards to Jane Boleyn. Was she with George and the royal party at Waltham, serving the Queen, or was she elsewhere? There is no way of knowing her movements. The reason for this is obvious. In a world in which men dominated, Jane was of no importance. She was not central to court politics like her in-laws. She is very much a shadowy figure in the background, and this has probably helped perpetuate the myth of her as a devious woman spying on those around her. As we shall see later, like her husband she was no wide-eyed innocent, but the view of her as purely vindictive and evil is surely wildly exaggerated.

Many people died during the sickness of 1528, including the courtier William Compton, one of Henry's favourites. The impact of the disease, and Henry's realisation that he had come close to losing Anne, confirmed the King's feelings. Anne, for her part, never wavered in her determination to be anything less than queen consort. She would have been fully aware of the callous disregard the King demonstrated towards his thrown-off mistresses, including her own sister. She was determined not to go down that path, and in this her brother supported her. Did Anne Boleyn eventually give in to Henry and agree to marry him because she genuinely fell in love with him, or did she agree to marry him to further the course of religious reform? It is impossible to tell. The underlying belief that religious reform was fundamentally right was strong in both George and Anne, and they would have recognised Anne's relationship with Henry as an opportunity to support it. By 1528 the die had been cast, and Anne was destined to be Henry's queen. His sister's relationship with the King would advance George's career and the cause of Reform, but at a huge cost.

Part 2 - Career and Influence

10 The Waiting Game (1527-29)

Henry VIII first instructed Cardinal Wolsey to begin seeking an annulment of his marriage to Catherine of Aragon in May 1527. On 17 May, the first formal steps were taken by means of a secret ecclesiastical tribunal that investigated the validity of the marriage. The trial took place at Wolsey's home, York Place, in Westminster. Wolsey called on the King to answer an objection which had been raised concerning his marriage to Catherine: that it was contrary to both God's law and ecclesiastical statute, and so could affect his salvation.[1] The trial was of course "stage-managed", resulting from the King's objections to the marriage rather than anyone else's, but although it was adjourned before it really got anywhere, it "enabled Wolsey to start a debate" on the marriage.[2] It appears that at this point Wolsey had no idea that the King had a new bride in mind and so wanted to get on with annulment proceedings as quickly as possible. While Wolsey's attention was on negotiating an alliance with France, Henry VIII took things into his own hands and began a campaign to obtain a dispensation from the Pope allowing him to marry again. Unfortunately,

Pope Clement VII was taken hostage by Emperor Charles V's forces during the Sack of Rome in May 1527 and was therefore in no position to assist Henry's cause, even if he had been inclined to do so. An application was made to him in August 1527 for a dispensation to enable Henry to marry again, but a favourable response did not seem likely.

Around the middle of that year, Anne left the court and returned to Hever. It was during this time that correspondence between the pair provides a snapshot of Henry's courtship of Anne, which was already in evidence at the time of the outbreak of sweating sickness (although the lack of dates makes it difficult to establish a precise timeframe). Anne was certainly at court at the beginning of May 1527 because she attended a reception at Greenwich for the French Ambassadors. It is likely she left court shortly after this. This was her second period of exile, the first being after the Percy affair. Eric Ives, Anne's biographer, believes that the first letter was written in the autumn of 1526, before Anne left the court.[3] This dates the letters to a period between autumn 1526 and the end of 1528, which is when Anne returned permanently to court. 17 letters written during this period survive. Henry's correspondence come from the hand of a man who notoriously hated writing letters, and are filled with words of love and devotion, and schoolboy-style doodles of the couple's initials. It is difficult to imagine when reading them that in less than ten years' time he would order the execution of the woman to whom he was writing, as well as that of her brother, who acted as the courier for many of the letters.

One of his first letters, written (as Ives surmises) in autumn 1526, is in a light-hearted style. Henry tells Anne that he "wishes for you instead of your brother".[4] George's duties brought him into close proximity with the King on a daily basis. The next two letters, written shortly afterwards, are more serious as Henry seeks Anne's love. The earlier letters demonstrate that Anne had not yet returned Henry's affections, which in turn shows that when the annulment was proposed, it was not purely because of

Anne Boleyn: Henry had no way of knowing that Anne would ever return his feelings. By Easter 1527, Henry was asking Anne to be his mistress, an "honour" she vehemently refused. It was not until August, when Anne had been at Hever for some months, that she succumbed to the King and agreed to become his wife, though not his mistress. This required her to remain at Hever for decency's sake, as it was no doubt anticipated that they would be married within months, rather than the five and a half years that it actually took. Knowledge of the annulment proceedings came as a bombshell to the court. Queen Catherine was extremely popular, not only at court but also with the general public. It was bad enough that the King was seeking to put her aside, but if it came to light that there was another woman involved, there would be a scandal.

In a number of Henry's subsequent letters, it is apparent that their bearer is often George Boleyn. In one, Henry writes, "the great affection I have for you has induced me to send you this bearer, to be better informed of your health and pleasure, and because, since my parting from you, I have been told that the opinion in which I left you is totally changed, and that you would not come to court".[5] He ends by saying, "beseeching you to give credence to this bearer in all that he will tell you from me"; it is more than likely that Henry is talking about George, since no mere courtier would be trusted with such personal information, and the circle of people who knew of the relationship between the King and Anne was limited. From the contents of this letter, it is also apparent that the King visited Anne at Hever reasonably regularly throughout this period. As one of his closest companions, George would have accompanied him, particularly as Hever was his home and Anne was his sister.

Henry was well aware of the closeness of the siblings. While in exile, Anne's one continuous link with the goings-on at court would have been her brother who she would have wanted to be with her, not only for news but also for companionship. By being the King's trusted courier, George had the ideal opportunity to travel to Hever reasonably frequently to see his sister, and to spend time at home being spoiled and pampered by her, and on occasions by his mother (who acted as chaperone to her daughter).

In other letters, Henry tells Anne that the bearer will provide her with more information than he has written, indicating that the bearer is fully conversant with the situation. In particular, there is one letter, probably written towards the end of 1528 in which Henry specifically refers to George: "I heartily recommend me to you, ascertaining you that I am not a little perplexed with such things as your brother shall on my part declare unto you, to whom I pray you give full credence, for it were too long to write."[6] Henry had sent George to impart some particularly bad news relating to the annulment proceedings, and obviously felt that this was better coming from George than through lengthy correspondence. In the same letter, Henry remonstrates with Anne over leaked information regarding a visit he was planning to make to her, blaming the leak on "lack of discreet handling". It is unclear whether he blames Anne or George for this. As George would have been aware of the contents of Henry's letters, and was travelling to and fro between Hever and the court, he may well have let slip something which he shouldn't. Whatever the circumstances of the leak, neither sibling could have been in doubt of the King's displeasure.

As we know from the fact that she was in London when the sweating sickness broke out, Anne was not at Hever for the whole of this period. She was regularly at court, but returned there permanently at the end of 1528, by which time the King's "Great Matter", as the annulment proceedings came to be called, was no further forward. It was the beginning of the end for Cardinal Wolsey. By now, it was common knowledge that the King was seeking to marry Anne Boleyn, and although she had been kept in the background, just as Jane Seymour was eight years later, now there was no attempt at subterfuge. Once again, George was propelled into being the brother of the King's new love, and this time a Boleyn was actually trying to usurp the Queen rather than just being a passing fancy. During the next four years, Anne, George, their father and their supporters took a more direct and aggressive role in the proceedings.

The immediate effect of Henry's quest for an annulment was to undo Wolsey's 1526 reform of the Privy Chamber. Those closest to Anne Boleyn were raised to positions of prominence, and during 1527 and 1528 the Privy Chamber reformed. As Wolsey had expelled the Boleyn faction in 1526, so now those same people returned to the fold. In early 1528, George Boleyn did not have the political weight of either Wolsey or Nicholas Carew, but in addition to her brother, Anne had the more weighty support of her father, and of the Dukes of Norfolk and Suffolk. With the three groups jockeying for position, there was a temporary stalemate. This was not helped by the fact the Boleyns and their allies could not put forward any positive ideas of how to proceed in a constructive way. In November 1528, the Duke of Norfolk, Thomas Boleyn and George Boleyn signed their names to a document to be presented to the Papal legate, Cardinal Lorenzo Campeggio, purportedly demonstrating that the annulment had the overwhelming support of the English people. The document later disappeared without coming to anything. Eventually, in June 1530, a deposition signed by the Spiritual and Temporal Lords of England, including George Boleyn as Baron Rochford, was sent to the Pope praying him to consent to the King's desires, and pointing out the evils that would arise from delaying the divorce.[7] However, until the arrival of Thomas Cranmer towards the end of 1529, the Boleyns and their supporters were clearly floundering.

Throughout 1528 and 1529, Henry continued to believe that the Pope would yield to him, and that it was only imperial obstruction that was preventing it. By the middle of 1529, Pope Clement VII was no closer to granting Henry a divorce than he had been in 1527, and Henry believed that by obtaining a favourable judgement in England the Pope would be given the excuse he needed to accede to Henry's wishes. Enormous effort was made over a number of years to convince the Pope that his predecessor, Julius II, had exceeded his powers when granting Henry a dispensation to marry Catherine when the marriage was against divine law. Henry could not accept that the Pope had no intention of granting him an annulment, and that this had nothing to do with imperial pressure. Yet in the meantime, in England, Wolsey's loyalty was being called into question. He arranged a hearing of Henry's cause in London in the summer of 1529, at the Legatine Court at Blackfriars. The hearing commenced on 31 May and was a public-relations disaster. Catherine ran rings around the court and her husband. She famously knelt before her husband giving an impassioned speech in which she stated that she "was a true, humble and obedient wife". She told Henry, "by me you have had divers children, although it has pleased God to call them out of this world, which has been no default in me". She swore when she married him that "she was a true maid without touch of man".

After her speech, Catherine got up, curtseyed to her husband and walked out of the court, ignoring those who tried to make her return to her seat and saying, "On, on, it makes no matter, for it is no impartial court for me, therefore I will not tarry. Go on."[8] Although the case went on without her, no final decision was made and the court was adjourned, never meeting again. On 16 July, the Pope ordered that the matter should be transferred back to Rome for determination. As the Pope was still the prisoner of Charles V, a resolution in Henry's favour was no closer than it had been two years previously.

Both Thomas and George Boleyn were present at the hearing at which Queen Catherine made a mockery of their pretensions. They would both have been humiliated by the result, as well as by Catherine's performance. She was a worthy match for Anne, and this alone would have antagonised George and his sister. In years to come, the pair displayed a noted dislike and mistrust of Princess Mary, who had inherited her mother's courage, intelligence, defiance and religious fervour.

Wolsey had staked everything on obtaining a papal dissolution of Henry's marriage and had been unable to comply.

He alone was blamed for the failure, and for the fiasco of the court hearing. He was hated and resented by his opposing factions for his wealth, power and, more particularly, his influence over the King. The Boleyn family's supporters exploited his failure to do the King's bidding, and both they and Catherine supporters worked together to destroy him. The Boleyns in particular began to put enormous pressure on Wolsey. Initially, Henry was still prepared to give his chancellor the benefit of the doubt, but in August the French ended their pressure to get Charles V removed from Italy, which would have resulted in the release of the Pope from imperial control. Although Wolsey continued to petition the King of France to provide more support, he failed. Any faith and trust Henry previously had in him dissolved. This was assisted and encouraged by Wolsey's opponents, who vilified him at every available opportunity. In truth, Wolsey, as Henry's servant, did everything he could to bring about his master's divorce, but he was in an impossible situation; "his role as *legate a latere* made it impossible for him to pursue to its logical conclusion the King's thesis in the matter of his divorce or to coerce the Pope or the English clergy to decide the suit in Henry's favour."[9] Wolsey was not foolish enough to be deliberately obstructive, whatever his personal feelings may have been, but, he could not perform miracles and he did appear to have been stalling. On 9 October 1529, a writ of praemunire was filed against Wolsey in the court of King's Bench, on 17 October he relinquished the Privy Seal, and on 22 October 1529 he was formally dismissed as Chancellor.

The possibility of Wolsey worming his way back into favour remained a threat, particularly should he be allowed any direct access to the King. Wolsey's two opposing factions presented Henry with a schedule of 44 charges against him, including, amongst a wide variety of alleged offences, acting on the alien authority of the Pope. The articles against Wolsey were dated 1 December, and were signed by all the leading courtiers including Thomas More, but excluding George Boleyn who was on embassy in France at the time.[10] Until the end of 1529, Thomas Boleyn and Anne exerted the most pressure, Thomas due to his political experience and acumen, and Anne through her influence over the King. George Boleyn was still a very young man of around 25, with no political power or experience, and his active involvement in policy and diplomacy did not begin until the end of that year. Despite this, as a leading member of the Boleyn faction at court, he provided a supportive role, and helped popularise his sister's cause with the younger members of Henry's court. Bearing in mind his religious convictions, George had more reason than most for seeking Wolsey's downfall. Although the draft charges did not bring about Wolsey's ultimate destruction, in April the following year Henry sent Wolsey to York as Archbishop. It was in reality a move by Henry to get Wolsey as far away from London as possible.

Wolsey had never personally supported the annulment of the King's marriage, and while in York he began communicating with Catherine and the Pope directly. When Henry discovered this in November 1530, Wolsey was arrested and charged with treason. He was ordered to be brought to London, where no doubt he would have faced trial and probable execution. However, he was already suffering from ill heath and never made it to London, dying on 29 November 1530 at Leicester Abbey while en route to the Tower. Once Wolsey's enemies had accomplished his fall, and there was no longer a need for unity, the two remaining factions once again divided into separate groups. Sir Thomas More, who as far as the Boleyns were concerned was hardly the ideal replacement, took over from Wolsey as Chancellor and Henry's right-hand man. More had previously assisted Wolsey in his efforts to stop Lutheran books being smuggled into England. Also emerging from the ashes was Thomas Cromwell, Wolsey's former employee.

Throughout this period of political upheaval, George Boleyn continued to work his way up the court hierarchy. Despite 1529 being a traumatic year on the political front, it was to be a rewarding year for the young Boleyn, and one which kick-started his diplomatic and political career. On 15 November 1528, George secured the position of keeper of the Palace of Beaulieu in Essex. The grant also provided the power of leasing for his lifetime. On 1 February 1529, he was appointed chief steward of Beaulieu, receiving £10 a year as steward and 3 pence a day as keeper of the New Park.[11] On 27 July 1529, he was also appointed governor of Bethlehem Hospital.[12] The hospital had been opened in 1247 as the Priory of St Mary of Bethlehem, and became a royal hospital in 1375. By 1377 it was catering for mentally-ill patients and had become known as "Bedlam".[13] The position of Governor was a valuable sinecure, requiring little work but providing much status. George remained governor of Bedlam until his death, after which the appointment went to Peter Mewys.

In October 1529, George was knighted. The exact date is unknown, but in September of that year he was still being referred to as George Boleyn, while by the end of October official papers were referring to him as "Sir". On 8 December, he took his father's title of Viscount Rochford upon his father being made Earl of Wiltshire. This was initially a courtesy title, but ceased to be so in 1533 when he was called to Parliament as a peer in his own right. Henceforth, George and Jane Boleyn became Lord and Lady Rochford, a title Jane retained following her husband's death. That same year, George was appointed as a Gentleman of the Privy Chamber[14] and in around 1530 became a member of the Privy Council, which was the court's central advisory and policy-making body, very different from the Privy Chamber. As a member of the Privy Council, George had direct influence over policy, although he was still extremely young. His advancement propelled him past older and more experienced courtiers, who understandably resented the young Boleyn upstart in the same way as they resented his sister. What made the jealousy worse was that neither brother nor sister was known for their humility. Despite their intelligence, neither of them had the sense to hide their pride and joy at their newfound power, and already-raised hackles crept even higher.

Prior to his ultimate destruction, Wolsey had attempted

to bribe George and other members of Anne Boleyn's circle of favourites. This was clearly at the suggestion of Thomas Cromwell, as can be seen from the contents of a letter written by Wolsey to Cromwell in December 1529: "All possible means must be used for attaining her [Anne's] favour... I commit me to your wise handling."[15] That same month, Cromwell made out the draft of a grant to George Boleyn, bestowing on him an annuity from Wolsey's estates of £200 out of the lands of the bishopric of Winchester, and of 200 marks (£133) out of the abbey lands of St Albans.[16] This was a transparent attempt to save Wolsey from total destruction by bribing Anne's brother and other favourites, including Sir Henry Norris, whose fee was increased from £100 to £200 in January 1530. Despite the ploy failing due to its inadequacy and belatedness, these grants to George transformed his financial position from that of a lowly courtier to that of a lord. The grant to George was made during his first foreign embassy, and would have been received while he was in France.[17] Cromwell knew that these bribes to Anne's favourites would do nothing to help Wolsey. The recipients were made fully aware that the grants were being awarded to them on Cromwell's advice, ensuring that they were indebted to Cromwell and not to Wolsey. Up until his downfall, George Boleyn had more reason than most to be grateful to the man who would do the most to destroy him. At the time of their own downfall, it is unlikely that either Anne or George would have missed the irony of Wolsey's fall; by 1536, it was they who were hated for their wealth, power and influence over the king.

Upon Wolsey's downfall, his palace at York Place fell into royal hands, with Wolsey handing it to Henry, along with Hampton Court Palace, in an effort to save himself. In addition to the rented house at Greenwich, and also the rooms he occupied at Greenwich Palace which enabled him to be on call to the King at short notice, George was now granted opulent rooms for his personal use at York Place. Financially, there is no doubt that George Boleyn benefited more than any other courtier from

Wolsey's disgrace.

In September 1529, about a month prior to Wolsey's downfall, Eustace Chapuys became imperial ambassador to England in place of Don Inigo de Mendoza. Chapuys was born in the Duchy of Savoy somewhere between 1489 and 1492, was educated at the University of Turin, and became a doctor of civil and canon laws. He remained in England until 1545, when he was forced to retire due to ill health. With his legal background, Chapuys was the ideal person to advise and defend Catherine of Aragon during the annulment proceedings, and he continued to be a close ally to the Princess Mary after her mother's death. As envoy to Catherine's nephew, Charles V of Spain, and as a staunch Catholic, Chapuys was one of the Boleyns' bitterest enemies. It is, however, from Chapuys' dispatches that a vast amount of information regarding this period is drawn. It must always be borne in mind that Chapuys is biased and that all his dispatches were designed to show Anne and those who supported her in an unfavourable light. As George Boleyn was so closely affiliated to his sister and so diligent to her cause, he also came in for mild criticism from Chapuys. His letters often refer to meeting George, who he disparagingly refers to as "the lady's brother", when attending court. Shortly after his arrival in England, a dispatch of Chapuys to the Emperor dated 25 October indicated that he had met "a civil gentleman, named Bollen [Boleyn] sent by the king to conduct me to the Palace". This would have been just before George went on his first foreign embassy, and the likelihood is that he is the "Bollen" referred to.[18] Later, in February 1530, Chapuys would again describe a meeting with George, referring to him as "exceedingly courteous".[19] At least in the early days, it appears that Chapuys actually liked George.

It was in 1529 that Catherine of Aragon needed the help of a man like Chapuys, as matters relating to the annulment began to move on, albeit slowly. Henry summoned his Reformation Parliament, in which Thomas Cromwell, Wolsey's previous employee, took a significant role.

11 The Reformation Parliament (1529-36)

In the aftermath of Cardinal Wolsey's fall, Henry VIII sought to assume direct control of the government, aided by a combination of advisers, including the Boleyns. With so many different voices advising him, Henry became indecisive, which resulted in a stalemate. Into this confusion stepped Thomas Cromwell. He appeared to be as evangelical as the Boleyns, as well as being intelligent, articulate and astute, and he had the loyalty of Wolsey's previous followers.

Thomas Cromwell was born in 1485 in Putney, London, and began working for Wolsey in August 1514. After studying law, he became a Member of Parliament in 1523. Cromwell assumed control of the group that had supported Wolsey, and with the help of the Boleyns, he was appointed royal councillor in late 1530. He would become Henry's chief minister in 1532 upon the resignation of Thomas More. It was to be Cromwell and Reformer Thomas Cranmer, who was lodging at Durham House in the household of

Thomas Boleyn, who would do the most to push forward Henry's annulment, legalise his marriage to Anne Boleyn, and make the break with Rome. It would also be Cromwell who would do the most to destroy the King's marriage to Anne, with the reluctant help of Cranmer, a little over three years later.

When the Pope refused to help Henry VIII with his quest for an annulment, the King and his advisers turned to Parliament and Convocation. The "Reformation Parliament" is the name given to the Parliament which sat from October 1529 to April 1536. One historian has gone as far as describing this Parliament as "the most important Parliament in English history".[1] It certainly changed English history, passing the main pieces of legislation which led to the English Reformation and which also made Parliament "omnicompetent", establishing that "no area involved in the government of the realm was outside its authority".[2] It also passed legislation concerning economic, social, legal and administrative reform.

The Reformation Parliament was established on the theory that England was governed by one supreme head, namely the King, and that all jurisdiction in the land, including that of spiritual matters, belonged to the King. It naturally followed that no foreign power could dictate English public policy – specifically, the Pope. It established that only law enacted by a monarch within a sovereign state was binding; hence, this sovereign power was supreme and gave the King and Parliament authority over church law. By putting Thomas Cranmer's original ideas into effect, Cromwell gave Parliament legislative precedence over the Church of Rome. Previously, Parliament was merely an advisory assembly dependent on the Crown for existence; now, by giving Henry absolute power in England, Parliament was transformed into an established institution with the power to legislate. This actually had a side effect that was not anticipated by Henry, and possibly not Cromwell either: when Henry succeeded in achieving the statutory authority of Parliament over the church, he also acknowledged Parliament's authority over the Crown. Henry would no doubt be furious to learn that today's constitutional monarchy, in which the Crown has no real statutory power, was unwittingly initiated by him. As one of the most tyrannical and domineering monarchs in English history, a man who revelled in his power, this seems particularly ironic.

The beginnings of the Reformation are woven throughout the history of the early 1530s, but for ease of reference, the purposes and achievements of the Reformation Parliament have been consolidated into this chapter, with particular emphasis on the legislation passed while George Boleyn was in attendance. Everything of consequence which happened from late 1529 to 1536 must be considered in light of the decisions made by the Reformation Parliament, and the statutes enacted as a consequence of those decisions.

In the summer of 1530, the King had planned to demand large sums of money from the English clergy for supposedly conspiring in Wolsey's alleged offences. By January 1531, he had already begun a number of exemplary prosecutions. Henry was offered a £100,000 bribe by the clergy in return for a pardon for any complicity. Although the pardon was initially for complicity in Wolsey's offences, the King later offered a pardon for the church's general exercise of "illegal" spiritual jurisdiction. On 7 February 1531, the King became more specific, demanding that the church immediately recognise him as "sole protector and supreme head of the English church and clergy". There could be no doubt that it was the Boleyn faction that advised the King in this matter, as demonstrated by the prominent part played by George Boleyn. Although George, now Lord Rochford, was not officially called to Parliament until 5 February 1533,[3] he maintained a prominent role in the Reformation from 1530 until his death.

Henry wanted his title of supreme head of the Church of England recognised without qualification, and it was George Boleyn, who he sent to persuade Convocation of the scriptural case for supremacy. The Convocations of Canterbury and York were the English church's legislative body which, like Parliament, was made up of two houses: the upper house of bishops and the lower house of general clergy. The Convocation of Canterbury ran at the same time as Parliament, and the King's articles were introduced to them on 7 February 1531, following which Convocation met on five consecutive days between 7 and 11 February. George Boleyn, by now a member of the Privy Council, was chosen by Henry to express his growing anti-papal sentiments and Parliament's arguments in favour of supremacy. He was sent to Convocation on the afternoon of Friday 10 February and delivered various tracts, one of which still survives today.[4] George announced to the legislative body that the King's "supreme auctorite grounded on God's word ought in no case to be restrayned by any frustrate decrees of popish lawes or voyed prescriptes of humanr traditions, but that he maye both order and minister, yea and also execute the office of spiritual administration in the church whereof he ys head".[5] Convocation did not want to deal with this 26 year-old envoy, they wanted to deal directly with the King but when they sent members of the lower house to see the King, they were turned away and instructed to deal with George. Henry, ever the coward, was happy to use the inexperienced young man as a buffer between himself and Convocation, and this was no doubt to the extreme satisfaction of the Boleyns. The position in which Henry was happy to put George can have done nothing to temper the young man's pride, and it is hard to imagine that Thomas Boleyn was unmoved by his son's extraordinary prominence at such tender years.

Convocation initially baulked at the idea of recognising Henry as head of the church, and eventually a suggestion was made, by one of Cromwell, Thomas Audley or even George Boleyn himself, to qualify the demand with the words "as far as the law of Christ allows". The following day, upon hearing the King's agreement to the limitation clause, the clergy agreed the amended wording, thereby accepting royal demands to recognise Henry as "Head of the Church of England, as far as the law of Christ allows". Although this was a victory for the Boleyns and their supporters, verbal acceptance by the clergy and actual compliance were two different matters, and any act of Convocation had to be agreed on by Parliament to be enforced.

By the end of May 1531, Henry warned the Pope that a continued insistence on him being summoned to a hearing in Rome would mean the destruction of papal authority in England. His threats had no effect on the Pope, who merely warned Henry that the case could no longer be delayed. Henry's fury at the Pope's unsympathetic stance was the catalyst for the final rupture between himself and Catherine in July of that year. Catherine's daughter had previously been taken from her as punishment for refusing to concede to the King's desire for the annulment, and now Catherine too was sent from court. Henry did not bid farewell to his wife of 23 years and never saw her again. His hardened resolve towards his wife and the Pope was to the enormous satisfaction of the Boleyns, who could eventually see an end in sight; however, it would be another 18 months before a marriage took place.

It was not until March 1532 that action was taken in Parliament to enforce Convocation's 1531 agreement to acknowledge Henry as head of the Church of England. On 18 March a petition entitled "Supplication against the Ordinaries" was presented to Henry. Its aim was the destruction of the clergy's independent legislative powers by alleging misuse of their spiritual jurisdiction. A party of leading courtiers - Norfolk, Exeter, Oxford, Sandys and Thomas and George Boleyn – was sent to the bishops and abbots. The clergy were well aware of the Boleyns' influence. The delegation of courtiers demanded submission of the clergy without any limitation or reservation. With the impending threat to strip the church of its powers, Convocation had no choice but to surrender. In a document entitled "The Submission of the Clergy", officially ratified on 16 May, Convocation recognised the King instead of the Pope as supreme lawmaker of the church.[6] Therefore, by 1532, Parliament was the only valid legislative body in England. This was a great triumph for the Boleyn faction and an important step towards the eventual break with Rome.

The submission of the clergy was given as the reason for Thomas More's resignation as Chancellor in 1532. It had been More who replaced Wolsey in October 1529, but his faith would not permit him to accept Henry as head of the church over the Pope. Following his resignation, Cromwell steered Parliament to more decisive action with regards to the annulment.

Despite his active involvement in the Reformation, George, Lord Rochford, was not summoned to Parliament until February 1533 at the age of 28. From then on, his attendance was highly impressive. For years he had helped popularise his sister's cause within the Privy Chamber, and upon his admission to Parliament he did the same with the younger peers, who were naturally more inclined to the idea of change. 1533 was an important year in Parliament. On 14 March 1533, the "Appeals Bill", prohibiting appeals to Rome on legal or other matters, was presented. The bill came before Convocation in April 1533, presided over by Thomas Cranmer, the newly appointed Archbishop of Canterbury. The bill was passed and the resulting act was entitled the Act Concerning Ecclesiastical Appointments and Absolute Restraint of Annates. It was this act that began the process of the transfer of authority from Rome to the King. At the time this act was passed, Henry's case for an annulment was still pending in Rome. Its passage meant that Parliament was sanctioned to seek a decision in England, and under pressure from the Crown, Convocation agreed that Henry's marriage to Catherine was invalid. Only a trial was needed to enforce this decision, and Cranmer presided over a special trial of the annulment proceedings at Dunstable Priory, Bedfordshire. On 23 May 1533, this court rubber-stamped Convocation's opinion, declaring the annulment of Henry's marriage to Catherine,[7] and on 28 May 1533 Cranmer confirmed the legality of Henry's marriage to Anne, which had taken place secretly on 25 January 1533. Henry VIII's "Great Matter", his quest for an annulment, had been settled in England, not Rome, and was sanctioned by Parliament.

In 1534, during the fifth session of Parliament, George's attendance rate was prodigious, particularly bearing in mind the fact that he was on a diplomatic mission abroad for a total of two months, and was also Lord Warden of the Cinque Ports from June onwards. Despite these other onerous duties, he attended more sessions in Parliament than many other Lords Temporal. Out of the Lords Temporal attending Parliament, only the Earl of Arundel, the Earl of Oxford and the Earl of Wiltshire, George's father, attended more frequently than George: on 45, 44 and 42 occasions respectively, with George appearing 41 times. The average attendance was just 22 out of 46.[8] George's high attendance demonstrates his commitment to his own career, as well as to Reform and to his sister's cause. His work rate from 1533 onwards, particularly from April 1534, was impressive. Never was there a year when attendance in Parliament had been more important, since it was in 1534 that the Acts of Succession and Supremacy were finally passed, as well as the Act Concerning Peter's Pence and Dispensations, which outlawed payments to Rome and gave the Archbishop of Canterbury the authority to grant dispensations. All Members of Parliament sitting at that time could safely say the decisions they made during that year changed the course of history.

The Act of Succession was passed in March 1534, and vested succession in the heirs of Henry VIII and Anne Boleyn. It required subjects to swear an oath, the Oath of Succession, renouncing any foreign authority and recognising Anne Boleyn as Henry VIII's wife, and their children as legitimate heirs to the succession. Refusal to take the oath was deemed treason in an updated Treasons Act. The Act of Supremacy was passed in November 1534 and came into force in February 1535, establishing the King's ecclesiastical authority. The Act of Supremacy declared, "Albeit the Kynges Majestie justely and rightfully is & oweth to be supreme hede of the Churche of England and so is recognysed by the Clergy of the Realme in their convocacions."[9] This was the final break with Rome. It was no longer the church "in" England; it was now the Church "of" England. Parliament removed the authority of the Catholic church in England and replaced it with domestic authority, with Henry VIII as supreme head. Parliament, influenced by Cromwell and the rest of the Boleyn faction, in particular Thomas Cranmer, and Thomas, George and Anne Boleyn, had used domestic statute to supersede the law of the church.

The Reformation Parliament did not meet during 1535, but was recalled in February 1536. There was rebellion and dissatisfaction among certain peers, such as Lords Darcy and Hussey, following the executions of Thomas More and Bishop John Fisher the previous year. In 1536 steps were taken to make Parliament co-operate by forcing attendance of all members. Those members who did not attend had to appoint a proxy. Previously, in January 1534, the proxy vote for Lord LaWarr, an adherent to the old religion, was held by George Boleyn. This had probably been arranged by Cromwell, who is recorded as witnessing the document.[10] [11] As George had completely opposite views to LaWarr, he no doubt used the vote in total opposition to LaWarr's wishes. In 1536, less than three months before George's arrest, George once again held LaWarr's proxy vote; LaWarr had submitted a blank proxy, saying he "had a wyndoe for to put in whom yt shall please the kynges highnes to apoynt".[12] The proud and ambitious Lord Rochford was undoubtedly delighted, but unfortunately for the Boleyns, a number of those peers who were either excused attendance at Parliament, or who simply did not turn up, later sat on the trials of Anne Boleyn and her brother; these men included Lord LaWarr. After George's death, LaWarr's proxy remained with Cromwell. This final session of Parliament saw the passing of the Act extinguishing the Authority of the Bishop of Rome, which made those giving any authority to the Pope (now known as the Bishop of Rome) liable to prosecution, and the Act for the Dissolution the Lesser Monasteries, which began the process now known as the Dissolution of the Monasteries. This Parliament was dismissed on 14 April 1536,

Good Friday, just under three weeks before George was arrested.

12 The League
of Schmalkalden

Running alongside the Reformation Parliament, and influential in England's Reformation itself, was the attempted alliance with Germany through the League of Schmalkalden.

The Schmalkaldic League was a movement formally established in Germany on 27 February 1531 by the country's most powerful Protestant leaders: Philip I, Landgrave of Hesse, and John Frederick I, Elector of Saxony. The League was created thanks to a treaty that established a defensive military alliance of Protestant princes against Charles V, the Holy Roman Emperor, who held the political power in Germany at this time. This alliance of Lutheran princes aimed to break with the Roman Catholic Church, and for the League to replace the Holy Roman Empire. The movement helped spread Lutheranism throughout northern Germany, and had a substantial influence on the English Reformation.

In the wake of England's break with Rome, Henry actively

pursued diplomatic contacts with the League, but following the downfall of the Boleyns, it was to end in failure. Henry VIII's evangelical advisers obviously steered him toward political contact with the League to advance their own religious interests. The generally accepted historical view is that Henry had no real religious interest in forming an alliance with the League, and that his motives were only to approach the Germans in time of necessity (for example, when Charles V and Francis I of France were making an alliance). However, this view of Henry is challenged by Rory McEntegart who proposes that Henry had a genuine interest in allying England with the League, and that there is no evidence to suggest he retreated from them as soon as foreign external situations improved. Like the members of the League, Henry had become disillusioned with the Pope and the Holy Roman Empire, so his interest was piqued by these men who were defying those religious and political powers, and defending their beliefs.[1] McEntegart also points out that although Thomas Cromwell was guiding policy at this time, "he was certainly not making it", and the King's thoughts and approval were always sought.[2] Whatever Henry's motivations may have been, it is clear that as his disillusionment with the Pope and the Emperor increased, so his attitude to the Protestant movement and the Germans who had previously challenged the Pope's supremacy became more and more favourable.

As for the Germans, their own inclination towards an alliance with their old enemy was greatly assisted by the presence and influence of the Boleyns and their supporters. The Boleyns were known evangelicals, and their closeness to the throne encouraged a positive view of the chances of a successful alliance. As early as its inauguration in February 1531, the League considered approaches to Henry VIII and Francis I with a view to forming an alliance in the event of an imperial attack. This resulted in letters being sent to England and France to test the water. Although in August Henry sent an ambassador, William Paget, to Germany to discuss the possibility of English support, this was a diplomatic embassy rather than a religious one, and it involved both Catholic and Protestant Germany. It was not until the dramatic domestic changes of 1533-5 that a more direct approach was made to the German Princes. In July 1533, six months after Henry had married Anne, and while George was in France on embassy, it was decided that ambassadors would be sent to Germany. Although these tentative initial overtures failed, with Cromwell at the helm England began steering towards the development of a diplomatic policy in Germany.

Throughout 1533 and 1534, George Boleyn's active involvement in the negotiations with the League was nominal. He was dispatched on four French embassies during those two years, and it was as ambassador to France that his particular talents were mainly employed. However, his active involvement in the Reformation Parliament brought him into contact with the concept of the German alliance, which was being pursued by Cromwell, at that point the Boleyns' greatest asset and champion. George's own evangelical stance meant that he could obviously see the merit in an approach to the Lutheran princes, and his involvement in the negotiations of the following year confirms his personal commitment.

By late 1533, embassies to Germany were being limited to discussions with those Germans opposed to the Catholic church. This was a fundamental policy shift from earlier in the year. The Germans were now being asked for their advice on how best to reduce the Pope's powers, and were also being asked to support the King's annulment. In May 1534 the English ambassadors stated that their embassy had:

> Unknown to the king, been promoted by some of the realm's distinguished councillors and people... who favour the gospel and have requested such an embassy will have greater cause to prompt the king, so that through this means, which the Almighty in his grace has now miraculously set

forth, the gospel might be brought into England,
and from a persecutor will be made a lover of the
word of God.[3]

If correct, this meant that a group of leading English
politicians had not only promoted the embassy to Germany, but
had also provided the ambassadors with secret instructions to
request that a German embassy be sent to England to lend weight
to the Reformist cause there. Indeed, the secret instructions went
further:

If it does not immediately achieve anything useful
with the king, it may still assist the advancement
of God's glory in the land and among the king's
people, particularly those who are around him;
and through this the king will be made aware of
our doctrine and belief.[4]

In other words, if the requested German embassy could not
convince the King, then it may at least have more effect on those
around him, who could then be manipulated into encouraging the
King towards their newfound evangelism.

As to the identity of these "leading politicians", McEntegart
gives full credit to Thomas Cromwell, who had been the
dominant influence in promoting the embassy in the first place.
What of the others? As one of the most outspoken evangelicals,
it is difficult to imagine that George Boleyn was not amongst
them. This is even more persuasive considering his scaffold speech,
in which he specifically stated that he "took upon [himself] great
labour to urge the king to permit the printing of the Scriptures
to go unimpeded among the commons of the realm in their own
language", and went further by saying, "I was one of those who did
most to procure the matter to place the Word of God among the
people because of the love and affection which I bear for the gospel
and the truth in Christ's words".[5] These words virtually mirrored
the ambassadors' secret instructions.

The Boleyns and other evangelicals at the English court saw the potential alliance with the Germans from a religious, as well as a political, stance, but there is controversy over Thomas Cromwell's motives. Some historians see Cromwell as a "man of conventional piety"[6] and a pragmatist who used the new evangelical beliefs for political means. However, his biographer John Schofield believes that Cromwell's religious views began to change in 1530, and that by 1533 there was "no doubt about Cromwell's Lutheran faith". Cromwell had links with known Reformers who were punished for reading heretical works; he asked Stephen Vaughan, who was on the continent at Henry VIII's bidding, to bring back works by Luther and Tyndale; he had Christopher Mont (one of Henry VIII's ambassadors) working in his house translating German works for him; and he was known for holding theological discussions at his home.[7] However, whatever his personal faith, while Anne Boleyn remained in favour it was in his best interests to share her family's religious persuasions, and by breaking with Rome he gave Henry what he wanted – namely, supreme power in his own land.

Although the 1534 embassy to Germany eventually failed, and the German offer to promote the gospel in England came to nothing, the English evangelicals had announced their presence to their German religious allies. They had also confirmed their wish for closer relations with the League, something that was further pursued the following year when George Boleyn took on a more high profile role in proceedings.

Philip Melanchthon was a German professor and theologian. He was also a friend of Martin Luther, and a leader of the Lutheran Reformation. It was Melanchthon who was given the thankless task of presenting to Charles V a statement setting out the Protestant doctrine, a statement with which Charles was singularly unimpressed. In early 1535, Francis I invited Melanchthon to France to discuss ways of reconciling the Roman and Protestant churches. News of this invitation reached England, causing Henry to fear an alliance between

France and Germany. To prevent this, an embassy was suggested
to intercept Melanchthon and divert him to England.[8] There
was some suggestion that George Boleyn would be one of those
sent to Germany. A remembrance of Thomas Cromwell written
some time in March states, "What shall be determined touching
my Lord of Rochford's going".[9] Although George did not go to
Germany, his active involvement in the proceedings is confirmed
by a letter dated 19 July 1535 written jointly by George and his
uncle, the Duke of Norfolk, to Cromwell. George and Norfolk
were with the court at Windsor for the start of the summer
progress. 11 days earlier, Henry had authorised Robert Barnes to
travel to Germany and arrange for Melanchthon to visit England.

Final arrangements for the embassy were discussed between
Henry and his councillors in the absence of Cromwell, who had
been called away to London. The plans were conveyed to him
in the letter from George and Norfolk. Although a joint letter,
it is deeply evangelical in tone, and the turn of phrase is most
definitely that of George Boleyn. The letter advised Cromwell
that two embassies were to be sent, one led by Robert Barnes
and Dereck Holt, and one led by Christopher Mont and Simon
Heynes. Barnes and Holt were to travel to Germany to meet with
Melanchthon and dissuade him from going to France because,
"the French King doth persecute those that will not grant unto
the Bishop of Rome's usurped power and jurisdiction... saying
unto him how much it should be to his shame and reproach to
vary and go now from that true opinion wherein he hath so long
continued". They were also to encourage Melanchthon to travel
to England instead due to "the conformity of his opinion and
doctrine here", and if that didn't convince him, "with the good
entertainment which undoubtedly he shall have here at his Graces
hands".

Heynes and Mont were to travel to John Wallop, Henry VIII's
ambassador in France, "in as secret a manner as they can, and
coming like his friends to visit him and not as sent by the king". If
Melanchthon had already arrived in France they were to dissuade

him, "of his continuance there", and to lure him to England. Finally the letter warns that the ambassadors are to be diligent, saying, "And to make an end, his Grace would in no wise that Barnes and Heynes shall tarry for any further instruction of the Bishop of Canterbury or any other". The letter finishes, "And thus fare you well, from Langley, in much haste". It is the phraseology alone which holds this letter out as George Boleyn's, even setting aside the evangelical tone. Norfolk remained an orthodox Catholic throughout his life, and though putting his signature to the letter, he obviously left the contents to his nephew.[10]

In the end, Melanchthon travelled to neither England nor France. The following year the fall of the Boleyns caused an outcry in Germany.[11] The German Protestants were fully aware that Anne and her brother were supporters of Reform, deducing that their downfall was due to anti-Protestantism and that they had been punished for heresy. Philip Melanchthon wrote to the Strassburg council on 19 June:

> [Since] the king has executed his second wife, who it is said was well inclined to the gospel....that before we send an embassy we take cause to send a man there, to ascertain whether the king is still of the same opinion and supports the gospel.[12]

This is not to say that further attempts were not made. There continued to be negotiations between England and Germany for a number of years, which ended with the farcical marriage between Henry and Anne of Cleves in January 1540. Despite Cromwell's best efforts, there never was an alliance between Germany and England, and his attempts to form one eventually resulted in his own downfall and execution in July 1540.

At the end of 1529, though, the consequences of the Reformation Parliament, and the attempted alliance with Germany, were very much in the future. In the meantime, negotiations with France and Rome continued. As well as his involvement in the Reformation Parliament, George Boleyn played an active diplomatic role in France, undertaking six diplomatic missions there between October 1529 and June 1535.

13 The King's Great Matter

Following the alliance of Cromwell with the Boleyns in late 1529, Henry VIII's annulment was pursued with commitment and single-mindedness. However, the Boleyns were now taking a more active role in proceedings.

In October 1529, George Boleyn became ambassador to France and shortly afterwards was sent on the first of his six diplomatic missions abroad. There can be little doubt that George's appointment was helped by the influence of his sister and the reputation of his father. Why else entrust such an important mission to a young man who was a complete novice in the art of diplomacy? Yet even with Anne's support, he would have been highly unlikely to have been given such an eminent position at such a young age unless he had demonstrated a capacity for fulfilling the role. He was Henry's representative abroad, and even for a future brother-in-law Henry would not have risked being potentially humiliated by an incompetent envoy. Jean du Bellay, the French ambassador who would become Bishop of Paris in 1532, had no illusions as to George's importance, despite his tender years. He warned the ambassadors in Paris to flatter Boleyn pretensions, saying that he should be given a good welcome and more honour than was ordinarily necessary: "Those who send him wish him to be received with more than ordinary honor. Penisson, whom you know, is sent to keep him company, and to 'servyr d'addresse;' but I warn you that the reception given to him will be well weighed."[1][2] The fact that George was to be shown more than ordinary honour was a mark of favouritism that no doubt owed more to his doting sister and father, a man the ambassadors in Paris knew well, than to the King.

Henry's trust in George as ambassador was tempered by his decision to send him to France with an assistant, Dr John Stokesley, the Dean of the Chapel Royal. Although George was notionally heading the mission, the truth of the matter was that his second-in-command Stokesley, a man in his fifties who has been described as an "expert canon lawyer",[3] would in reality be the envoy making the decisions, and would effectively serve as George's mentor. Despite George's grand title, he was actually being sent to France to gain experience, and to learn from Stokesley and the other experienced diplomats. This was to be a steep learning curve for the 25 year-old, but one that he grasped with both hands. George was no fool, and he must have realised why a man as young as himself had been given such an opportunity. As a proud young man he would have been determined not to fail, and to prove his capabilities in his own right rather than as the lucky brother of the King's new love. There was also an added financial incentive. As ambassador, George received an income of £2 per day, which was a huge salary for a young courtier previously on an income of £100 per year. This income is stated in the state papers to be paid "in prest and advancement of his diets at 40s. a day, for four months, 240l." George's high favour is shown in the fact that George received 40 shillings a day for food, whereas Stokesley only received "26s. 8d. a day, 160l."[4] As a man of intelligence, George would have quickly realised that diplomatic missions abroad were highly lucrative, as well as prestigious.

The principal object of George's first foreign embassy was to persuade the universities of France to find in favour of Henry's divorce from Catherine. The instructions were issued to George at the start of October, prior to him being knighted and ahead of him becoming Viscount Rochford. The instructions specifically refer to him as George Boleyn and do not contain the prefix "Sir", but they do confirm that he had at last been reappointed to the Privy Chamber:

> Instruccions geven by the Kinges Highnes to his trusty and right welbeloved Counsaillours George Boleyn, oon of the Gentlemen of the Kinges Privey Chamber, and Mr John Stokesley, Doctour of Dyvynite, whom His Grace nowe sendeth on Ambassiate to his derest brother cousin and perpetuel alye the Frenche King...[5]

The party of ambassadors eventually left England towards the end of October. While in France, George received his father's title of Viscount Rochford on 8 December, the same date upon which his father became Earl of Wiltshire. When George first arrived in France, he and Stokesley were instructed to have an initial interview with the resident ambassador, Francis Bryan, who George was to replace for a season to enable Bryan to return to England. Quite what the highly experienced and older Bryan thought of being replaced by a 25 year-old is unknown. George was then to attempt to convince King Francis I to support the mission. George and Stokesley took a large train of courtiers with them to France in order to present well to the French court, and to reiterate to Francis the importance of the mission. When the English envoys met face to face with the King, they received a favourable reception, and he gave them his verbal support, insisting he would use all his efforts to assist Henry. Armed with the King of France's verbal support, George and Stokesley had no reason to believe that the academics would do anything other than capitulate and give the required opinions in favour of divorce. Du Bellay also believed that the academics would rule in their favour and that George and Stokesley would soon be able to head back to England with good news.[6] Unfortunately, the ambassadors were in for an unpleasant surprise. The opinions were entirely unfavourable, which meant more direct intervention from Francis was needed.

On 16 January 1530 Stokesley wrote to George's father, now the Earl of Wiltshire, regarding George travelling to see Francis I. Stokesley's letter refers to "the unlernyd Spanyard Doctour Petre Garray", a Spanish theologian who was in Paris speaking to the academics on Catherine of Aragon's behalf.[7] Despite the French King having verbally indicated his favour towards the divorce, the university theologians, headed by Noël Béda, trustee of the Paris Faculty of Theology, had thwarted his wishes and compiled a long list of signatures against the divorce. The bulk of Europe was under imperial control, and the University of Paris was hard to win over. In his letter to Wiltshire, Stokesley went on to say, "And one of our devises that my lord your son doth now solicite, is to have very effectual letters to him, as well from the French King as from the said Admiral his promoter." George had been sent to try and procure the direct intervention of the French King by means of a written missive. By then, the French court had left Paris and gone to Dijon, so George set off from Paris on 16 January to ride to Dijon accompanied by the train of courtiers who had been sent to France to accompany him. His aim was to persuade Francis to write to Pierre Lizet, the President of the Parliament of Paris, a man of great power and influence both in Paris and with the Sorbonne. Stokesley surmised in his letter to Wiltshire that the mission would fail, as Charles V was holding Francis's two eldest sons as hostages. He felt it was highly unlikely Francis would make any direct move, which would, in the circumstances, have the effect of antagonising Charles. George therefore had an uphill struggle in eliciting Francis's direct intervention. Yet the importance of obtaining his support was paramount to the success of the mission. In his letter to Wiltshire Stokesley continued:

> If my Lord [of Rochford] speak of our desires, we
> shall revoke their subscriptions [of the Doctors]
> and bring them to our hands, and set those simple
> Doctors again at their liberty, without brute or
> suspicion of any partiality on the French king's
> party; and, if the king and his counsel deny
> our requests, my Lord your son will spent him
> somewhat straightly.

In other words, George was to use every method at his disposal
to get Francis to provide direct support. And to the surprise
of all, that was exactly what Francis did. George succeeded
in obtaining from him a letter instructing President Lizet to
dissuade the theologians from disobeying him, and threatening
them with punishment if they did so. Francis's letter is written in
the strongest possible terms, saying he is much dissatisfied with
those who gave an opinion on the King of England's divorce,
and insisting that the fault must be corrected. He advises Lizet
that if there is an insistence on consulting the Pope, this must be
prevented, as it "would be against the rights and privileges of the
Kingdom."[8] Francis also promised George that if Beda continued
to oppose Henry VIII's annulment, he would be banished from
France.[9] Remarkably, George, an inexperienced diplomat, had
been successful in persuading the King of France to put his
full weight behind Henry's cause, irrespective of the fact that
Catherine of Aragon's nephew was holding Francis's sons hostage.
But there was a catch: presentation of the letter was to be deferred
until Francis's sons had been returned.

Francis I had married Louis XII's daughter, Claude of France,
in 1514. Salic law prevented Claude from acceding to the throne
of France on the death of her father in January 1515, but her
husband and cousin Francis, Duke of Angoulême, inherited the
throne, becoming Francis I of France. Francis was considered to
be the first Renaissance king of France. He was a poet, though not
of great talent, and he sought to bring culture to a war-obsessed

France. Although he was ten years older than George Boleyn, they shared the same love of hunting, sport and amusements of all kinds. Francis was witty, amiable and intelligent. These attributes together with his love of poetry and culture gave him much in common with the young English lord, while George's mission gave him easy access to Francis, who probably enjoyed the witty and charming Englishman's company. In addition to his more admirable attributes, Francis was also frivolous, selfish, unstable and inconsistent. These weaknesses of character made him an easy target for coercion.

Francis was initially favourable to the Protestant movement that swept through Europe following Martin Luther's denunciation of the corruption and self-indulgence of the Roman Catholic Church. This was partly due to the influence of his evangelical sister, Marguerite of Angoulême, whom Anne Boleyn had encountered during her time in France as a child and young adult. His favourable attitude to Reform made him a useful ally, and assisted George Boleyn in his negotiations. Francis's attitude changed in October 1534, however, following the Affair of the Placards, in which notices were put up on the streets of Paris and other major French cities denouncing papal mass. A notice had even been put on the King's bedroom door, and the violence of the Reformists pushed Francis into denouncing the Reformed faith. From then on, he viewed the movement with suspicion and as a plot against him, and thereafter persecuted followers, in direct opposition to the Boleyns and their religious convictions. His religious and political inconsistencies made him a fickle friend, and Henry VIII never completely trusted him.

Some of George Boleyn's success when dealing directly with Francis was down to the character and personality of the young man himself. As we have already seen, George Boleyn was a charmer, as well as having the presence of mind to play on Francis's weaknesses. In addition to this, the French court was well known for its entertainment and jollity, an environment well suited to the young Boleyn who loved the trappings of court society. It is far easier to negotiate successfully with somebody with whom you have a good relationship, and George used his charm and wit as much as his advocacy skills to win over the French King. As confirmation of George's intimacy with, and enjoyment of, the French court, he took his time in leaving Francis at Dijon, and did not arrive back in Paris until 5 February. On 27 January 1530, at Dijon, there is record of a payment of 2445 livres and 13 sous to goldsmith Pierre Mangot from Francis I's treasurer for a gold chain for George Boleyn. This lavish offering either served as a gift to a royal favourite or a sweetener to keep him happy.[10]

In January 1530, George's father Thomas Boleyn, Earl of Wiltshire, received instructions from the King to travel on embassy. His mission was to approach Emperor Charles V, who was about to meet Pope Clement VII for his imperial coronation. This mission was an attempt to win Charles over in the "Great Matter" of the King's quest for an annulment. It amounted to a comprehensive re-launch of his pursuit of an annulment and a last-ditch attempt to gain Charles's support. Wiltshire probably received Stokesley's letter of 16 January while en route to Italy. Wiltshire travelled to Italy with Thomas Cranmer, whose original plan it had been to try and obtain academic opinion abroad, and who had therefore instigated George's mission to France. Wiltshire and his party stopped in Paris where they visited the Sorbonne, which had the most prestigious faculty of theology in the world. George's journey to Francis to obtain a letter of support took place virtually simultaneously with his father's journey to Paris. George returned to Paris on 5 February and met up with his father the following day.

When Wiltshire eventually departed from Paris he took Stokesley with him. Wiltshire later had his own meeting with Francis on 19 February at Moulins,[11] in which he sought to persuade Francis to send the letter that George had encouraged the French King to write. He was unsuccessful. On 27 February, the Bishop of Tarbes, Francis's ambassador in Rome, wrote to Jean de Breton de Villandry, regarding "the matter of Mons. de

Boulan" and of the Emperor's greatest fear being that Francis would favour the English King. Francis held back at this point.[12] The letter was eventually presented in June 1530 (dated 17 June even though it was written some five months previously) and although it took five months between negotiations and action, George Boleyn's stubborn persistence paid off. Francis's letter was later used to great effect in reversing the decision of the universities. As for Wiltshire, he eventually departed from France, arriving in Bologna on 14 March, accompanied by Stokesley and Cranmer.

It was Thomas Cranmer, a man close to the Boleyns, who together with Cromwell assumed control of the matter of Henry's divorce following the fall of Cardinal Wolsey. Cranmer was a Reformer, having met the Lutheran scholar Andreas Osiander while in Europe. He became acquainted with the English ambassadors, Edward Fox and Stephen Gardiner, earlier in 1529, when he had first suggested to them that Henry VIII's problem was theological, and proposed that Europe's faculties of theology should be consulted. Henry had met Cranmer in October 1529, and that meeting resulted in George Boleyn and John Stokesley being sent to France later that month. Following the demise of Wolsey, it was Cranmer's radical idea to deny papal supremacy and to promote Henry as head of the Church of England. He wrote an account of his ideas while housed with the Boleyns at Durham Place, and placed these before Henry prior to travelling to Italy with Wiltshire. He enjoyed a close relationship with all three of the evangelical Boleyns, which was probably another reason why George Boleyn was specifically chosen as ambassador in October 1529 to put into practice Cranmer's idea of consulting the European theologians.

Cranmer appeared to have a genuine love for Anne Boleyn, which was extended to her brother. In October 1533, he wrote to George asking him to request that his uncle, the Duke of Norfolk, appoint a particular person as secretary to the Duke of Richmond, Henry VIII's illegitimate son. Cranmer asked this favour in return for appointing the gentleman's brother to his own service at the previous request of George. His letter makes clear that the approach to Norfolk would be more effective coming from George than from Cranmer directly, saying, "and that the rather at this my request ye do therein the more effectively, as your discreet wisdom in that behalf doth think best for his furtherance". Cranmer addresses his letter to "my very singular good Lord, my Lord of Rochford".[13] The familiarity between Cranmer and the Boleyns is obvious from the tone of the letter, as is the affection. Cranmer was a great asset to the Boleyn allies, and it was through their influence that he was appointed Archbishop of Canterbury in 1532 after the previous Archbishop William Warham died.

Cranmer's ideas were not entirely new to Henry. In mid-1529, Anne had shown him a pamphlet by William Tyndale entitled *The Obedience of the Christian Man and How Christian Rulers Ought to Govern*. The pamphlet stated, "The king is in the room of God and his law is God's law", and went on, "One king, one law is God's ordinance in every realm".[14] In other words, the King's law is God's law, and if the church ruled the Princes of Europe then this was an invasion of the divine order. This would of course have appealed to the vain and egotistical Henry, as it was essentially preaching the divine right of Kings. *The Obedience* gave a realistic alternative to Rome's judicial and administrative control. Link this with *The Supplication of Beggars*, which George Boleyn had requested his sister show to Henry, and the makings of the Reformation are clear: the combination of divine right with Lutheran principles, restoring the proper God-given status and power of the King, who would then reform the church and bring it back to the true Biblical purity. Implementation could prove somewhat more difficult. That, of course, is where Cromwell proved so effective, steering the Reformation from the end of 1529 until the Act of Supremacy in 1534.

As could have been predicted, Wiltshire and Cranmer were unsuccessful in winning Charles V over to Henry's cause. During his meeting with Charles, Wiltshire raised Cranmer's argument of the authority of scripture versus the authority of the Pope, but irrespective of Wiltshire's arguments Charles would not be moved, and decided that the affair should be determined by the ordinary course of action in Rome. Wiltshire had to go home embarrassed and empty-handed. Worse still, he was served with a citation for Henry to appear in Rome to have his cause tried there, as had been ordered by the Pope the previous July. The only concession Wiltshire could obtain was that the Pope would agree to a six-week delay.

Once his father and Stokesley had left him in Paris, George longed to return to England. He and his train had spent Christmas and New Year with the French court in Paris, which was well-known for its entertainment and frivolity, but there was a world of difference between being in Paris with the joys of the French court and to being alone in Paris with a group of middle-aged theologians. He was lonely and bored. He was also making no progress with the theologians because, as we have seen, presentation of Francis's letter to the Dean and Doctors of theology had been deferred until the release of Francis's sons. George's frustration was obvious. Towards the end of February he wrote a bitter letter to Dr William Bennett (who he addresses as "Mr Doctor"), an ambassador on embassy with George's father. First, he asks for news from Italy, "but I would hear the truth of everything as it is, without any manor covering"; then he goes on to complain that despite having obtained Francis's letter, he still could get no definitive answer from the French at that time: "I would I could send you some news from hence that should give you pleasure. I can know none anyway that I can work; they of this country say nothing, whether it be because they cannot, or else they will not, I cannot tell." George was also deeply disappointed that nobody at home was taking the trouble to write to him, and complained:

> I can send you no news from home; there is no
> good fellow will take the pain to write, they be so

merry as a good fellow said to me the other day. Our country folks have so many pastimes they have no leisure to write. I trust in short space to be at home to pass time as other of my friends do; whether I shall forget to write or no, I cannot tell. I pray you commend me to all folks there, to my Lord elect (Stokesley) specially to the bishop of Worcester (I was his guide from Notley to Oxford); to all other as you will and think best.

He signed it, "Your friend."[15]

Despite being homesick, George was able to joke that once returned and enjoying the English pastimes with his friends, he might have time to write to his fellow ambassadors, but then again he may not.

One of Anne Boleyn's earliest biographers, Paul Friedmann, who always chose to believe the worst of Anne and her brother, suggests that George was recalled to England due to him being totally unfit for the role of ambassador.[16] There is no evidence to support this assertion, however. As can be seen from George's expenses of 40 shillings a day (totalling £240), it was only ever intended that he be in France for four months. The facts do not support Friedmann's suggestion that George's attitude alienated Francis, and that his arrogant and foolish boasting detracted from his missions abroad. George was sent on six foreign embassies, and of those the majority were particularly tricky. Would Henry realistically have continued to send his brother-in-law on sensitive embassies to the King of France, whose support Henry was desperate to elicit, if Francis had taken an aversion to the young man? Although George obviously had no desire to extend his stay in France, this is not evidence of his incompetence, merely a sign of a homesick young man wanting to be with his friends.

Curiously, George's letter to Bennett is full of indecipherable code, which had obviously been devised by the ambassadors as a precautionary measure prior to leaving England. Other letters of the age contain some similar cipher, but this letter includes an unusually large amount. George's letters are normally short and to the point, but it would appear that he took boyish glee in the cloak-and-dagger machinations of foreign policy. He returned to England in late February 1530, having spent his intended four months in France, two weeks before his replacement arrived. John Wellisbourne replaced him initially on 14 March, followed later by the original ambassador, Francis Bryan, an experienced courtier and diplomat. Despite George's success with Francis I, his age alone obviously meant he did not have the gravitas of seasoned diplomats such as Bryan. He was not sent on embassy again for another three years. By then, he would be a seasoned 28 year-old courtier with the necessary skills of a politician and diplomat, and not one who necessarily needed to rely on charm, personality and persistence, or the reputation of his father and sister.

During the period between early 1530 and early 1533, and despite his diplomatic role coming to a temporary halt, George, now Lord Rochford, continued in Henry's service as a trusted courtier. He maintained a high profile in the Privy Chamber, was a constant companion to the King (as we have seen), and took an active role throughout the duration of the Reformation Parliament. During the same period, the matter of the King's annulment rumbled on. The annulment itself has been discussed in great depth in other books regarding Henry VIII and his complicated love life. Although a précis of the annulment negotiations is unavoidable, bearing in mind George's involvement in most aspects of it, discussion here is confined to the areas in which it specifically refers to or involves George Boleyn.

During 1530, pressure continued to be put on the Pope to alter his attitude, but Henry, a man used to getting his own way, was coming to the end of his tether. In October, a proposal was put to Parliament that the Archbishop of Canterbury be empowered by statute to hear the case for the annulment, irrespective of papal prohibition. In December Henry wrote directly to the Pope demanding that he allow his cause to be decided in England, having refused the citation to appear in Rome for a hearing. The Pope's lack of sympathy was pushing Henry towards an eventual break with Rome, as devised by Cranmer at the end of 1529. Matters came to a head in February 1531 when, as we have seen, Convocation accepted Henry as head of the church in England. Yet despite this Henry continued to spend time and effort on blocking a hearing in Rome. He was still not prepared to push forward with his "God-given" rights, and this caused further delay. This was partly due to the Archbishop of Canterbury's refusal to defy papal authority, and partly due to the King of France's attempts to bring England and Rome together, which raised English hopes of a breakthrough.

Whatever the reasons for Henry's delay, Chapuys wrote of increasingly anti-papal tirades from Anne and her father.[17] He makes no mention of such outpourings from George Boleyn, who, despite his commitment to the cause, appears to have taken a less aggressive, or at least a less vocal, approach than either his father or his sister. There is no mention at all in any extant record of George Boleyn showing his temper or exhibiting a violent side to his nature. He was forceful, dogmatic, and perhaps argumentative, and certainly fought his corner, but seemingly never with open aggression. Although Thomas Wyatt refers to his pride, George is never accused of having a temper to match that of his fierier sister. Two volatile individuals rarely maintain a close and enduring friendship like that between Anne and George, even if they are related. Anne and Henry were both passionate people, and as we know that relationship eventually ended in disaster. Anne regularly clashed with her own father, whose temperament resembled his daughter's. If George had been as tempestuous as Anne they are unlikely to have been as close as they were, even though their interests meshed.

Eventually, in April 1531, Wiltshire published the opinions of the European universities, which his son had canvassed on his mission to France in October 1529. Despite his success with

Francis, the universities had not reversed their opinions while George had been in France. It took until July 1530 for this to happen. The publication formed part of a collection of documents entitled *The Collectanea Satis Copiosa* (The Sufficiently Abundant Collections), which was written and collated by Thomas Cranmer and Edward Fox.[18] The full title, "The determination of the most famous and most excellent universities of Italy and France, that it is unlawful for a man to marry his brother's wife; and that the Pope hath no power to dispense therewith", speaks for itself. *The Collectanea* confirmed what the Boleyns had been telling Henry all along - that each state had its own jurisdiction, independent of the Pope. It went further by stating that Henry had no superiors on earth, including the Pope, and therefore he already exercised supreme jurisdiction in his realm.

Yet Henry VIII still prevaricated in pushing forward his advantage. Despite the frantic efforts to rid himself of her, over the Christmas and New Year period 1530-1, the King and Catherine of Aragon remained on reasonable terms, irrespective of her continuing implacability towards an annulment. She was still at court, and at times she even dined with Henry. It was not until July 1531 that there was a final break between Henry and Catherine. Although George was out of the country over Christmas 1529-30, as one of the King's closest aides he would certainly have been at court on other occasions when the Queen was present. He had travelled to Waltham with Henry and Catherine in June 1528, at the time of the sweating sickness outbreak, and was certainly at court for the Christmas festivities of 1530-1. George was royal cupbearer and would in any event have been present on all state occasions to serve the King. Catherine would have known George Boleyn since he was a little boy, and would have been fully aware that his sister was the woman attempting to usurp her. Under normal circumstances it would be incredibly awkward to be forced into the company of a woman whose husband is in a relationship with your sister, particularly when that woman is Queen of England. George, however, was a Boleyn, with a self-confidence and self-assurance bordering on the arrogant, and with a total belief in himself and his own family. Brazening out a difficult situation was unlikely to be a problem for him. After all, Anne was not the first of his sisters to have caught the King's eye. George had been playing "the little brother in the middle" for years.

During this period of indecision and uncertainty, courtiers began to take sides as Catherine's supporters realised they had helped oust the power-crazed Wolsey only to have him replaced by Anne. Nicholas Carew had always been a Boleyn opponent, albeit a covert one. He was now joined by the likes of Charles Brandon, Duke of Suffolk, and later the Duke of Norfolk himself. On the surface, as long as Anne remained in the King's favour, these people had no choice but to continue supporting her, but once that situation changed, the Boleyns would discover exactly where their supposed allies' loyalties lay. These were all powerful enemies to acquire. The defection of certain courtiers was obviously due to their abhorrence of Reform, about which the Boleyns were so passionate, and their allegiance to Catherine, but some of it had to do with a dislike of Anne personally. As her influence grew, so did her temper, pride and haughtiness. She treated important and powerful men with arrogance and contempt, believing herself to be invulnerable. Although there is no extant record of her brother demonstrating the same behaviour, he was invariably linked to his sister by his unerring support of her, and by his own air of pride. They were raised together, and they would eventually fall together.

By Christmas 1531 matters were no further forwards and opinion was turning against Anne. By now, Henry had been formally separated from Catherine for six months, and neither she nor her ladies were at court for Christmas. Despite his formal separation from Catherine, and the fact that Anne was now acting the part of queen-in-waiting, the issue of the annulment was no further forward. It was to be a miserable Christmas for everyone. The New Year of 1532 brought the re-opening of Parliament, which refused to accept that matrimonial causes were a Crown matter rather than a church matter. This meant the

Boleyn approach was now the only alternative; eventually, after a year of prevarication, Henry was propelled into taking matters into his own hands.

As we have seen, in May 1532 Convocation was forced into acknowledging Henry as head of the Church of England by enforcing the earlier agreement of 1531 regarding the Submission of the Clergy. This revolutionised Anne's position. Thomas Audley replaced Thomas More, who had resigned as Chancellor, and Thomas Cromwell became the key man in Parliament. George was one of the two noblemen in the Privy Chamber, and Wiltshire was Privy Seal. There were now Boleyn family members and supporters in all areas of government and the court. A marriage seemed imminent, and to emphasise the point, on 1 September 1532 Anne was created Marchioness of Pembroke, making her the first female peer in her own right.[19] A ceremony was held at Windsor Castle, during which Anne was conveyed to the King, and in the presence of the noblemen of the day, "the king invested her with the mantle and coronet".[20] It is not known whether her brother was present at the ceremony. Although his father and uncle are listed as two of the witnesses, George's name is not mentioned, but it would be surprising if he were not in attendance. The title marked the approaching end of the long drawn-out affair.

In the autumn of 1532, a conference was held in Calais between Henry VIII and Francis I in a face-to-face meeting.[21] Ostensibly the meeting was to discuss the defence of Christendom against the Turks, but in reality it was to discuss the steps necessary to bring about the marriage of Henry VIII and Anne Boleyn, and to enlist the King of France's active support. Francis I's sister Marguerite of Angoulême, the Queen of Navarre, was to have been hostess but she was ill. This resulted in a delay in the travel arrangements while it was decided who should replace her. The journey to Calais should have taken place in July, but did not begin until 11 October. Anne was present as were a large contingency of courtiers. The Dukes of Norfolk, Suffolk and Richmond had 40 men each in attendance on them. The Earls of

Surrey, Oxford, Derby and Wiltshire, together with the Bishops of Winchester, London, Lincoln and Bath had 24 men each. Then there were the Lords Montague, Grey, Sandys, Rochford, Daubeney and William Howard. There were also 48 knights, including John Dudley, Edward Seymour, William Fitzwilliam, William Kingston, Anthony Browne and Richard Page, and 30 unnamed esquires. This was an extremely lavish affair. Nothing of the kind had been seen since the Field of Cloth of Gold meeting in 1520, and it confirmed the importance to Henry of obtaining Francis's support.

The meeting between Henry and Francis took place on the 21 October in the company of the King's men, including George Boleyn. It would have been the first time George had come into contact with Francis since February 1530. No ladies were present on this occasion. Henry and his entourage rode to Sandingfield to meet Francis, while Anne and her ladies remained at Calais. The French and English then rode on together to Boulogne where Francis entertained them royally. This was essentially a royal stag party, and it lasted four days, with much wine, women and song. On 25 October, they rode back to Calais, where the French were entertained with equal lavishness. According to the chronicler John Stow, there were 8000 people present at, and around, the festivities. It was not until 27 October that Anne met the French King. That evening, a masked ball took place, at which Anne danced with Francis before she and her ladies were unmasked. In addition to Anne, the ladies present on this occasion were Anne's sister Mary Carey, Lady Derby, Lady Fitzwalter, Lady Lisle, Lady Wallop and George's wife Lady Rochford. This was the only formal occasion upon which George and Jane Boleyn would have travelled abroad together, although Jane would have remained throughout with Anne's train while George obviously followed the King on the 21st to his meeting with Francis, and to the four days of entertainment at Boulogne.

When face to face with Henry, Francis appeared sympathetic to Henry's cause and was prepared to give a guarantee of French protection against Charles V. By now, Henry was not prepared to wait on the Pope any longer and his only concern was to prevent an excommunication. Although Henry disingenuously promised Francis that he would take no immediate steps to marry Anne, it was clearly his intention to do so upon their return to England. Chronicler Edward Hall records that the couple married on Thursday 14 November 1532, St Erkenwald's Day, the day after they arrived back in England. Certainly some type of pledge must have been made to Anne, because it was either in Calais, or shortly after their return to England, that her relationship with Henry was finally consummated and the couple began living together.[22] Given Anne's stance during the previous seven years, it is highly unlikely that she would have surrendered her honour to the King unless an assurance of marriage had been made.

14 Foreign Diplomat

Henry VIII officially married Anne Boleyn on 25 January 1533 in a secret ceremony at Whitehall.[1] Following his meeting with Francis, Henry decided to seek papal consent after the marriage, presumably believing the Pope would not object after the deed was done. The wedding itself was a very private affair with only Anne's parents, brother and two favourites mentioned by Chapuys as being present.[2] Chapuys does not name these two favourites, but Nicholas Harpsfield later recorded that Henry Norris and Thomas Heneage attended, along with Anne Savage, Lady Berkeley.[3] There is no specific mention of either Mary Boleyn or Lady Rochford being in attendance. Although she was Anne's sister, Mary Boleyn's absence is easily explained. She had been the King's mistress, and her attendance may well have caused embarrassment – indeed, she may have chosen not to be there.

The absence of George's wife at the wedding of his beloved sister is more difficult to explain, but the King may well have wanted to keep the ceremony as private and low-key as possible. As George's wife, though, Jane must surely have known about the wedding.

Although it was rumoured that Archbishop Cranmer performed the marriage ceremony, Cranmer dispelled these rumours in a letter to Archdeacon Hawkyns, and it appears that it was Dr Rowland Lee, the King's chaplain, who officiated.[4] It was now essential that matters progress as quickly as possible. Although nobody could have known for sure at the time of the marriage, Anne was already pregnant. It has been suggested that Elizabeth was conceived in Calais, but if she was born on or around her due date then she was conceived in mid-December, a month after the couple's return. When the wedding party came out of the small chapel, Anne was Queen Consort and George was brother-in-law to the King of England. More importantly from their perspective, shortly afterwards, when Anne's pregnancy was confirmed, they believed they would be mother and uncle to the next King of England. Their excitement and relief at the successful conclusion of a campaign that had started seven long years ago had to have been tangible. They had no way of knowing that their troubles were just about to begin.

It was not long after the marriage that George's diplomatic career was once again given a kick-start. Throughout the protracted annulment negotiations, Henry relied heavily on the alliance he had formed with France, and it was this reliance on Francis I which provided George with all his experience in foreign diplomacy. English foreign policy had previously been to maintain neutrality between France and Spain, while encouraging disputes between them and not forming a firm alliance with either, but with the Emperor in league with the Pope, the annulment had thrown this policy into chaos. Henry needed an alliance with France in order to obtain a legal justification for his second marriage, and became hell-bent on securing Francis's in his "Great Matter". It was only Henry's continued obsession with Anne that protected her and the rest of her family from those who continued to support Catherine and Catholicism, and who could not countenance such an alliance. France was seen as the old enemy by many people in England, including Cromwell and the Duke of Norfolk.

Despite his defiant marriage, Henry was still seeking papal approval, and negotiations with Rome continued. Irrespective of this, the marriage effectively threw away the agreement Henry had with Francis, who later complained, "as fast as I study to win the Pope, ye study to lose him".[5] By the beginning of March 1533, Henry realised he could not keep Francis in ignorance of his wedding any longer. On 11 March, George Boleyn received a warrant from the King to travel to France and give a message to Francis informing him that Henry and Anne had married, and to ask Francis to order his representatives in Rome to join those of England in urging the Pope and Cardinals to accept the marriage as a fait accompli.[6] As Henry had previously induced Francis to assure the Pope that he would take no immediate steps to marry, it was anticipated that the French King would not take the news well. George's instructions, therefore, are full of hyperbole and self-justification. It was anticipated that his mission would last for 14 days, for which he received a huge income of £106, 13s, 8d.[7] Amusingly, when on foreign missions the ambassadors' income is denoted as being for their diet. It would indeed have been a feat had he managed to consume food worth just over £106 in a period of two weeks. George left for France on 13 March, arriving on the 16th.[8] [9] The details of the mission were kept secret, much to the annoyance of Chapuys, and there was much speculation at court as to the reason for the embassy.

For Henry to have chosen George for a foreign mission to Francis, in the sure knowledge that the French King would not take kindly to the news being imparted, is a testimony to the confidence Henry had in his brother-in-law and George's relationship with the French king. But there was obviously the additional advantage of George being Anne's brother and therefore best suited to break the news of his sister's marriage to Francis. George had already developed a good relationship with the Francis and his sister Marguerite during his first mission to

France. Perhaps it was hoped that George's natural exuberance, and his obvious delight in the marriage of his sister to the King of England, would be infectious.

His specific instructions were to present Francis with letters written by the King, "and express the delight he [Henry] feels at the friendship and offers of service," - especially regarding Francis asking for Henry's advice concerning the marriage of the Duke of Orleans with the Pope's niece. He was required to tell Francis that, according to his advice given at their last interview, and out of Henry's anxiety to have male issue for the establishment of his Kingdom, Henry "has proceeded effectually to the accomplishment of his marriage, trusting to find that his deeds will correspond with his [Francis's] promises, and that he will assist and maintain the King in the event of any excommunication from the Pope." This was in fact untrue, as Francis had given no such advice. George was instructed to further advise Francis that by demanding that Henry appear before him, the Pope was threatening his royal dignity: "that a prince should not submit to the arrogance and ambition of an earthly creature [i.e. the Pope] and that this would pervert the order which God ordained", and would be as prejudicial to Francis as to Henry. Therefore, by playing to Francis's own egotism, George was to demand that Francis refuse to allow the Pope to proceed against Henry. He was ordered to request that Francis should not consent to the marriage of the Pope's niece to his son, unless the Pope held that Henry's cause was just. If not then "the friendship of princes was nothing but dissimilation". Finally, he was charged with a discussion of Scottish issues, which were to be explained to Francis by George himself.[10]

Henry was attempting to bend Francis entirely to his will. He even went as far as providing George with a letter that Henry proposed Francis should send to the Pope, urging him to grant the English king's divorce on account of the scruples which he entertained in consequence of his pretended marriage to Catherine. The intended letter included a threat to the Pope that failure to comply would result in Francis, as well as Henry, being obliged to have recourse in other ways and means, "which would be less agreeable to the Pope".

Unsurprisingly, George had a poor reception from Francis, who was unhappy with Henry's hasty decision to marry first and receive papal blessing later. Francis felt that Henry had duped him into being used as an instrument to deceive the Pope, and he was also angry at being expected to bend to Henry's will. George, as Henry's mouthpiece, was in an unenviable position. He, as much as Henry, must have anticipated the negative reaction his news would initially provoke, because he appears to have gone into the discussions with Francis particularly forcefully. Enemies of the Boleyns erroneously blamed his poor reception on his unreasonable behaviour. The reception was purely down to Henry's deception and subterfuge, and his attempts to coerce Francis into a cause of action designed solely to assist the English King. In reality the young Boleyn, in compliance with Henry's confidence in him, actually managed to turn the situation around within a matter of days by deploying "uncommon audacity and obstinacy".[11] Before leaving France, George was presented with a litter and three mules, which was a wedding gift for his sister from Francis. George arranged to bring them home with him so that he could present them to Anne himself.

After informing Francis of the marriage of his sister to Henry, George, as per his instructions, strongly urged Francis to write a letter to the Pope in support. This seemed almost a replay of January 1530, when George had convinced Francis to write to Pierre Lizet for the support of academic opinion. By requiring Francis to support every move he made, Henry was running the risk of permanently alienating the French king. Sure enough, Francis was initially indignant at the suggestion and refused to write, feeling himself being used by "his good brother" the English king. A letter written by Francis to the Bailly of Troyes and dated 20 March confirms his indignation. Francis wrote that he had "already written about the arrival of Viscount Rochford, who has begged him, in the name of the King of England, to write a letter to Cardinals Tournon and Grammont, according to a memorandum".[12] However, Francis did not think it was reasonable, and said he had told Lord Rochford that he could do nothing to break the affair. Francis was due to have an interview with the Pope, of which he hoped Henry would be a part. However, George Boleyn persisted, and eventually persuaded Francis that the Pope was encroaching on his own sovereign rights. As in January 1530, Francis composed a further letter, although somewhat different in tone to the one suggested by Henry, requesting that the cardinals urge the Pope to pronounce in favour of the English King. In his letter, Francis states that Rochford had come from the King of England and informed him of the Pope's refusal to admit the excusator. Francis indicated that this would be an insult to all Christian princes. and that the cardinals must urge the Pope to admit Henry's excusator in accordance with the privilege of him and other princes. He warned that at present, princes barely suffered the Pope to infringe on their privilege and pre-eminences; any refusal would seem a further attempt to suppress these. Refusal would further cause displeasure to Francis, and should not be proceeded with until the hoped-for meeting between the Pope and the two kings.[13] Francis gave a copy of the letter to George to show Henry, to establish whether Henry was happy for it to be dispatched.

George Boleyn obtained this result in less than four days, again by his boldness, audacity and obstinacy. This was a personal triumph for him, much to the disgust of the Bishop of Paris, Jean du Bellay, who vented his anger in a letter to the ambassador of France in London dated 20 March. In it he strongly criticised George Boleyn for being "such an unreasonable man", but although furious with his success, in his letter du Bellay gives grudging praise for the respect Rochford commanded at the meeting, and the skill with which he supported the discussion.[14] It has to be remembered that in March 1533 George Boleyn was still only about 28. He had been sent to France to coerce the

French king into a course of action that Francis was not overly happy to take. Failure would result in the disappointment of the King of England and his own sister, not only in the outcome, but also in him personally. The pressure would have been enormous. It was inconceivable that he could go home completely empty-handed, hence his dogged persistence. It may also explain the unreasonableness that he is accused of exhibiting. Francis was already angered by Henry's marriage, which had taken place in direct opposition to the assurances given by Henry only three months previously. Attack is often the best form of defence, which may well have resulted in George responding to his cool reception with a seemingly unreasonable forcefulness.

Francis's letter in support of Henry was returned to England by courier, and George remained in France for a further two weeks, indicating that whatever displeasure Francis may have felt, this was not directed at George personally. George's remaining in France may have been because his instructions did not solely relate to his sister's cause, but included orders to communicate with Francis regarding the marriage of the Duke of Orleans to the Pope's niece, and the differences between England and Scotland. Alternatively, it may partly have been because, self-satisfied with his success, George took his time returning home, determined to enjoy the delights of the French court. He did not arrive back in England until 8 April. There is a dispatch from Chapuys dated 16 April saying George had arrived from France eight days previously, and that George's servants had proudly informed Chapuys that their master "had received in France 2,000 cr. as a present for the good news he had brought of his sister's marriage".[15] It is clear that George left Francis on good terms, whatever the Boleyn enemies may have chosen to believe.[16]

Whether smugly self-satisfied with the result of the French mission or not, in reality, the small success George had achieved in France had no practical effect. Despite attempts to use Francis as a means of intimidation, the Pope remained unwavering. Irrespective of the Pope's continuing refusal to relent, due to

Anne's pregnancy, and also to the intervention of Cranmer, matters that had taken six years to get to this point now started to move quickly. On 23 May 1533, Cranmer declared Henry's marriage to Catherine void, and five days later he declared the marriage of Henry and Anne to be valid, thereby stripping Catherine of her title as Queen. By having his marriage with Catherine declared void, Henry was in effect declaring his own daughter Mary a bastard, with no concern for her feelings or the feelings of her mother.

As we have seen, it was also in May that Cranmer instigated the break with Rome, thereby making Henry head of the Church of England. The break would be completed by the Act of Supremacy in 1534. This was the beginning of the English Reformation, and the end of England as a Catholic country.

Matters were now put in hand to have Anne crowned queen, and the date for her coronation was set for 1 June.[17] Unfortunately, having devoted much of his career to bringing it about, her brother was not able to attend his sister's moment of glory. Less than two months after returning from France, George was sent back. In May 1533, accompanied his uncle, the Duke of Norfolk, and a large contingency of courtiers so that they could both be present at the meeting scheduled between Francis and the Pope.[18] Henry had chosen a contingency of men who would be acceptable to Francis, and clearly George Boleyn was considered to be one of them, having spent considerable time with the French king on previous missions.

The Duke of Norfolk headed the mission, accompanied by George and Sir Francis Bryan, both of whom Francis already knew as ambassadors, and Sir William Paulet and Sir Anthony Browne, who were both close friends of Henry VIII.[19] They were ordered to attend the meeting so as to prevent any hostile reaction against Henry, and in particular excommunication. Hence George missed the coronation of his sister, which must have been an enormous disappointment for both of them. Anne would have wanted her only brother and most loyal supporter to share the momentous occasion with her, and George must have been hugely disappointed not to have shared the limelight after all his conscientious hard work. It is an indication of the importance Henry placed on having his newly-acquired brother-in-law in attendance at the proposed meeting between Francis and the Pope that he was prepared to have him miss his own sister's coronation. But there was of course another reason for George's attendance at the meeting: Anne trusted him above all others. The siblings obviously agreed that having a Boleyn at the meeting outweighed the importance of George being at the coronation.

Whether Anne wrote to her brother regarding her coronation is unknown, as there are no surviving letters between the siblings. However, George's wife Jane attended both the coronation and the coronation banquet as one of Anne's ladies, so would have been able to report back to him. George also received a letter from Anne's new chaplain Edward Baynton. On 9 June, just over a week after the coronation, Baynton wrote to George in France informing him that the coronation had been "performed honourably". Baynton humorously wrote:

> The pastime in the Queens Chamber was never more. If any of you that be now departed have any ladies that they thought favoured you, and somewhat would mourn at parting of their servants, I can no whit perceive the same by their dancing and pastime they do use here.[20]

Such entertainments in the queen's chambers would later be used as evidence against Anne and her supposed lovers, particularly her brother, who was later lambasted at his trial for having the indecency to dance with his sister. But whilst the King remained happy with his new wife, it was just seen as amusing and light-hearted fun, which of course was exactly what it was. Baynton was one of the men who would later investigate the Queen for her indecorous behaviour and supposed adultery, obviously forgetting his own earlier acceptance of her behaviour as innocent fun. Knowing his sister better than anyone, George no doubt read Baynton's words with wry amusement, little appreciating the horror that would be unleashed on himself and his sister in less than three years' time.

Baynton had suggested that the courtiers who travelled in George's train would not be missed at home due to the joyous entertainment in the new queen's chambers. A number of Henry's courtiers attended the French court at one time or another, particularly his favourites such as Charles Brandon, George Boleyn, Thomas Wyatt, Francis Bryan, Nicholas Carew, and the King's precocious young son, Henry Fitzroy, all of whom were dashing, high-living young men, leaders of fashion, and in some cases of culture. In a world in which foreign travel was limited, ambassadors were sent on embassy with a large group of young courtiers keen to alleviate boredom with the excitement of new experiences. These young men returned to England exuding an arrogant sophistication, which was the envy of those who remained at home. When they came back they were "all French in eating, drinking and apparel, yea, in French vices and brags".[21] Because of this, all young courtiers wanted the opportunity to be part of an ambassador's train in order to see the world and become like Anne Boleyn's elegant and sophisticated brother. Therefore, when George went abroad, he travelled with a large contingency of courtiers keen to emulate him. It would be naive to think that the entertainment these young men would have enjoyed while in France or Italy was all polite dinner parties. They were recklessly determined to get as much enjoyment as possible out of the experience, and more importantly, they travelled without the hindrance of wives. A wild and debauched social life could fit in nicely with high politics and diplomacy, if the right balance could be struck.

In addition to the honour of representing King and country abroad, and to the financial rewards of a foreign embassy, there can be little doubt that George derived enormous pleasure from his trips to France as English envoy. Judging by his reputation as a high-living womaniser, both at home and abroad, but also by his growing reputation as a competent politician and diplomat, he seems to have established an excellent balance. By 1533, he had developed into a fine diplomat and politician like his father before him. This was not just Boleyn arrogance, but a fact recognised with reluctance by the entire court. As Cromwell conceded in 1536, it was not a good idea to underestimate George Boleyn.

On the mission that began in May 1533, George and his train of courtiers, including a retinue of 160 horsemen, had the dubious company of the Duke of Norfolk. When they passed into France, the Duke was accompanied by the Duke of Richmond, the King's illegitimate son, who was with him for the experience of foreign travel and to be introduced to the King of France. The Duke of Norfolk, George's uncle, was a particularly odious individual. His own biographer, David Head, describes him as having an unpleasant personality: "Being feared and respected might have been all Norfolk expected, for there is little evidence that he was loved by anyone."[22] He was as ruthless and self-seeking as any courtier of the age, and was neither trusted nor trustworthy. His own wife said of him, "He can speak fair to his enemy as to his friend".[23]

Thomas Howard was born in 1473 and succeeded his father as 3rd Duke of Norfolk in 1524. He had been Lord Treasurer of Ireland from 1520 to 1521, and became Lord High Treasurer in 1522 upon his father's retirement. Although he was a staunch Catholic throughout his life, he was happy to support the King in his desire to marry his niece, Anne Boleyn, as long as it was profitable for him to do so. Once the tide turned against her he assisted in her destruction, and that of his nephew. In fact, his loyalty to the Boleyns waned long before their eventual downfall, due mainly to his jealousy and bitterness when his fortunes did not increase in line with theirs. What he failed to see was that his prospects were always to be limited by his own character and his obvious need for power. There were few people more repellent than Norfolk, even in the sixteenth century. Ultimately, Henry was bound to those people he liked and trusted, and although Norfolk was a useful tool, he was not a member of the King's inner circle, and never would be. He lacked the natural wit and charm of his Boleyn in-laws, and this failure would always limit his influence with the King.

George went on two missions to France with his uncle, and whatever his personal views may have been, continued to work closely with him as late as July 1535. George may very well have loathed Norfolk as much as his sister did. Norfolk once complained that Anne spoke to him worse than a dog. Her brother George was more reticent, but in 1534 when Anne's relationship with Norfolk completely broke down, Norfolk complained to Chapuys that both George and Anne were exhibiting signs of mistrusting him.[24] It was upon their return from France in August 1533 that the King's illegitimate son married Norfolk's daughter, Mary Howard, when they were both just 15 years old. This marriage provided Norfolk with a prominent link to the King. Although Anne herself had encouraged the union, once her relationship with Norfolk completely broke down, both she and her brother had cause to regret the potential power the marriage gave to their untrustworthy uncle.

When the English contingent arrived in France in May 1533, they remained in Calais for a number of days awaiting instructions. Upon hearing from Henry that a meeting between the Pope and Francis should be prevented unless a favourable decision could be assured, the English party travelled on to Paris. There they had two long meetings towards the end of June with Francis's sister, Marguerite, who displayed great kindness to the ambassadors.[25] Marguerite was predisposed towards the evangelical movement, meaning she had much in common with George, and while in conversation with Norfolk and his nephew, she confirmed that she would encourage her brother to support Henry. The meeting between Francis and the Pope was scheduled for July 1533 in a small town in the south of France. Given the age's difficulties with communications, it had been necessary for

Henry's ambassadors to leave England at least a month in advance to ensure they arrived in time for the meeting - hence George's departure from England on 28 May, missing his sister's coronation by just four days.

After their discussions with the Queen of Navarre, the party travelled to Riom, where they eventually met up with Francis on 10 July. The meeting with the Pope had been scheduled for the 15th, but had been put off due to the oppressive heat. The English party proceeded with Francis through a number of small French towns on what was similar to the English equivalent of the summer progress. Six days passed during which the French and English enjoyed a relaxing break in the South of France, under the guise of "negotiations". During that time, the English were treated to lavish entertainments by their French hosts, who had been ordered to treat the English envoys with honour "as would have been the very person of my Lord the Dauphin."[26] This could best be described as a short holiday from the rigours of politics, no doubt thoroughly enjoyed by George Boleyn and the other young men who travelled with him. During the break Norfolk was taken ill, and on 16 July it was suggested that he travel on to Lyon and remain there whilst the French court continued its travels, with a view to the court joining him in Lyon later. Norfolk took leave of the court, arriving in Lyon on 21 July where on the way the party narrowly escaped disaster. Sir Anthony Browne, who was with the English contingent, wrote to Cromwell on 24 July:

> Also, Sir, you shall understand that the 21st day of this month we arrived at this town [Lyon] and before our arrival, three legs off, at a village called Griesves, my Lord of Norfolk dined and his company, and all with him the bishops of Paris, Monsieur Morrent, with divers others; and after dinner, because the weather was wet, were under a great tree, and sat there and had a [collusion] with fruits and drink; and so departed; and within half

an hour after, rose a great thunder and burnt the
same tree; and also at the same time was burnt one
of the French king's archers, which stood within
three yards of him, with the thunder, and no else,
thanks be to God.[27]

It would seem from this account that the whole party was very
nearly struck by lightning. It was perhaps an omen of things to
come. It is uncertain whether George Boleyn was with Norfolk at
the time or whether he had remained with Francis and the French
court. He would certainly not have wished to leave Francis's
lavish entertainments in order to enjoy the pleasure of his ageing
uncle's company. It is far more likely that the younger courtiers
such as George, Francis Bryan and Henry Fitzroy remained with
Francis. Whatever their movements, George's fun was about to be
curtailed in a dramatic fashion.

On 11 July, the Pope declared Cranmer's proceedings null and
void, and pronounced a sentence of excommunication on Henry.
The sentence was delayed by six weeks to allow Henry to set aside
his unlawful marriage with Anne and return to Catherine of
Aragon. News of the sentence of excommunication reached the
English party in Lyon on 25 July and Norfolk is said to have nearly
fainted when he heard. Either George was already with Norfolk,
or else Norfolk quickly recalled him from Francis, because upon
hearing the news he immediately sent George back to England,
presumably thinking that the shock would be better if delivered
by the Queen's brother. From George's point of view, the sentence
of excommunication may have proved disastrous. There must
have been a fear in the back of his mind that the Pope's sanctions
might force Henry to relinquish Anne and abandon the anti-papal
legislation that was to be finalised the following year. As we know,
none of this happened - but it must have been a very anxious young
man who returned to England with the news. It took George only
three days to get back to England, arriving at Windsor on 28 July.
A dispatch from Chapuys dated 30 July confirms that George

had arrived two days earlier: "I have not been able to discover the cause of Rochford's coming, who arrived 2 days ago from the place where he found Norfolk, in great diligence."[28] George remained in England awaiting further instructions, which came on 8 August. The instructions to Norfolk and George remained the same - namely that all possible means be used to prevent a meeting between Francis and the Pope until such time as the Pope acceded to Henry's wishes. The communications set out arguments that the ambassadors were to use to dissuade Francis from the meeting.[29]

As soon as George received these instructions, he must have immediately returned to France since he was back with Norfolk by 12 August. If they could not persuade Francis to abandon the meeting, the English ambassadors were ordered to return home.[30] Although no meeting between Francis and the Pope had taken place by the time George and Norfolk left France at the end of August, Francis refused to abandon it altogether. By now, the King of France was almost entirely alienated by Henry's insistence on his support, and by Henry's demands that Francis fight his battles for him. Francis refused the English delegation's requests to abandon the proposed Papal meeting completely, saying that arrangements were too far gone to call it off and that it was in Henry's interests for it to go ahead as it would be hard to "buy another such opportunity".[31] The only concession Francis made was to continue to offer to mediate between Henry and the Pope, and he did actively encourage English assistance in his negotiations with the Pope. Although Henry insisted that Francis's intervention was not needed, in reality the bull of excommunication meant Henry's gamble of marrying first and obtaining papal consent later had not paid off. His cause, at least as far as Rome was concerned, now seemed lost, and in addition to this his alliance with France was in severe jeopardy. Although George was to attend three further embassies to France, once that alliance failed completely in mid-1535, his diplomatic career would once again come to a grinding halt.

15 Uncle to a Future Queen

By the time George returned from France at the end of August 1533, Anne was heavily pregnant, and there were already rumours circulating that the King had begun having affairs. If Henry expected Anne to endure this, as Catherine had done, he could not have been more wrong. The rumours originated through Chapuys, who later admitted that he had got things wrong, and dismissed an argument between Anne and Henry as merely a lover's quarrel.[1] Not even Henry would have risked upsetting Anne while she was pregnant with the long-awaited Prince, and in any event there is no evidence to suggest that the marriage was in difficulties as early as August 1533. There is no realistic suggestion that the King's eye had started to wander until the autumn of 1534, by which time the rumours may have had an element of truth, although again they originated almost exclusively from Chapuys. In the autumn of 1533, there was no reason to suppose that even the birth of another useless girl could turn Henry against Anne. Despite the disappointment of the child being a princess rather than the anticipated prince, Anne was still young enough to have more healthy babies, and everyone, including the King, was convinced that the next child would be a boy.

Although George missed the coronation of his sister, he was present at the christening of his niece, Elizabeth. Princess Elizabeth was born on 7 September 1533, having been conceived the previous December, shortly after Anne and Henry returned from Calais. She was christened on Wednesday 10 September at the Church of Observant Friars, Greenwich. Thomas Cranmer was appointed godfather to the future Queen Elizabeth I, and the Marchioness of Exeter, Dowager Marchioness of Dorset and Dowager Duchess of Norfolk stood as godmothers. As Anne was recovering from childbirth she was not present, and it was customary for the King to be absent. The Dowager Duchess of Norfolk carried Elizabeth and the train of the baby's mantle was held by her grandfather the Earl of Wiltshire, the Earl of Derby and the Countess of Kent. On either side of the Duchess walked the Dukes of Norfolk and Suffolk. John Hussey, William and Thomas Howard, and Elizabeth's uncle George, Lord Rochford, all supported a canopy over the baby.[2] [3] The Boleyns were determined to put a brave face on the event and it would still be some time before the lack of a son would destroy their equanimity. For now, everything in the garden appeared to remain rosy for them, provided Anne had a son at some point.

Nevertheless, the birth of a daughter was a huge disappointment to everyone. It was hardly surprising that shortly after the christening of the new princess the treacherous Duke of Norfolk became more and more familiar with the imperial ambassador. This familiarity with Chapuys resulted in the complete breakdown of the relationship between Norfolk and Anne Boleyn during 1534. On 15 September, just five days after the christening of Elizabeth, Norfolk and Chapuys attempted to have a private conversation, but had not banked on the presence of Norfolk's annoyingly perceptive nephew. Chapuys wrote to Charles V about the attempt at subterfuge:

> At my departure from court I begged Norfolk
> would allow me to speak with him apart, which
> he showed no inclination to do for the reasons
> already mentioned [i.e. Anne's suspicion of
> him]. He therefore sent the brother of the Lady,
> as I understand from a man who heard him, on
> a message to the king's chamber, who returned
> almost immediately after so as to cut short any
> conversation which we might be engaged in.[4]

The vigilant George rushed back in order to prevent a conversation between his uncle and the Boleyns' bitterest enemy. Norfolk may very well have complained that Anne and George were becoming increasingly suspicious of him, but it was hardly unmerited. The siblings had just cause to be concerned over their uncle's rapidly decreasing loyalty. His daughter was now married to the King's only surviving son, albeit an illegitimate one, and there was limited incentive for Norfolk to continue supporting the Boleyns - although as long as the King commanded it, he would continue to do so. The birth of a daughter caused much smug satisfaction among Boleyn enemies, and both Anne and George must have been aware of that.

Sixteenth century queens had a duty to have sons, and not to do so was considered a failure, as it had been with Catherine. Yet in the sixteenth century, there was a high level of childlessness, and a high child mortality rate added to the problem. George and Jane Boleyn were married for around 11 years and had no children, or at least none that survived. There is no record of Jane actually conceiving let alone giving birth, although it is possible that there were miscarriages. By the time of her marriage, Anne was approximately 31, which, although certainly not too old to have further children, would have reduced the likelihood of her conceiving, particularly as she did not have her first child until she was about 32. Added to her problems was the issue of Henry's potency. This was later raised at George Boleyn's trial, which confirmed that rumours regarding the King's potency did circulate, and perhaps there were periods when Henry suffered sexual dysfunction. All of this put enormous pressure on Anne, who would only be fully acknowledged as queen if she produced a son. The stress and pressure alone would have made it even more difficult for her to conceive. Yet despite this, Anne did apparently have a strong maternal bond with Elizabeth. Although the child was moved to her own household shortly after her birth, her mother regularly visited her.

At the time of Elizabeth's birth, her half-sister Princess Mary was living at Beaulieu Palace in Essex. Mary had resided there for several years, but after the birth of Elizabeth she was made to leave the property in order for her to become part of her half-sister's household. This was basically a punishment for her refusal to recognise Elizabeth as heir to the throne. According to Chapuys, Mary had to be forcibly removed from Beaulieu by Sir William Fitzwilliam, the Duke of Norfolk and Henry Norris. Previously, in 1529, George had been granted the Chief Stewardship of the Honour of the Palace of Beaulieu. Beaulieu, situated in Boreham, near Chelmsford, was originally named New Hall. It had belonged to the Earl of Ormond and had been inherited by George's father upon the Earl's death in 1515. Thomas had quickly sold it in 1517 for £1000 to Henry VIII, who had loved the property since he had first set eyes on it. The King greatly improved the property and renamed it Beaulieu, meaning, "a fair place". After Mary was made to leave, it was given to George who also loved the place, and wasted no time in moving in his household and some of his furniture.[5] Acquiring Beaulieu as a home was a great coup for George. It was not only a signal of Henry's approval; it also brought one of the Ormond estates back into the Boleyn fold. And Beaulieu was now a truly splendid property, having had thousands of pounds spent by Henry, including a tennis court.[6] George and his wife now lived in regal splendour.

Irrespective of George's delight at the acquisition of Beaulieu, there remained the vexing problem of Mary. Her loathing of

Anne, and her obstinacy in acknowledging Anne as queen and Elizabeth as heir to the throne, cannot have been helped by ousting her from the home she had lived in for years, or the fact that it was then handed over to the brother of the woman who had usurped her mother.

When Mary joined Elizabeth's household, she was under the charge of Elizabeth's governess, Lady Anne Shelton, who was also Anne and George's aunt. According to Chapuys, the Duke of Norfolk and George Boleyn rebuked Lady Shelton for treating Mary with too much kindness and respect, saying the girl should be treated like the bastard she was.[7] As with most of Chapuys' reports, there is no supporting evidence, and no indication as to the source of his claims. He was regularly fed information by Boleyn enemies, and obviously swallowed any criticism with relish. Although George had a natural antipathy towards Mary, this was not true of his uncle. Norfolk was prepared to facilitate a marriage between his niece and his monarch if that was the will of the King, but his natural allegiance was toward Catherine and Mary. That said, this would not have prevented him from carrying out the King's orders with respect to Mary. Chapuys' dispatches frequently give Anne Boleyn sole responsibility for Mary's treatment; yet it was Henry who was determined to break his daughter's will. The rebuke, if it was in fact made to Lady Shelton by George and Norfolk, was provoked by to the King's increasing hostility towards his proud, obstinate daughter. As Anne's aunt, Lady Shelton could not be seen to fail the King. It was not until Henry's harshness towards Mary continued, and even worsened, following the Boleyn siblings' deaths, that the girl learned that her treatment was not solely due to Boleyn manipulation.

Although it was the King's command that Mary should not be allowed to call herself Princess, Mary's stubbornness did remain a thorn in the Boleyns' side. They needed Mary to accept Elizabeth as the rightful heir. Although Henry's marriage to Catherine had been pronounced null and void, at the time of Mary's birth the marriage had still been considered legal. In canon law this meant she was not subsequently judged to be illegitimate, and she would remain heir to the throne in the event of Henry's death, irrespective of the Act of Succession passed in March 1534. This was a direct threat to Anne's daughter and George's niece, and the Boleyn instincts was to fight.

At his trial, George publicly exhibited his commitment to his niece in dramatic and courageous style; when it came to protecting his family's interests, he, like the King, was not beneath putting pressure on a 17 year-old girl, albeit through a third party. But in George there was also the voice of reason. It had been him that had warned Anne, following her threat to have Mary killed, that this would insult the King. He may have gone so far as to put pressure on Mary to accept Elizabeth as rightful heir, but he would sensibly go no further. Anne did make three separate attempts to befriend Mary, two in 1534 and one in January 1536 when the girl's mother was on her deathbed, but unsurprisingly these attempts were all rejected. Mary's justified rudeness caused even more resentment from Anne, which in turn caused more resentment from Mary.

All of this would have been irrelevant if Anne had given birth to a son. There would no longer have been any argument as to the succession because a son would automatically have taken precedence over all previous daughters. Unfortunately for the Boleyns, of course, that never happened.

16 French Alliance
Put to the Test

On 12 October 1533, the Pope finally had his meeting with the King of France, the meeting which Francis had previously refused to abandon.[1] This took place in the presence of the English ambassador, Bishop Stephen Gardiner, who had taken over from Norfolk and George Boleyn as Henry's chief representative at the French court after their return to England in August. The only concession Gardiner was able to obtain at the meeting was that the Pope would agree to delay putting into effect his censures on Henry, in particular the excommunication, by a further month.

Henry was a proud and arrogant man who was effectively being blackmailed by Rome into submitting to its will under threat of excommunication. Henry could also be a shallow, egotistical man who allowed himself to be easily influenced if the advice being given would ultimately result in him getting his own way. Playing on his ego and desire for Anne, the Boleyns and their supporters, in particular Thomas Cranmer, manoeuvred

him towards an absolute division of the English church from
the authority of Rome. As King of England, why should Henry
be bound by any other jurisdiction? There commenced a game
of bluff between London and Rome, with the Pope threatening
censures and excommunication on Henry, and Henry threatening
a break with Rome. Henry was a born-and-bred Catholic, and his
basic religious ideals remained the same throughout his life - hence
his dogged determination to influence the Pope to agree to the
annulment. George and Anne Boleyn were genuinely interested
in, and motivated by, Reform; the break with Rome took place
not because of a similar commitment from Henry, but because he
needed to reform the church in order to get his own way.

George and Anne played on the King's self-centred egotism
to get their own way. As his wife, Anne could influence Henry.
Up until his fascination with her diminished, she could speak
to the King in a way that nobody else would dare; the rest of the
Boleyn faction could only advise. However strong Anne may have
been though, particularly for a woman in the sixteenth century,
no single person could have done what she did on her own. She
needed her friends and family behind her. Her brother, through
love as well as selfish motivations of his own, provided her with
a level of committed support through ten long years that enabled
her to challenge the religious convictions of a nation. It was his
strength of character, so similar to her own, that resulted in Anne
asking for him following her arrest, and the same strength of
character that necessitated his own death.

1534 was to prove an eventful year. On 23 March, Rome voted
unanimously for the validity of Henry's marriage to Catherine.[2]
This meant that as far as Rome was concerned Henry's marriage
to Anne was invalid, and Henry was a bigamist. This also meant
that Rome deemed Elizabeth illegitimate. From the Boleyns'
point of view, this made the eventual break with Rome essential.
The French cardinals had absented themselves from the Rome
vote and therefore, although on the one hand King Francis I was
supporting Henry's cause, on the other hand he was only prepared

for this to be passive, not active. Events in Rome coincided with the passing of the Act of Succession in London, making only the children of Henry and Anne legitimate heirs to the throne.

The Act of Succession, and the Act of Supremacy passed eight months later, were major triumphs for the Boleyns, but this is not to say that Henry and Anne did not continue to have problems. There was the ever-present question of the Princess Mary, in addition to the fact that Anne was still without a son. Anne's unpopularity was growing, and this was exacerbated by the political situation abroad. Although Henry relied on the alliance with France, Henry and Francis never completely trusted each other. Henry's lack of trust was exacerbated by Francis's failure to provide active support for Henry's cause in Rome, as demonstrated by the French cardinals absenting themselves from the March vote.

Henry VIII's matrimonial difficulties caused huge upheaval to England's foreign policy. Had Henry maintained his policy of neutrality between France and Spain this would have secured England's safety abroad. His marriage to Anne and his treatment of Catherine, Charles V's aunt, ensured reconciliation with the Emperor was impossible. In addition to this, Henry's alliance with France was under constant pressure and suspicion. This suspicion as to the King of France's loyalty resulted in a further embassy to France for George Boleyn. In April 1534, George was chosen, along with Sir William Fitzwilliam, to undertake a further mission to obtain an audience with Francis and his sister, Marguerite, the Queen of Navarre.[3] Their instructions were to urge Francis to abandon his alliance with the Pope and actively declare himself against him; to suggest that Francis should invade Milan, but without taking subsidies from the Pope; to urge Francis to adopt similar legislation as had been passed in England against the Pope's supremacy; to arrange a meeting between the two Kings, the Queen of Navarre and Anne in the near future; and to further urge Francis to refuse to give the hand of his daughter to the King of Scotland.

Their mission was kept secret and was not generally known in the court, again much to the annoyance of Chapuys. They departed on 16 April with Chapuys frantically trying to find out the purpose of the embassy. On 17 April, George and Fitzwilliam wrote to Lord Lisle regarding a delay caused by bad weather:

> This shall be to advertise [you] yesterday we took our passage at Dover with a very stout wind to have landed at Calais. Howbeit, when we were somewhat off the shore, the wind uttered at northeast, so as we co[lde] not fetch Calais, but were forced to land at a village [five miles] from this town [Boulogne- sur-Mer] called Utterselles: by reason whereof, considering the haste of our journey, we could not conveniently [see your] lordship at this time. Nevertheless at our return we w[ill] not fail to do...[4]

Due to the delay, although the envoys left for Calais on 16 April, they were unable to meet with Francis until the 21st at Coucy-le-Château. Upon their arrival, George and Fitzwilliam received a warm welcome from Francis and his sister, and a lavish reception party was arranged for them.[5] On this occasion, though, Francis had no intention of agreeing to English demands. The warm greeting towards Henry's representatives was partly an extravagant attempt to soften the blow of their eventual failure. Although they became aware of the French king's attitude early on in the negotiations, neither George nor Fitzwilliam was prepared to give up without a fight, and four days of negotiation followed. George Boleyn in particular would have wanted to successfully negotiate with Francis for an outcome satisfactory to Henry. To go home a failure would certainly raise allegations of his incompetence from his envious rivals, which in turn would lead to the inevitable malicious comments about his royal connections. George's position was that of having to work three times as hard for the same amount of respect. As can be seen from his manic work ethic throughout the early 1530s, he was not a man to sit back and take advantage of his position. His pride alone would not allow him to do so.

Yet despite his persistence, Francis was not prepared to invoke anti-papal legislation in France. The envoys were only successful in obtaining Francis's agreement to a further meeting with Henry. On 24 April, four days after entering into discussions with the English diplomats, the French king prepared a memorandum setting out the various demands of Henry's diplomats and his answers to them: regarding abandoning his alliance with the Pope, he had no such alliance and so could not break it; this was not an appropriate time to invade Milan, but if he should ever do so he would not put himself under obligation to the Pope for the sake of subsidies; although willing to do so in principle, he saw no reason why he should follow a similar course to the anti-papal legislation that had been passed in England and cause trouble in his kingdom, although he did not blame Henry for doing so; he had no objection to the proposed meeting with his "good brother"; and he was happy to refuse the hand of his daughter to King James V of Scotland.[6]

Francis was understandably concerned that by following Henry's example, he too might receive a sentence of excommunication and that it could result in war on France's borders. In those circumstances, he asked what Henry would do for him. George and Fitzwilliam returned to England two days after receiving Francis's response, firstly to advise Henry of the outcome of the negotiations, and secondly so that arrangements could be put in place for the royal meeting.

As promised in their joint letter of 16 April, George and Fitzwilliam visited Lord Lisle and his wife on their way back to London. Lady Lisle presented him with "dotterals" (plovers) as a gift to his sister. We know of the gift due to a letter written by John Atkinson to Lady Lisle on 5 May saying:

And the Queen did appoint six of your dotterals
for her supper, six for Monday dinner, and six for
supper. My Lord of Rochford presented them his
self, and showed her how they were killed new
at 12 of the clock in Dover, of the which she was
glad, and spake many good words toward your
ladyship's good report, as I was informed by them
that stood by.[7]

It was a mark of the siblings' closeness that gifts for Anne were
often initially presented to her brother in the knowledge that they
would reach the Queen safely. The letter also raises the spectre
of the lack of privacy within the court. As with every aspect of a
sixteenth century queen, the gift was presented by George to his
sister in the public arena. Their conversation was overheard by a
number of people standing by and was reported on. This was a
minor example of the smothering suffocation of court life for
Anne. How could a woman under such close scrutiny possibly
have acted in the manner of which she was later accused? This
close scrutiny also makes an even greater mockery of the theory
regarding George Boleyn's sexuality. Rumours of his womanising
abounded, but there were no contemporaneous rumours of
homosexuality, which there surely would have been if he had acted
in a way considered inappropriate for the brother-in-law of the
King. George remained a trusted diplomat and confidante of the
King right up until his arrest.

When George and Fitzwilliam returned to court, Henry
chose to view their mission as a success. Although the French king
would not invoke anti-papal legislation, the fact that he indicated
a willingness to follow "his good brother" with similar measures
to those declared in England, and that he confirmed his agreement
to a further meeting with Henry, meant that his response was
generally interpreted favourably in England.

Shortly after George's return from France, Henry gave a
grand dinner in honour of him and Fitzwilliam, and in front of

the entire court proclaimed that "he was bound to give thanks to God for having so entirely conciliated to him such a good brother and friend as the King of France, who was always ready to share his fortune and conform his will, which the said Rochford and Fitzwilliam confirmed."[8] Of course, this was not correct. The English representatives and Henry himself were being fobbed off by the French king, but Henry was determined not to see it that way, and that same month he wrote to his ambassador in France, John Wallop:

> We greet you well, signifying unto you that, perceiving by the respect of our right trusty and right wellbeloved counsellors the Lord Rochford and Sir William Fitzwilliam knight, Treasurer of our Household, the hearty zeal, propence good mind and will of our good brother the French king towards us and our realm ministered and showed in such brotherlike and friendly sort as nothing unto us can be more joyous or acceptable, you shall on our behalf give our said good brother our most entire and hearty thanks for the same. And touching his gentle, loving, most prudent and amiable answers in all things by us incommended and given in charge to our said counsellors, as well concerning our meeting as otherwise, you shall declare to our said good brother that the same are unto us so great, thankful and so heartily desired on our part that nothing can be to our greater joy, comfort and contentment.[9]

The reality was that whatever Francis had told Henry's envoys, he had no intention of invoking anti-papal measures. Later, Francis's continuing refusal to go down the English route of royal supremacy confirmed Henry's suspicion that he could not fully trust him. But upon George Boleyn's return to England in May 1534, Henry showed no outward sign of discontent. On the contrary, he had proclaimed to the court his contentment with the results of George's fourth embassy, and had rewarded George with the offices of Constable of Dover Castle and Lord Warden of the Cinque Ports.[10]

Despite failing to persuade Francis to invoke anti-papal legislation, it was again George Boleyn who Henry chose as ambassador to travel to France in July.[11] His instructions were issued on 7 July 1534 and he left England three days later.[12] George was instructed to have an initial meeting with the Queen of Navarre to elicit her help in encouraging her brother to support Henry, and to postpone the royal meeting which had been scheduled to take place the following month until the following spring. He was to say that, although Anne was anxious to meet the Queen of Navarre, she wished the meeting to be deferred due to being far gone with child. On 10 July, Sir Edward Ryngeley wrote to Lord Lisle confirming that although the King had been due in Calais at the end of August, this was now somewhat in doubt and that the King was waiting "till the return of my lord of Rochford out of France."[13]

As in March 1533, when he had imparted to Francis the news of his sister's marriage, Anne's brother George was obviously the most suitable person to undertake the task of advising Francis of her second pregnancy. But in addition to this, he had already established a good relationship with the Queen of Navarre on previous embassies, due mainly to their joint commitment to Reform, and it was no doubt felt that George was the most likely person to encourage her into persuading her brother to provide support for Henry's cause.

There was an element of subterfuge in the instructions that made the meetings George was to have with Francis and Marguerite less than straightforward. The instructions from Henry state that George was to tell the Queen of Navarre that Anne wished to defer the meeting, but that Henry was so anxious to see the French king that he would not put the meeting off on Anne's account. George was to say that Anne wanted Henry by her side due to her advanced pregnancy, and he was instructed to "press this matter very earnestly", and say that Anne, "with much suit", had obtained leave for George to go to France instead of the King, "Rochford being her brother, and one whom her grace knoweth well will, to the utmost of his power, without offence to the king's highness, endeavour himself to her graces satisfaction in this behalf."[14] The instructions then go on to say that Anne hoped she might be able to go to Calais the following April. All this meant that George was to make clear to Marguerite that although his sister was desirous of meeting her, it was Anne alone who wished to postpone the meeting due to her pregnancy, and that it was nothing to do with Henry. The instructions clearly confirm that Anne's brother was astute enough to promote his sister's best interests without compromising Henry to any degree.

After seeing Marguerite, George was then to proceed to the French court for a meeting with Francis. His instructions included a number of matters, but he was again to request, on Anne's behalf, the postponement of the meeting, "using such ways and means as the queen of Navarre approves", and adding, "as of himself", that he thinks it would be advisable to agree to it, "as the time [Anne's impending confinement] shall shortly be here". Again, he was to ensure that Francis was aware that the request to postpone the meeting was coming solely from Anne, "the said Lord Rochford even so tempering his communications with the French king in this matter as he smell[?] not the king's highness to be overmuch desirous of it, but all in the queen's name."[15]

The instructions also state that George was to have further communication with the French king on issues that are not contained in the written instructions, but which have been discussed directly between the King, George and Anne: "He hath received more ample and full instructions... by mouth..." This shows a depth of trust in his brother-in-law that the King confirms in the body of the instructions themselves. These instructions also show the respect and affection in which the King held him, containing the following paragraph:

> First the Kings Majesty, knowing the approved
> wisdom fidelity and diligence, which is and ever
> hath been in the said Lord Rochford, with the
> propence good will mind and heart to serve his
> Highness in all things that may tend to his Graces
> contentment and pleasure, hath now appointed
> the said Lord Rochford, as one whom his grace
> specially loveth and trustith."

George arrived back in England on the 27 July bringing
with him confirmation that Francis had agreed to postpone the
meeting until the following year. As an example of how hopelessly
wrong Chapuys could be with the information contained in his
dispatches, he wrote to the Emperor on the day of George's arrival
saying, "The King has not been glad of the appointment of the said
Landgrave, nor of the news reported from France by Rochford,
among which is the delay of the interview till April."[16] The reality
was that George's instructions had actually been to get the meeting
postponed to the following April, which does exemplify how
dangerous it is to rely too heavily on the information contained in
Chapuys' dispatches.

In the end, the proposed meeting between the two kings and
queens never did take place. The meeting was rescheduled on a
number of occasions, but was eventually scheduled to take place in
May 1536. For obvious reasons this was cancelled. Less than two
years after George's return from France, Henry happily sacrificed
the brother-in-law he "specially loveth and trustith", in order
to get rid of the wife of whom he had tired. Like a child with a
favourite toy, when Henry no longer cared for Anne, both she and
her brother were thrown away. George Boleyn's years of loyalty
and devoted service were entirely forgotten in the King's haste to
remarry.

17 Lord Warden
of the Cinque Ports

During 1534 and 1535, and into 1536, the Boleyns maintained their strong position at court, and George Boleyn continued to be shown high royal favour. At the start of 1534, the Captain of Guisnes Castle, Lord Sandys, was taken grievously ill. Guisnes was the stronghold that guarded the last outpost of England on the continent - the city of Calais. Although Sandys eventually recovered, for a time it was believed he would die. On 4 April 1534, John Husee wrote to Lord Lisle, "And since my last letter I have perfect knowledge that if he had deceased my Lord of Rochford had been Captain of Guisnes."[1] The position was a highly prestigious and lucrative one. The salary was 2 shillings a day, and a 40 mark reward, with allowances, making a total of over £1000 a year. Lisle himself sought to exchange his deputyship of Calais for the captaincy of Guisnes, but Henry had already earmarked the position for his brother-in-law. This was later reaffirmed in a further letter of Husee's to Lord Lisle dated 11

April, when he states that Cromwell himself confirmed "that my Lord of Rochford hath grant of the same long agone."[2]

Due to Lord Sandys's recovery, the captaincy remained with him, but instead George was made Lord Warden of the Cinque Ports and then Constable of Dover Castle on 16 June 1534, positions he retained until his death.[3] The official grant was made on 23 June, but the appointment must have been known well before this because on 11 June Sir Edward Ryngeley wrote to Lord Lisle, "We have a new Lord Warden of the Ports, which is my Lord of Rochford."[4] Again, this position was highly sought after, but George Boleyn was in the right place at the right time to be granted it. The date of the grant suggests that it was a reward for George's efforts in France on his fourth diplomatic mission that April, which Henry chose to perceive as successful. This coincided neatly with the death of Edward Guildford, the resident incumbent, on 4 June.

The Cinque Ports is a group of port towns on the southeast coast of England. The original five were Sandwich, Dover, Hythe, New Romney and Hastings, but Winchelsea and Rye were also added. The port towns were of strategic importance for the defence of the country from potential foreign invasion. As such, they were responsible for the fitting-out and manning of ships for the transport of the King's army, and defence of the coast. In return, they received extensive immunities and liberties, which they guarded jealously. Every ambitious man in England wanted the distinction of being granted the position of Lord Warden, so much so that the post was held by princes of the realm such as Edward I, the Duke of Gloucester (later Richard III) and Henry VIII himself prior to becoming King. Ominously, the Duke of Buckingham had held the post prior to his execution in 1521 on trumped up charges of treason.

The post of Lord Warden of the Cinque Ports dates from at least the twelfth century and is now a ceremonial office. In the sixteenth century, it was the most powerful appointment of the realm. The Lord Warden had "lieutenant's powers of muster" and admiralty jurisdiction along the coast, and served as the Crown's agent in the ports. His responsibilities included collecting taxes, arresting criminals and returning writs. He held court in St James' Church, near Dover Castle, and the jurisdiction was similar to that of Chancery. The merging of the Constableship of Dover Castle with the office of Lord Warden meant that the Lord Warden also had a garrison at his disposal. Even today, the position of Lord Warden and Admiral of the Cinque Ports is the most ancient military honour available in England. More recent holders include William Pitt, the Duke of Wellington and Winston Churchill. Queen Elizabeth II currently holds the position.[5] Following George Boleyn's death, the post was handed to Thomas Cheyney, who was actually earmarked for the post on 8 May 1536, seven days before George even stood trial.

The appointment was made by the Crown, and the Lord Warden's first loyalty was to the sovereign, who was often intolerant of any rival jurisdiction. This resulted in the Lord Wardens having conflicting loyalties, because they were also bound by their oath of office to maintain and defend the ports' liberties. The ports looked to their Lord Wardens to be their protectors against external pressures, in particular those exerted by the Crown. This was not an easy balancing act for any Lord Warden, let alone one who was the King's brother-in-law.

George Boleyn's position as Lord Warden meant that when he was not abroad on embassy, much of his time would have been spent in Dover. His influence is referred to in correspondence between England and Calais. The post was not a sinecure, and he was not merely a figurehead; he took a very active role. For example, in April 1535, two men, Robert Justyce and his son James, were ordered to make certain payments together with further penalties for other misbehaviour, including a verbal refusal to make payment to the complainants as ordered. On 8 May Sir Richard Dering wrote to Lord Lisle complaining that he was being blamed by the Justyce's for the making of the order, when it was in fact "my Lord Warden's own personal act and judgement, sitting in court, and sitting with him then there present Sir William Haute and Sir Edward Ryngeley, knights and divers other gentlemen", whereby George "commanded them both to prison".[6] Dering goes on to say that George:

> Not only at his departing from the Castle did straitly command me, but also by his several letters in like manner did command me that they both should satisfy the said parties complainants their demands adjudged and also pay the penalties and moreover be bound with sufficient sureties for their good abearing before they should depart out of prison.

Eventually, the two men paid the sums they were ordered to pay, less sums which the complainants relaxed, and were thereby released by Dering, even though they had not given the sureties George had ordered. Dering also discharged them from part of the penalties they had been ordered to pay.

The fact that the complainants themselves relaxed part of the judgement suggests that the amount awarded by the young Lord Warden had been excessive. Upon hearing the judgement, Robert Justyce had exclaimed that "he would rather be cut in two with a sword than pay the demands the complainants adjudged or pay the penalties" - hence the Lord Warden's decision to command them to prison. Robert Justyce had been foolish enough to challenge the authority of George Boleyn in a court full of high-ranking officials, and such audacity could not be allowed. The fact that George sentenced both father and son to prison confirms our view of him as a young man capable of a single-minded ruthlessness, particularly when openly challenged. In this instance he went further. Not only did he verbally reiterate his orders to Dering, he also did so in several letters. This was not simply a question of making an example of the men. George was obviously furious, and he pursued the matter with a single-mindedness bordering on the vindictive. By the tone of Dering's letter, and from his actions, he clearly thought the Lord Warden had over reacted. He wrote to Lisle, "Of my own zeal, good will, and contrary to the commandment of my said Lord Warden, I have... set them both at liberty". However, he does express anxiety as to the "non-doing", of the Lord Warden's commandments.

Dering's letter raises a further issue of note. In heraldry, a cognisance was a mark worn by servants of a noble house, confirming the family by whom they were retained. George had commanded that in all towns of the ports no servant was to wear the cognisance of anyone other than the King or himself. Dering beseeches Lisle "not to take displeasure with me for doing of my said lord and master's commandment." This appears to exhibit a breathtaking arrogance on the part of George Boleyn, but the King had clearly given him direct authority to make such a commandment. Be that as it may, it is not difficult to see how the Queen's brother acquired a reputation for pride and arrogance, or how his downfall was not entirely mourned by some of his contemporaries.

For George Boleyn to have undertaken the position of Lord Warden would be today's equivalent of appointing a 30 year-old with no legal experience as a leading High Court judge. The Boleyn self-assurance and self-confidence meant that the high responsibility was merely viewed as a challenge to be embraced. To be able to undertake the role with panache and competency would further endorse the perception held both by the court and the general public that the Boleyn brother was an intelligent and gifted young man in his own right, not one who had to rely on his sister for preferment. Ironically, success for George Boleyn was more essential to his pride and self-respect than for any other courtier. As a favoured brother of the Queen Consort, it would have been easy for him to rest on his laurels. But pride and exuberance do not sit easy with lethargy and idleness. He lived in a world of treachery and backstabbing. He had to prove himself, and in order to do that he had to be better than anyone else. This probably added to the view of him as being arrogant; how much of this was due to a defensive response to the situation he was in, and how much to his natural personality and character, cannot be known.

George clearly embraced the role of Lord Warden. Examples of writs he issued and examples of his influence are contained in the state papers. On 23 June 1535, a matter of days after returning to England following a mission to France, a writ was issued by George to the bailiff and jurates of Romney and Old Romney, to provide a jury at Lyde on Thursday 1 July. The writ was issued from Dover Castle. The bailiffs and jurates duly sent the names of 12 jurors according to his writ. The presentation of the jury on 1 July concerned "lead, wine, sugar loaves, &c. found at Weis end, Langard, Brockes end, the Forland, the Nasse, &c".[7] A similar writ was issued by the Lord Warden on 3 August to produce a jury on the seashore at Lyde at 10 a.m. on 12 August.[8] On 15 September 1535, a verdict was given at Newcastle before George Boleyn by Sir John Heron and his fellows, regarding Sir Humphrey Lisle and Alex Schafto who had absented themselves from the Warden's court on account of indictments that had been found against them by freeholders of the country.[9] The energy and efficiency required to fulfil the duties of Lord Warden, while still maintaining a political and ambassadorial role and a high court profile, confirm what a hardworking and remarkable young man George Boleyn was.

Ominously, George is also mentioned in his role of Lord Warden in a letter written by Lord Lisle to Cromwell dated 2 July 1535. It was regarding the issue of the forfeiture of wool. Lisle writes, "As touching the forfeit of wools, I assure you, if I had not prevented the same before, my Lord of Rochford had had it himself; and so he showed me when I came before him, or else he had been sure of it! Wherefore mine only trust is in you above all creatures..."[10] It was becoming apparent to anyone in the know that Cromwell sought to be the sole source of all benefits, and that suits to the King that did not have his support should be prevented. He had expressed dissatisfaction to Lisle who had prevented forfeiture without seeking Cromwell's express authority. Lisle's defence was that if he had not done so then Lord Rochford would have carried out the action instead. By July 1535, Cromwell sought to be the sole intermediary with the King. Although Cromwell could bully the likes of Lisle, George Boleyn, as with Henry Norris and Francis Bryan, was not so easily subdued. Although the issue of the forfeiture of wool is a minor one, it does not bode well for future events.

The relationship between Anne Boleyn and Cromwell has been well documented, but there was at times a rather fraught relationship between George Boleyn and Cromwell. This is further emphasised in an earlier letter sent by George to Cromwell on 26 November 1534. It is worth quoting in full because it exemplifies Cromwell's attempt to undermine the young Lord, and George's unrestrained indignation:

> On Sunday last the mayor of Rye and others were with me at court, and I have taken such order and direction with them as I trust is right and just. I have commanded the mayor to return to Rye, and see the matter ordered according to the order I have taken in it before. He now advertises me that you have commanded him to attend you, and not obey this order. If you have been truly informed, or will command the mayor to declare you the order I have taken, I trust you will find no fault in it. Touching the last complaint put up to you by one of London, I never heard of it before; but when the mayor goes down he may cause the other party to appear before you at your pleasure.[11]

Cromwell had countermanded one of George's orders given as Lord Warden, and this was something the young Lord was not prepared to tolerate. The young man was not only angry, but also probably humiliated at being made to look as if he were subservient. The tone of the letter is quite obviously self-righteous indignation. Dangerously, he was not afraid to show his anger to the King's chief minister, or to make no attempt to camouflage his displeasure. In 1534, Cromwell had taken him for granted, but he would not do so 18 months later.

Figure 1 - George Boleyn's cipher

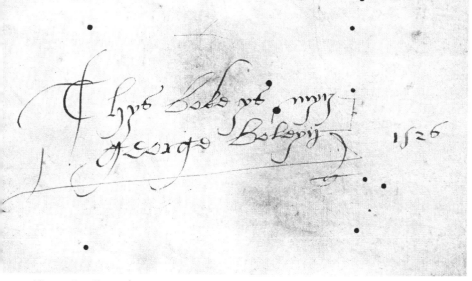

Figure 2 - George's inscription in Les Lamentations de Matheolus

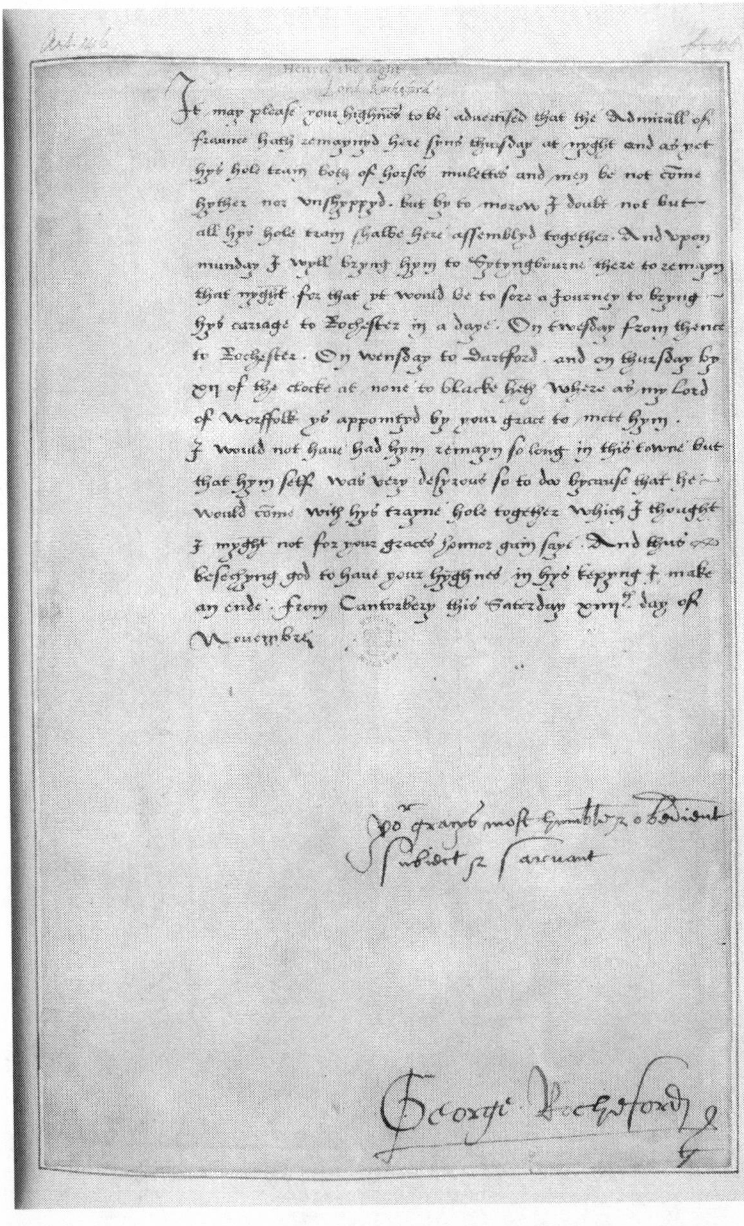

It may please your highnes to be advertised that the Admirall of ffraunce hath remaynyd here syns thursday at nyght and as yet hys hole trayn both of horses muletts and men be not come hyther nor unshyppyd. but by to morow I doubt not but all hys hole trayn shalbe here assemblyd together. And upon munday I wyll bryng hym to Sytyngbourne there to remayn that nyght for that yt would be to sore a journey to bryng hys cariage to Rochester in a daye. On twesday from thence to Rochester. On wensday to Dartford. and on thursday by on of the clocke at none to blacke heth where as my Lord of Norffolk ys appoyntyd by your grace to mett hym. I would not have had hym remayn so long in this towne but that hym self was very desyrous so to doo bycause that he would come with hys trayne hole together which I thought I myght not for your graces honor gaynsaye. And thus besechyng god to have your hyghnes in hys kepyng I make an ende. from Cantorbery this Saterday xiiij day of Novembre

Yor graces most humble & obedient
subiect & servant

George Rocheford

Figure 3 - Letter from George Boleyn to Henry VIII

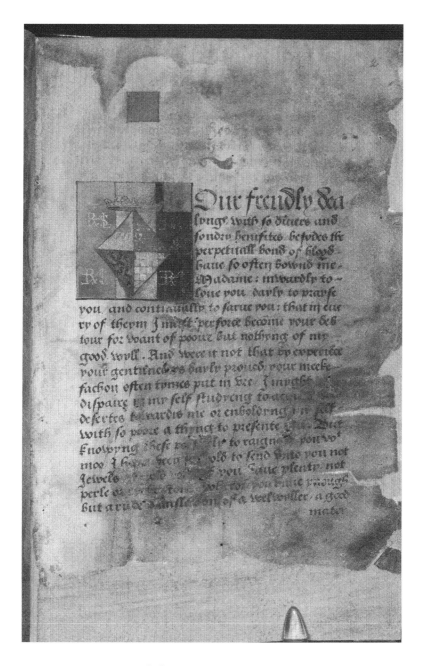

Our frendly dea

longe, with so diuers and
sondry benifites besydes the
perpetuall bond of bloud
haue so often bound me
Madame: inwardly to
loue you darly to prayse
you and continually to serue you: that in eue-
ry of therm I muct perforce become your deb-
tour for want of poour but nothyng of my
good will. And were it not that by experiece
your gentlenes darly proued, your meeke-
faction often tymes put in vre, I myght
dispaire of my self studreng to acqt
desertes towardis me or enboldrng it fo[r]
with so poore a thyng to presente you. But
knowyng these roll elly to raigne in you vo[?]
moo I haue ben bold to send vnto you not
Jewels ... you haue plenty, not
perle ... you haue ynough
but a rude tansle[?]on of a welwiller, a good
mater

Figure 4 - George's dedication and preface to Les Epistres

Figure 5 - Engraving of Anne Boleyn

Figure 6 - Engraving of Henry VIII

Figure 7 - Engraving of Thomas Cranmer, Archbishop of Canterbury

Figure 8 - Engraving of Thomas Cromwell

Figure 9 - Engraving of Thomas Howard, 3rd Duke of Norfolk

Figure 10 - Engraving of Francis I of France

Figure 11 - Engraving of the marriage of Anne Boleyn and Henry VIII

Figure 12 - Engraving of Hever Castle

Figure 13 - Engraving of the arrest of Anne Boleyn

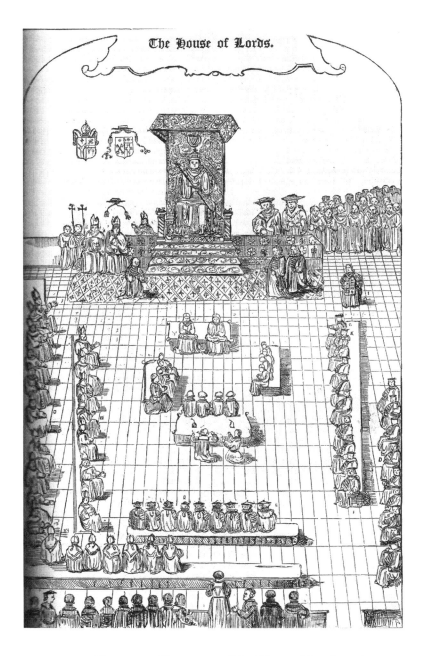

Figure 14 - Engraving of the House of Lords in the reign of Henry VIII

Figure 15 - Tower of London

Figure 16 - Chapel of St. Peter ad Vincula, Tower of London

Figure 17 - Tower Hill scaffold memorial

Figure 18 - Dover Castle

Part 3 - The End of an Era

18 Crisis at Home and Abroad

In July 1534, George Boleyn was riding high. He was promoted to positions of trust and importance far beyond his years - he was still only around 29 to 30 years of age. The King does not appear to have had anything but confidence in his young brother-in-law; at no time was his competence challenged, save by Boleyn enemies abroad. Yet despite George's influence and importance continuing to blossom, by the middle of that year cracks were starting to show in the Boleyn stronghold.

Anne appears to have lost a baby through a premature stillbirth in the summer of 1534. At the time, her brother was in France obtaining a postponement of the meeting scheduled to take place between the French and English Kings because of Anne's pregnancy. The stillbirth, would have been extremely distressing news for George's return home. He would have left England on a high, his sister pregnant with the anticipated future King of England, only to return home to a highly distressed and emotional Anne, her dreams momentarily in tatters, and a disappointed King. Then, according to Chapuys, in the autumn of 1534 George's wife, Lady Rochford was banished from court, supposedly for conspiring with the Queen to have a rival removed: "the young lady whom this king has been accustomed to serve".[1] It has been suggested that this lady was Jane Seymour, but this cannot be correct as the King's interest in Jane did not begin until much later. On 13 October Chapuys reported that Lady Rochford had plotted with Anne to pick a quarrel with Henry's new fancy and force her to withdraw. However, as Chapuys himself acknowledges, he regularly got facts wrong, and in addition to this his communications were always slanted to show Anne in a bad light. This could have simply been wishful thinking on his part. If there were a lady at court who had taken the King's fancy, it would appear that the relationship was purely superficial because it obviously did not last long. Even Chapuys himself admitted that not too much importance should be placed on it, since Henry was fickle and Anne knew how to manage him. Irrespective of the seriousness of the relationship, it was a sign that the King's affections had started to stray. Anne was no Catherine; she would not put up with it quietly.

With regards to Jane Rochford's role in all this, if the story is true it shows that Anne was close enough to Jane to confide in her and seek her help with what was surely a delicate matter. However, it may be that Anne chose her as an ally simply because she was George's wife, and therefore a member of the family who could possibly be trusted more than an outsider. Lady Rochford's banishment is mentioned in two dispatches from Chapuys. In the second, dated 19 December, he confirms that his previous information regarding her was correct. If true, and Jane Rochford was not only banished but also banished for the reason given by Chapuys, there is no record of her return to court. Up until the arrest and trial of her husband, there is no further mention of Lady Rochford; she may have been present at a demonstration in favour of the Princess Mary, which took place in the summer of

1535, but her name is actually not mentioned in the account of the demonstration and subsequent imprisonments. The story of her involvement comes from a note in the margin of that account mentioning "Millor de Rochesfort et millord de Guillaume".[2]

It was also in the autumn of 1534 that George's eldest sister, the widowed Mary Boleyn, became pregnant and secretly married William Stafford, a man of inferior rank and status. From the Boleyns' point of view, Mary, being the Queen's sister, had betrayed and embarrassed them by her shameful behaviour, and by not seeking her family's permission to marry. Anne, as queen, was now head of the Boleyn family, and should have been consulted. Anne was so furious with her sister that she banished her from court as soon as the marriage came to light. It is not certain whether the sisters ever met again. Chapuys suggests that Mary's banishment was justified because she "had been found guilty of misconduct, it would not have been becoming to see her at court."[3]

Shortly after her banishment, Mary wrote to Cromwell begging him to speak to her various relatives for financial support, saying, "Pray my lord my father and my lady to be good to us... and my lord Norfolk and my brother... I dare not write to them, they are so cruel against us."[4] It is clear that Thomas and George Boleyn shared Anne's anger at Mary's pregnancy and poor marriage choice. Thomas's reaction was probably due to losing the chance of placing Mary in a marriage that would have proved more beneficial to him. Anne and George's anger was most likely to have been caused by pride. The nobility were not expected to marry for love; marriages were made for family advantage. Mary could not be allowed to flaunt her pregnancy around court to the embarrassment of her relations. The siblings' fury at their sister's indiscretions can only have been exacerbated by her decision to write to an outsider to intervene on her behalf with her family. The Boleyns would have been mortified that Mary chose to ask Cromwell, a mere commoner, to help her and to become involved in their family affairs. Whether George ever saw Mary again after her banishment is something we will probably never know.

Mary Boleyn, like Jane Rochford, is a difficult woman to pinpoint. Extant records are virtually silent with regard to her movements. There is no way of really knowing what Mary's relationship with George was like, but bearing in mind his ability to cut her off following her banishment, they were probably not close. Likewise, she made no known attempt to contact him following his arrest. Mary's character and personality was very different to her brother's, and George seems to have been able, whether unconsciously or by design, to distance himself emotionally from anyone whose character or views he could not or would not understand. That ability probably owed itself more to his belief in his own infallibility than anything else, as he seemed to be unable or unwilling to accept that anyone of worth could possibly disagree with his view of the world.

Despite the banishments of Jane and Mary, in the autumn of 1534 Anne and George Boleyn had far more important things on their minds. On 26 September 1534, Pope Clement VII died and Cardinal Alexander Farnese was created Pope Paul III. On 15 October, Sir Gregorio da Casale, Henry VIII's agent in Rome and a man well known to the Boleyns, wrote to George advising him that the whole of Rome was rejoicing in the death of the Pope, and that the creation of Paul III had given the greatest pleasure.[5] Paul III was considered friendly towards Henry and ill-disposed to the Emperor. Despite the passing of the Act of Supremacy in November, Henry still held some vague hope of an eventual reconciliation with Rome, but only on his terms. His terms were for the Pope to ratify the annulment of his marriage to Catherine and the validity of his marriage with Anne. The appointment of the new Pope renewed the possibility of reconciliation between England and the Holy See. However, it later became apparent that the new Pope's terms for such reconciliation remained the same as those of the previous Pope.

September 1534 brought fresh hope of a more amicable relationship with France. Despite the King of France's annoyance at Henry's bombastic attitude during the summer of 1533, Francis was prepared to make fresh efforts to renew a good relationship with Henry. The prospect of an improved relationship with France was greeted favourably by Henry, as well as by Anne and George. Unfortunately for them, this renewed optimism was painfully dispelled two months later.

In November 1534, a mission from the King of France, headed by Philippe de Chabot, Seigneur de Brion and Admiral of France, came to the English court. The possibility of renewing good relations with France was of significant importance. England was becoming more and more isolated from her European cousins, all because of Henry's matrimonial problems, a fact which could not have failed to escape the Boleyn siblings and their father. Both Anne and George had been heavily involved in attempting to postpone the meeting between the Pope and Francis the previous summer, and therefore the French Embassy was met enthusiastically and with some relief. When Henry sought a courtier to escort the French Admiral from the coast to the court, it was George Boleyn, as one of his leading courtiers and someone who knew members of the French court, to whom he entrusted the job. The importance of the mission is exemplified in a letter written by George to Lord Lisle from Dover on 6 November:

> This shall be to advertise you that I have sent this bearer, the king's servant, only to bring me foreword how and after what sort the Admiral doth purpose to pass the sea, and whether he will send his train, mules and carriage over before, or else to come himself first; the knowledge whereof should be of great furtherance to me in entertaining him here.[6]

Every courtesy was to be extended to the Admiral, and George was given the task not only of escorting him to London, but also of entertaining him on the way. The Admiral arrived at Dover on 11 November with a huge train of men and 350 horses, for all of whom George had responsibility. The administrative logistics were a nightmare, and that day a harassed George Boleyn wrote to his uncle, the Duke of Norfolk, who had been appointed to meet George and the Admiral at Blackheath:

> This my letter shall be to advise your Lordship that the Admiral arrived this day at ten of the clock at the Downs, and there I, with such gentlemen as be commanded by the king's grace to give their attendance to accompany me, met with him at his coming to land, and from hence we brought him to Dover, where he rested for this first night; and the next day to Canterbury, and there he has desired that he may tarry Friday all day, so that his train may meet with him there, which be now scattered some at Dover, some at Sandwich and some at other places.[7]

The visit was too important for the Admiral's wishes not to be accommodated, despite the additional onerous administrative difficulties this caused George. Doing so also resulted in him arriving in London later than planned. An already-harassed George Boleyn pre-empted any personal criticism from the King for this tardiness in a letter to Henry dated 14 November, in which he described the journey with thinly disguised irritation:

> It may please your highness to be advertised, that the admiral of France hath remained here since Thursday at night, and as yet his whole train both of horses, mules and men, be not come hither nor unshipped. But by tomorrow I doubt not but all his whole train shall be here assembled together: and upon Monday, I will bring him to Sittingbourne, there to remain that night, for that it would be too sore a journey to bring his carriage to Rochester in a day. On Tuesday from thence to Rochester. On

Wednesday to Dartford; and on Thursday, by 12 o'clock at noon, to Blackheath; where as my Lord of Norfolk is appointed by your grace to meet him. I would not have him remain so long in this town, but that himself was very desirous so to do, because that he would come with his train whole together, which I thought might not for your graces honour gain saye. And thus, beseeching God to have your highness in his keeping, I make an end.

From Canterbury, this 14th day of November

Your graces most humble and obedient subject and servant,

GEORGE ROCHEFORD"[8] (See Figure 3)

The undertaking of bringing the Admiral from the coast was too important for it to be placed in the hands of anyone other than a highly trusted individual, and George Boleyn was clearly acutely aware of this. The letter is earnestly written by a young man obviously eager to please the King and gives the impression of someone anxious to explain where any fault may be perceived. George clearly took his assignment extremely seriously, allowing the Admiral to travel only a single stage per day to ensure his comfort. At the same time he is keen to explain to Henry that the reason they have remained in Canterbury so long is by the specific request of the Admiral himself.

It was this enthusiasm, devotion, competence and, above all, loyalty which continued to endear him to the King. Yet almost exactly one year after this letter was written, George was supposed to have had sex for the first time with his sister. And at the same time as the above letter was written, George was supposed to have not only known of Anne's alleged affairs with the other four accused men, but to have actively encouraged them. Therefore,

Henry's "most humble and obedient subject and servant" was, according to his later prosecution, already committing treason at this point.

Unknown to Henry, one of the purposes of the Admiral's visit was to enforce the marriage, which had been arranged in 1518, between Henry's eldest daughter Mary and the Dauphin. The desire by the French to enforce the match was on the understanding that Mary remained legitimate, which would mean the undoing of the Acts of Succession and Supremacy. This came as an unpleasant surprise to Henry and as utter horror to the Boleyns. During his conference with the Admiral of France, Henry would not agree to the marriage between Mary and the Dauphin, but instead made a counter-proposal of a marriage between Princess Elizabeth and the Duke of Angoulême, the French king's third son. The counter-proposal was rejected. The desire by the French to enforce the marriage of Mary to the Dauphin was an indication that they were putting Mary's claim to the throne above Elizabeth's. The French stance shocked both Anne and her brother, who had previously thought that any support they may have received from abroad would be from France.

Unfortunately for them, the French embassy had come one month after the "affair of the placards", which had completely turned Francis I against the evangelical movement.[9] Not even his evangelical sister Marguerite could thereafter dissuade him from actively persecuting those who favoured the new religious ideals. Francis was well aware of the Boleyns' evangelical faith, particularly from his close association with George Boleyn over the years. From being tolerant of Reform, and a potential ally of the Boleyns, Francis had come to distrust the very ideals that they embodied. Francis knew that any child of Anne's would promote Reform, but that Mary would return England to Catholicism. The Boleyns had lost a possible ally, and no longer would George Boleyn be able to rely on a good relationship with the French king. Having left Francis on excellent terms in July 1534, George never met the French king again.

It is ominous that a month after the French debacle, during December 1534 an incident occurred that provided the first indication that George Boleyn might be out of favour with Henry VIII. According to Chapuys, that month George had a heated discussion with his cousin, Francis Bryan, who had previously been a staunch ally of the Boleyns.[10] Bryan was a notorious character, christened "the Vicar of Hell" by Cromwell. He was questioned in May 1536 as a possible victim of the plot against the Boleyns, but managed to escape without being arrested and charged. At some time in his life he lost an eye, the circumstances of which are contradictory. Like George, Bryan was a gifted poet and diplomat who was sent on numerous missions abroad by Henry. His reputation as a hell raiser made him popular with the King, with whom he was on intimate terms throughout his life. It was Francis Bryan, together with Henry Norris and George Boleyn himself, who were considered to be the three courtiers most influential with the King during the early to mid-1530s. On 13 August 1535, John Worth wrote to Lady Lisle requesting that she write to "Master Norris or to Francis Bryan, or to my Lord Rochford, in desiring them to get me a bill assigned of the king for the check of my wages for a three years."[11] It was clearly recognised by everyone that if a particular favour was required of the King, then these three men were the people to mediate.

In a dispatch from Chapuys dated 19 December, he wrote gleefully that "It is true that Rochefort's wife was sent from Court for the reason that I have heretofore written, and the said king recently showed disfavour to the said Rochefort in some question he had with master Bryan."[12] As with most of Chapuys' reports, there is no other corroborative evidence, and therefore the circumstances cannot be verified. Chapuys gives no indication of what the quarrel was about, probably because he was ignorant of the details. Whatever the substance of the quarrel, it was serious enough for the King not only to have intervened, but also to have sided with Bryan against his brother-in-law. Chapuys clearly ties the King's siding with Bryan to the banishment of George's wife, as if Chapuys is suggesting the King's disfavour at her bad behaviour was being taken out on her husband.

It is often suggested that Bryan deliberately faked the quarrel with George in order to steer clear of trouble at the time of Anne's downfall. Although this is a possibility, it seems unlikely bearing in mind the date of the altercation. Bryan was certainly a survivor, but in December 1534, despite the loss of their second child and the King's wandering eye, there was no realistic suggestion that Henry's marriage to Anne was in serious difficulties. Yet whatever the nature of the quarrel, it may well have been from this moment on that Bryan's allegiance to the Boleyns altered. Certainly by May 1536, he was securely on the winning side, making the timing of his argument with George highly fortuitous.

If Chapuys was correct, and George was out of favour with the King, the disfavour was clearly temporary because the following year he chose George to renegotiate the marriage of Elizabeth in place of Cromwell who was ill. At the time of the quarrel, though, George would have been embarrassed and humiliated. He may well have seen any altercation with his cousin as a private family matter. To have an argument aired in public, and to have the King side against him, would have been mortifying, particularly as this would have been the first time the King had ever shown displeasure towards him personally. It has also been suggested that the King and Bryan deliberately engineered the quarrel to enable the King to side against George, thereby showing his general displeasure with Anne, while using George as a scapegoat. This seems unlikely, but if true, it was a dreadful portent of things to come.

The last six months of 1534 were particularly difficult for the Boleyns. Anne had miscarried, her sister and sister-in-law had been banished from court, Henry had begun to pay attention to other women, an alliance with France could no longer be relied upon, and even George was temporarily out of favour. The following year would prove no better.

1535 was a particularly brutal and savage year, and the Boleyns come out of it with little credit. In February 1535, the Act of Supremacy, which had been enacted the previous November, came into force and steps were immediately taken to enforce compliance. This was the start of four of the most brutal and barbaric years in English history, as those who opposed this act and the Act of Succession were tried and executed as traitors. Many people were martyred in the name of religious reform, which to a large extent had been instigated by the Boleyn siblings and their supporters. There is no proof that either of the siblings actively supported these deaths, which were ordered by Henry and Henry alone, but just as the court later turned a blind eye to the deaths of the Boleyn siblings, so Anne and George appeared indifferent to the sufferings their commitment to Reform was causing. George Boleyn passionately believed that religious reform was fundamentally right, yet by achieving it, honourable men were being murdered. He must have prayed that the legislation would pave the way for Reform as he had envisioned it, rather than becoming merely a means of granting absolute power to an already egotistical monarch.

On 4 May 1535, George was present, along with his father, uncle (Norfolk), Henry Norris and other courtiers, including Henry's illegitimate son, at the executions of three prominent Carthusian monks. The Carthusians are a Roman Catholic order of monks and nuns, and like Thomas More and John Fisher, they refused to swear an oath to the Acts of Succession and Supremacy. Three priors were put to death - John Houghton, Robert Lawrence and Augustine Webster, respectively priors of the London Charterhouse, Beauvale and Axholme – and a Bridgettine monk, Richard Reynolds of Syon Abbey. They were hanged, drawn and quartered at Tyburn. Between 1535 and 1536, 18 Carthusian monks were executed for defying the new legislation.

In 1532, Thomas More had resigned his post of Chancellor. His Catholic faith meant he felt unable to embrace the belief that the Pope was only the Bishop of Rome, and that he had no authority over the Christian church as a whole. Likewise, the English Catholic Bishop John Fisher was unable to recognise Henry as head of the Church of England. Fisher had initially been arrested in March 1533 for supposedly alleging that when George Boleyn travelled to France he had taken with him large sums of money to be used as bribes.[13] Fisher was later set at liberty, but the following year he was again arrested, this time for refusing to sign the oath of succession acknowledging Anne's children as legitimate heirs. He was also unable to accept that Henry could be the law of God on Earth. Fisher was sent to the Tower on 26 April 1534, shortly after the Act of Succession came into force. He stood trial on 17 June and was beheaded five days later. The death of Fisher resulted in the Pope activating Henry's excommunication, which had been threatened three years previously.

Thomas More's opposition went back even further. He had refused to make a request to the Pope to annul the marriage of Henry and Catherine, and in 1533 had refused to attend Anne's coronation. On 13 April 1534, he also refused to sign his allegiance to the Act of Succession, and four days later he was arrested. More stood trial on 1 July 1535 and was beheaded on 6 July. Both Thomas and George Boleyn were present at More's trial as part of the special commission to hear the case, and witnessed his courageous and spirited defence. More died saying, "I die the king's good servant, but God's first."[14] Although More died a martyr and has been canonised, while he was Chancellor he had six Lutherans burnt at the stake for heresy, a death infinitely slower and more painful than the death he suffered. His was the sanctimony of those religious zealots in any era of history who genuinely believe they can commit any atrocity provided it is in the name of God.

Upon More's death, George had no compunction in accepting a grant of one of More's Kentish properties, Oteham Manor.[15] The grant was made on 10 April, but in a letter dated 4 May and addressed to Henry Norris, Thomas, Prior of Michelham, confirmed that less than a month later George sold the property.

He may well have sought to get rid of it, and its connotations, as quickly as possible. Alternatively, and more likely, he may simply have needed the money. In his letter, the Prior confirms that the yearly rent of 25 marks had been received by the Prior and his predecessors for over 200 years, including during the short period in which George Boleyn had the benefit of the property, "my Lord Warden being owner". George sold the manor to William Kenslye, and under the terms of the indenture was entitled to retain the rent for himself. The Prior was attempting to elicit Norris's help in asking George to "reform his indenture".[16] Whether the usually honourable George did in fact do so is unknown. There is certainly no mention of any rent being received by him from the manor of Oteham in the schedule of his income taken at the time of his death and there is no record of George ever being sued (the Prior had been threatening possible court action), which suggests the original indenture was reinstated.

In less than a year's time there would be a frantic rush to apply for grants of George's confiscated assets following his own execution. The sixteenth century was a brutal era of history, particularly under Henry VIII, and only the fittest survived. The mere fact that the Boleyns maintained their power base for so long leads to the inevitable conclusion that they were prepared, and perfectly able to play the system with a hard and brutal determination of their own. The deaths of the Carthusians, including More and Fisher, as with Elizabeth Barton and her associates 12 months earlier, should have acted as a forbidding warning to the nation of things to come. Their deaths were all due to their refusal to submit to the King's will, and the constant threat of Henry's increasing paranoia and egotism hung over the country.

The brutal deaths of the Carthusians caused disgust and horror throughout the country, and the presence of the Boleyns at the executions evoked further disgust. Failure to attend, however, regardless of religious persuasion, would have amounted to a direct challenge to the authority of the King. Just as it was the duty of the jury to find the Boleyns guilty in a little over a year's time, and likewise the duty of courtiers to attend their subsequent executions, the Boleyns had no choice.

In May 1535, following his attendance at the deaths of the Carthusians, George went on a further mission to France, intending to put pressure on Francis I to make a more public commitment to Anne's cause. He was also charged with renegotiating the match between the King of France's third son and Princess Elizabeth, which had initially been mooted the previous November to the Admiral of France. The English were also seeking an agreement that the boy should live and be educated in England prior to the marriage. Thomas Cromwell was originally intended to be the representative of the Crown, but had become ill. The responsibility therefore fell to George Boleyn, who once again attended with his uncle, the Duke of Norfolk, who was already in France. George arrived on the 20 May, a day after his uncle and two days before the arrival of Admiral Chabot, the principal French delegate.

Cromwell's absence caused some comment. On 5 May, Chapuys wrote, "Rochford, the lady's brother, will go in place of Cromwell. Many think that Cromwell excused himself of the charge in despair of the issue."[17] It was being insinuated that Cromwell had feigned illness, knowing the mission would fail, which it did. On 22 May, George and Norfolk met Chabot, the Admiral of France, at Calais, and neither side was prepared to compromise. In particular, the French would not countenance Francis's third son, the Duke of Angoulême, being educated in England prior to the proposed marriage with Elizabeth. Chabot was furious at the whole idea and threatened to abandon the negotiations, so George was quickly dispatched to England for further instructions, leaving France on 24 May and arriving in London the following day.[18] En route to England, George met up with William Fitzwilliam who wrote to Cromwell on 25 May informing him of his conversation with George:

This day I met my Lord of Rochford by the way,
who showed me part of his charge. And surely,
Sir, I not only cannot a little marvel to hear that
the Admiral arrived at Calais on Saturday [22nd
May] and was ready to depart from thence again
upon Monday, and that he makes so light of the
matter; but also much more marvel that he should
in effect answer to all the points of our charge.
And we had instructions to proceed with him by
degrees and to make a pause at the first, and if it
were for a day or two. And when we had brought
him to the point of desperation in that behalf,
then he and we to devise the best remedies that we
could, and thereupon declare the king's pleasure
in the second degree.[19]

There was clearly deep concern in the English camp as to the
arrogant, unhelpful attitude of the French delegates, who were
not prepared to discuss any compromise, and indeed seemed
keen to depart rather than negotiate further. Bearing in mind his
particular personal interest in the matter, it is not surprising that
it was George who was chosen to report the matter to the King
and obtain his further instructions.

It is a sign of the closeness of brother and sister that prior to
reporting to Henry, George's first thought was to see Anne to
inform her of the situation.[20] It is also a sign that they, as much
as Henry, were behind the negotiations regarding Elizabeth's
marriage. According to Chapuys, George arrived in London on
25 May, went straight to Anne, and had a long private discussion
with her. Chapuys wrote, "He cannot have brought back from
Calais anything agreeable to himself; for I am told by the Master
of the Horse [Nicholas Carew] that, both then and several
times since she has been in a bad humour, and said a thousand
shameful words of the King of France, and generally the whole
nation."[21] The French alliance had been put to the test and it had

failed miserably. England needed a foreign ally, and now the only alternative was reconciliation with Spain (to which Anne was a major obstacle). This joined with Anne's failure to produce a son, and with Henry's infatuation with Jane Seymour (which began early the following year), spelled the beginning of the end for the Boleyns.

George was detained in England as long as possible, but was eventually sent back to France at the start of June with instructions for him, Norfolk and their team to "firmly stand" on the previous demands but, if pressed, to consent to the Duke of Angoulême spending at least six months to a year in England before his marriage to Elizabeth. The instructions confirmed that prior to George's departure there had been a lengthy and detailed meeting of the counsel, "whereof was present the said Lord Rochford who can by mouth thoroughly instruct the said ambassadors of the same points, as the case shall require."[22] Again, as with George's mission of the previous summer, detailed written instructions were unnecessary. The King had enough faith in his abilities to dispense with the requirement. The intractability of the two sides meant that the meeting in Calais broke down abruptly on 17 June following lengthy and increasingly heated debate, and George and his team departed for England on 24 June. It was an ignominious homecoming for George Boleyn, following a mission that had ended in complete failure. Tragically, this was to be his final mission abroad.

While George was involved in the French negotiations in Calais, matters relating to the Cinque Ports obviously continued. On 28 May, the mayor of jurates at Rye wrote to Cromwell confirming that in the Lord Warden's absence abroad, his father had on his behalf opened various letters addressed to his son and had shown them to the King's attorney.[23] In the early days of the King's infatuation with Anne, Thomas Boleyn was in the forefront of all matters concerning his daughter as one of Henry's leading diplomats and courtiers. Gradually, he was pushed further and further into the background as his son and daughter took hold of their own destinies. It was his son who was sent to France on five separate occasions between March 1533 and June 1535. It was his son who was appointed as Lord Warden of the Cinque Ports in June 1534, one of the most prestigious appointments in the land. Thomas Boleyn was reduced to deputising for George in his son's absence, by opening letters on his behalf. Was Thomas proud of his son's achievements, or was there an element of resentment? He had been an exacting and domineering father throughout his children's formative years and into their adulthood, but by 1535, his influence over his clever children had waned. He was a proud, arrogant man, and a courtier by nature, just as his children were courtiers by nature and design. Was it pride he felt when he saw them eclipsing him, or resentment at his waning influence?

By mid-1535, there was near total alienation from France. Francis was now totally opposed to religious reform following the demonstrations in France, and Europe was appalled by the deaths of More and Fisher. Any influence or connections George may have held at the French court, and any good relations he may have had with the French king, were now well and truly in the past. By early July, Francis was even making anti-Boleyn comments. He criticised Anne on how "little virtuously she has always lived", and indicated how "she and her brother and adherents suspect the Duke of Norfolk of wishing to make his son king, and marry him to the king's legitimate daughter."[24]

In England, there was growing support for the Princess Mary. In the summer of 1535 there was a public demonstration at Greenwich in her favour, which had been aided and abetted by some of the ladies of the royal household who were not on duty.[25] According to a letter written by the Bishop of Tarbes to the Bailly of Troyes in October 1535, when Mary left Greenwich, "a great troop of citizens' wives and others, unknown to their husbands, presented themselves before her, weeping and crying that she was princess, notwithstanding all that had been done. Some of them, the chiefest, were placed in the Tower." A note in the margin of this letter says "Millor de Rochesfort et millord de Guillaume", which has been used to back up the idea that George's wife was one of the ringleaders who was sent to the Tower. Jane's alleged banishment from court had taken place the previous autumn, and the demonstration took place during the royal summer progress at which George was present, so her participation may have been out of frustration and anger at her continued estrangement. However, the usually vigilant Chapuys did not pick up this story, and likewise there is no record of Jane Rochford being incarcerated in the Tower prior to the fall of Catherine Howard in 1541. If true, her actions would have caused irreparable damage to the Rochfords' marriage and by taking such action, Lady Rochford would have been putting herself in open opposition and conflict, not only with Anne, but also with her own husband and the King, whose command it was that Mary should not be treated as Princess. In addition to anger, George would also have felt embarrassment and humiliation at his own wife being imprisoned for openly defying him, his family and the King.

Jane's good relationship with Mary following the deaths of George and Anne confirms the loyalty and affection she had for the princess despite the fact that her husband had been one of Mary's bitterest enemies. Jane must have maintained this loyalty and affection for Mary throughout her marriage to George; yet it is very difficult to imagine her taking such drastic action, which would have been completely against her own best interests. Jane was as much of a self-serving survivor as her in-laws, and putting her liberty, marriage and career on the line for her moral beliefs seems an unlikely thing for her to do. Besides, she became Jane Seymour's lady-in-waiting after the Boleyns' deaths. Henry was highly unlikely to have allowed her to resume such a prestigious position if she had previously spent time in the Tower for openly defying him. Weighing up the evidence, her involvement in the demonstration is improbable.

Despite the continued problems at home and abroad, during the summer progress of 1535 Anne and Henry appeared to be particularly "merry" together, and it was during October of that year that Anne became pregnant for the third time. It is notable that Anne managed to fall pregnant while she was relaxed and more confident of the King's love. The pressure on her to have a son was enormous. But the enjoyment of the summer progress, and being away from the suffocating confines of London, meant the dazzling Boleyns failed to notice a young woman named Jane Seymour. Even if they had, they would simply have dismissed her as a plain, quiet creature unworthy of their attention.

19 Oncoming Storm

In September 1535, Henry VIII's court stayed at Wolf Hall, the home of Sir John Seymour and his family, while on royal progress. Seymour's son Edward was already a member of the Privy Chamber, and was therefore well known to Anne and George Boleyn. The court stayed at Wolf Hall between 4 and 10 September, demonstrating the favour the Seymours enjoyed at this time. Although this visit is often used in novels as the setting of Henry VIII's first meeting with Sir John's daughter, Jane was already known to the King, and he was in any case accompanied by Anne on this visit. Jane had served Catherine of Aragon, and had moved into Anne's employ sometime in 1535. It is not known when Jane caught the King's eye, but initially his interest in her was notional. It was simply a case of courtly love at a time when Anne was pregnant.

The King's particular interest in Jane did not become apparent until January 1536, and she was not mentioned in any of Chapuys' correspondence until 10 February.[1] As late as 1 April 1536, Chapuys referred to Jane as a lady "whom he [the King] serves", referring to the courtly love tradition of a knight serving a lady, an innocent flirtation rather than a serious affair.

Jane Seymour was born around 1508, which made her only about seven years younger than Anne. However, there could not have been two women more different in temperament and personality. Where Anne was intelligent, quick-tempered and passionate, Jane appears to have been docile and submissive. Ironically, if Jane had survived long enough, the King may well have become bored with her. Instead, she was fortunate enough to become pregnant before that happened. As a result, she died as the sainted mother of the long-awaited prince.

But at the time of the royal progress, and over Christmas and New Year 1535-6, everything continued to appear favourable for the Boleyns. Despite the disaster in France, they were proud, triumphant and seemingly blessed with the King's favour. Anne was once again pregnant, and the family went into 1536 with renewed optimism. But three incidents at the start of 1536 proved to be disastrous, particularly for Anne and her brother.

Firstly, on 7 January 1536 Catherine of Aragon died. Upon hearing the news, Henry is supposed to have cried, "God be praised that we are free of suspicion of war!", because he now had no quarrel with Emperor Charles V, Catherine's nephew. Then he dressed in yellow and paraded the two-year old Princess Elizabeth to mass "with trumpets and other great triumphs".[2]

The Boleyn family were also delighted at the news, and Chapuys surmised that Thomas and George's only wish was that Mary would "keep company with her mother".[3] This may or may not have been true. The Boleyn position would certainly have been far stronger with Mary dead, but she was still the King's daughter. Irrespective of Thomas and George's private thoughts, it would be unlikely that either of them would have been foolish enough to have expressed those thoughts out loud in the public arena or in front of those people likely to report it to Chapuys. What Catherine's death really meant was that there was no longer any obstacle to reconciliation with the Emperor, save for Anne herself.

Clearly the Boleyns had not envisaged this at the start of 1536, as they seemingly maintained the King's favour. Of course foreign policy had never previously affected the Boleyns' position, and it would not have done so in 1536 if Anne had retained the King's love. But then the second event, namely the flowering of Henry's interest in Jane Seymour, coincided with the third and final event which altered everything.

The joy at Catherine's death was short-lived. On 24 January Henry suffered a bad fall from his horse, a fall which could have killed him. Five days later, on the very day of Catherine's funeral, Anne suffered her second miscarriage, losing Henry's longed-for son.[4] Anne is supposed to have blamed the miscarriage on her anxiety over Henry's fall, and also her emotional stress at his affection for Jane Seymour. Anne's response to Henry's relationship with Jane was in stark contrast to that of her predecessor, Queen Catherine. Where Catherine turned a blind eye, Anne ranted and raved. Henry had been enchanted by her passion and intelligence while they were courting, but now that she was his wife she was expected to behave differently. A feisty mistress was one thing, but a feisty wife was something else and would not be tolerated.

Nicholas Sander, a Catholic recusant writing during the reign of Anne's daughter, Elizabeth I, described how Anne miscarried "a shapeless mass of flesh". However, Sander was only 6 years old at the time of the miscarriage and was writing nearly 50 years after the event; there was no mention of a deformed foetus in 1536. Chapuys, chronicler Edward Hall and Charles Wriothesley (Windsor Herald and brother of Thomas Wriothesley, who was close to Cromwell at this time) simply mention a miscarriage, with Wriothesley and Chapuys adding that it was a boy.[5] Not only was there no mention of a deformed foetus at the time, it was also not raised in the aftermath of the miscarriage, or indeed at the subsequent trials of the four commoners and the Boleyns. This puts paid to the fanciful theory that Anne's five alleged lovers were invented in order to shift the blame for the miscarriage from Henry VIII, since a deformed baby was a sign of sexual misbehaviour in the parents. The suggestion that George Boleyn was arrested so that an incest charge could be used to accuse him of being the father of the abomination is nonsense. Why go to the trouble of bringing him to trial and then make no mention of the alleged deformed foetus? The miscarriage was the final nail in Anne's coffin, though, not because the foetus was supposed to be particularly repulsive, but because Henry now believed he would have no sons with her and that his second marriage was as cursed as his first. Also, Catherine of Aragon's death meant that the King could put Anne aside without being forced to return to his first wife.

As with any woman, Anne would have been highly emotional after her miscarriage, particularly bearing in mind Henry's callous derision, and lack of support and understanding. Probably for the first time, there was a genuine fear that Henry would abandon her as he had Catherine. George Boleyn's trial alleged that he was always with his sister. Brotherly concern for bereavement was twisted into something sinister. No doubt George did spend a lot of time with Anne, particularly after her miscarriage, in order to comfort her and give her the emotional support that her husband was incapable of providing. Gradually over the last year of their lives, Anne relied more and more on her brother for support and reassurance. Although she could rely on her father's loyalty, this was because by promoting his daughter's course he was also promoting his own. While George of course benefited from Anne remaining in power, the siblings provided each other with the demonstrative affection their father did not. George genuinely cared for his sister, and she reacted by seeking out his company more and more frequently as her hold over the King became more and more tenuous.

Irrespective of her innocence of the crimes with which she was later charged, Anne had already suffered one miscarriage in the summer of 1534. Henry now believed that his wife, who was by now about 35, was no more able to give him a son than Catherine had been. He had annulled his marriage to Catherine, broken with the Church of Rome, lost the esteem of a large number of his subjects, isolated England as far as foreign policy was concerned, and lost the respect of half of Europe for Anne's sake, yet she had not borne him the promised son. The Boleyns had let him down.

Opponents of the Boleyns, led by Nicholas Carew, seized on the opportunity of the King's waning love for Anne, and his growing affection towards Jane Seymour, to restore Mary to her rightful place. The deaths of More, Fisher and the Carthusians had hardened opinions against the Boleyns, and support for Mary was growing. Carew was backed by powerful members of the Privy Chamber, including Edward Seymour, Jane's brother. These people plotted to bring Anne down by pushing Jane Seymour forward as a possible replacement. They may also have whispered malicious gossip about Anne to a King who was suddenly receptive to it. Just how aware Anne and George were of the machinations against her is uncertain. George, as a member of the Privy Chamber and Privy Council, must have been fully aware of the opposition from certain fellow members, but he could not have envisioned the possibility that either he or Anne were in physical danger.

What of the chaste and virtuous Jane Seymour in all this? She did not have Anne Boleyn's ambition or intellect; Jane merely did as she was told, which was the very characteristic that endeared her to the increasingly egotistical King. She was perfectly willing to be used to destroy the Boleyns and was coached by her ambitious brothers and other members of the anti-Boleyn faction to win the King's love. But when the Boleyn family's opponents began working towards bringing them down, they were looking at the validity of a divorce or annulment, not a charge of treason. Not even the most ardent anti-Boleyn opponent considered execution as a realistic proposal. After all, who would think that a husband who had been so passionately in love with his wife would consider killing her? The end result astounded everyone.

By April 1536, if not before, the King's great affection for

Anne had eventually run its course, and at some point he must have approached Thomas Cromwell with regard to the possibility of an annulment. Wolsey had been put in the same position of seeking an annulment for his royal master nearly ten years earlier, and he had died a failure with a treason charge hanging over his head. Cromwell did not wish to end up in the same position as his previous employer, and he proved to be a far more deadly enemy than the long-dead Wolsey. If Anne caused as many problems as Catherine had, then perhaps an annulment was not the answer. Providing Henry would agree to allow him to proceed, there were other ways of getting rid of her. For Henry to have actually agreed to Cromwell's plot against her, his love for Anne Boleyn must indeed have turned into a great hatred.

The response of Anne and George to the threat was, as it had always been, to fight. George deliberately maintained a high profile at court. He retained the King's favour almost to the last. As we have already seen, when the King chose a peer to cast the proxy vote of Lord LaWarr at the session of Parliament beginning on 4 February 1536, it was George.[6] Even in early March, royal favours continued to be bestowed on him. His father's lease of the Crown honour of Rayleigh in Essex was extended on 3 March for a term of 30 years, and George was brought in as joint tenant with a 20 per cent rebate on the £100 rent.[7] Despite the making of this grant to the Boleyns, an inventory was prepared of all grants made by the King to the father and son from 1523 to 3 March 1536.[8] This has led to speculation that charges of treason were being mooted as early as the beginning of March, and that Thomas Boleyn had initially been considered as a possible victim.

Meanwhile, Anne's increasing vulnerability was exacerbated by foreign policy. Cromwell favoured an imperial alliance, and now that Catherine was dead the only obstacle was Anne. The renewed possibility of reconciliation with England and the Empire could also be used to dampen the King of France's increasing arrogance towards England. On 8 January, Cromwell wrote to the English ambassadors in France stating that Catherine's death had removed "the only matter of the unkindness" between Henry and the Emperor, and instructing them to keep themselves "more aloof and be the more fraught and cold in relenting to any of their [France's] overtures and requests."[9] This coincided with relations between France and the Empire becoming colder and colder; the death of poor Catherine meant that both foreign powers were at last soliciting England's friendship. In April 1536, Charles V offered imperial support to Henry in an attempt to ally with England. This was proposed with a view to combating the French threat to the imperial position in Italy. Following this olive branch, Anne and her supporters suddenly took a more pro-imperial stance. Anne and George were buoyed up by optimism that, following the disappointment of the French negotiations the previous year, reconciliation with the Empire had become a possibility. Unfortunately for them, the Emperor's terms were that he would only support Henry's marriage to Anne in return for Mary being recognised as heir to the throne.

The pressure on the Boleyns was becoming intense, as it became apparent that any potential alliance with the Empire was conditional on Elizabeth's succession being put into jeopardy. Their greatest hope was that the French had not been entirely alienated. The meeting between the French and English kings, which had been postponed on so many occasions, had been rescheduled to May 1536, and unsurprisingly it was George who was instrumental in making the arrangements. Henry was at last in a position of being able to play France off against Charles V, and in the middle of April it was still intended that the meeting take place. On 17 April, George wrote to Lord Lisle in Calais regarding the proposed meeting, asking for his assistance in the arrangements. This letter is set out in full below, because although it is very brief, it is the last letter written by George Boleyn preserved in the state papers:

> My Lord Deputy, as heartily as I can I commend
> me unto you, certifying you that the King's Grace

is minded to be at Dover within this fortnight: praying you to be so good unto me as to help my servant, the bringer hereof, to all such things as he shall need for my provision, as I shall be ready at all times to do you like pleasure. And thus praying you to think no unkindness in my short writing in great haste, I make an end.

From Greenwich, the xvijth day of April.

Yours assuridly to my power

George Rocheford[10]

Although he apologises for the brevity of the correspondence, this is in fact typical of the majority of George Boleyn's letters, save for those written jointly with another person. Few of them are particularly long. Most are written in a rushed, breathless style. With all the worries and concerns at the time, in this particular letter the reader can actually sense the harassment and anxiety of the author. A month later, George was dead.

For the first time since his marital problems had taken over foreign policy, Henry VIII was able to invoke the position he had always intended to take – that of neutrality between France and the Empire - but this was very nearly jeopardised by Thomas Cromwell. On 18 April, Charles V's ambassador, Eustace Chapuys, was summoned to court by Cromwell to discuss an alliance with the Emperor. By doing so, Cromwell had overstepped the mark: he exceeded his instructions to maintain cordial, non-committal relations with Chapuys. Such rashness emphasised Cromwell's leanings towards the Empire, and his actions caused a major rift between him and Henry.

When Chapuys arrived at court he was greeted enthusiastically by the Lords of the council, "especially Lord Rochford". Chapuys must have felt some wry amusement at the apparent enthusiasm of the young lord. George's potent charm was used to maximum affect, making strenuous protestations of his desire for an alliance with the Empire. Chapuys somewhat sarcastically told him that no doubt "he had as great pleasure in what was taking place as any other, and that he would assist as in a matter for the benefit of the whole world, but especially of himself and his friends". Despite the recognition of George's selfish motives, Chapuys reluctantly accepted that George displayed much amiability towards him, and that in turn he did likewise, although "avoiding all occasions of entering into Lutheran discussions, from which he could not refrain".[11]

George then conducted him to mass, where Chapuys was manoeuvred into his first-ever meeting with Anne Boleyn. He had been asked by Henry, through Cromwell, to kiss Anne's hand, which he refused to do. However, George managed to place Chapuys behind the door through which Anne would enter and, on entry, Anne swung round to the ambassador and bowed. The unwilling Chapuys was forced to reciprocate, thereby recognising Anne as queen. Following the meeting, Anne, the King and the rest of the court ate in Anne's lodgings, leaving Chapuys kicking his heels. George kindly took him to the King's Presence Chamber and entertained him with the other principal men of the court. Chapuys' meeting with Anne had obviously been stage-managed, not only by Anne and George, but also the King. It is hard to credit that the King could continue plotting so closely with his wife and brother-in-law on 18 April, and that barely one month later they would both dead.

After dining with George Boleyn, Chapuys had a private meeting with Henry, and set out to him the Emperor's terms that Mary must be returned to the succession before an alliance could take place. Henry was furious, and was openly rude to the ambassador. He wanted Anne recognised as queen unconditionally, with no acknowledgement of Mary as heir. The King's attitude no doubt lulled the Boleyns into a false sense of security, but this had nothing to do with loyalty to Anne. Henry was merely furious with the Emperor's attempt to interfere with domestic affairs and policy. Henry's refusal to negotiate with the Emperor and his ambassador caused an angry quarrel between himself and Cromwell, who was orchestrating the attempted alliance. Chapuys describes Cromwell's regret being so great "that he was hardly able to speak for sorrow, and had never been more mortified in his life, than with the said reply." Cromwell may well have blamed Anne's influence and her pro-French position for Henry's refusal to negotiate with the Emperor, and he would definitely have seen her as a threat to himself and his policies. On 2 April 1536, Passion Sunday, Anne's almoner John Skip had preached a controversial sermon about King Ahasuerus being deceived by his adviser, Haman, but Queen Esther saving the day.[12] It was a public attack on Cromwell, Henry VIII's right-hand man, and the advice he was giving the King. Cromwell was being threatened by the Boleyn contingent just as Wolsey had been.

Irrespective of his argument with Cromwell, Henry was well aware that there could be no reconciliation with Charles V while Anne lived. In turn, while there was no reconciliation with the Empire, there could be no effective policy of evenly balancing the Empire and France. Anne had failed to give him a son, he had fallen in love with another woman, and Anne's very existence was the only obstacle to England following the foreign policy that Henry had always envisaged. Henry must have considered his options, and then given leave for Cromwell to proceed against his wife. After his argument with Henry, Cromwell took to his bed for a few days, feigning illness, and began plotting. Anne had become a liability and a very real threat. When he returned to court, the ruination of Anne Boleyn and her family was planned and implemented in less than a month.

St George's day, 23 April, brought the first outward sign that the Boleyns were losing their influence. George was expected to receive the Order of the Garter, the pinnacle honour of the realm, and his sister strongly supported him. George had been nominated the previous year and had received a reasonable amount of support, but James V of Scotland had beaten him by two votes.[13] Despite Anne's championing of George, much to the delight of Chapuys the honour in 1536 actually went to Sir Nicholas Carew, a known opponent of the Boleyns and the man who was coaching Jane Seymour.[14] Carew beat George soundly, receiving twice as many votes, and even Thomas Boleyn had voted for him.[15] The choice was at least in part dictated by the King's earlier promise to Francis I that Carew was next in line.[16] In truth, if Henry had wished for George to be awarded the honour then no previous promise made to the King of France would have prevented him granting it; furthermore, if the King had always intended to honour his promise to the King of France why did he allow George's name to be put forward in the first place? Henry must have known that by allowing George's name to be put forward, and then awarding the position to an opponent of the Boleyns, he would bring public humiliation to his brother-in-law. George was forced to swallow his very public slight, and hold his head high as the court digested the implications of the King's choice. Up until now, George had been the golden boy, and he was completely unused to personal failure and rejection. The King's decision must have hit him hard. Yet neither Anne nor George could possibly have foreseen the manner of their eventual downfall.

It is probable that soon after Anne's miscarriage the King determined that he wanted the marriage to end. His jousting accident must have reminded him of his mortality and the urgent need for an heir. Henry now had a realistic alternative to Anne: Jane Seymour. He wanted to be rid of the wife he blamed for not providing him with a son, just as he had wanted rid of Catherine, and to move on to Jane, who came from fertile stock, with her mother having given birth to nine children. Henry wanted his next marriage to be accepted unconditionally without any suggestion of it being invalid, or any inference that its issue was illegitimate. The only way of ensuring this was for Anne to die, because, as with Catherine, she would never have agreed to an annulment.

It is inconceivable that at any time Cromwell acted of his own volition. He may have been given a relatively free hand in devising a plan, but to plot against a queen was unthinkable, and would have been treason. Cromwell may have come up with the answer, but it was the King who set the wheels in motion. The solution has become one of the best-known stories in English history. Anne was to be charged with treason, together with those who were closest to her; that, of course, included her brother.

On 24 April, the King approved the setting up of two commissions of oyer and terminer to investigate crimes committed in the counties of Middlesex and Kent.[17] These were set up by Cromwell and Thomas Audley, the Lord Chancellor. Just eight days later, Anne and George Boleyn were arrested for crimes committed in those two counties. On 27 April, writs were issued summoning Parliament to meet at Westminster on 8 June.[18] When it eventually met, the reason given was to settle the succession and to repeal statutes favouring Anne. In other words, Parliament was summoned to discuss these issues five days before Anne had even been arrested and charged. There can be little doubt that the whole purpose of the commissions was to ensnare Anne. George had failed to receive the Order of the Garter on 23 April, the day before the King had approved the special commissions; Henry had to have been aware, well before the special commissions had reported back to him, that George was going to be brought down with his sister. And if Henry was aware of that prior to receiving the results of Cromwell's investigations, then he must also have been aware of the details of the intended plot, even before it had been fully concocted.

The incest charge brought against George Boleyn is one of the most cynical and spiteful attacks on an individual in English history. He was accused for a number of reasons. Firstly, the charge was brought in order to bring further shame and dishonour to Anne's name. For Henry to have been cuckolded by his wife would bring him public humiliation, especially if she was found guilty of adultery with just one man, but if she was found to have had sex with a number of men, including her own brother, then Henry would be viewed not as a laughing stock, but as a wronged man, unlucky to have been married to an evil and perverse woman. The saying "throw enough mud and it sticks" was as true in the sixteenth century as it is today. In reality, because of George Boleyn's performance in court, the incest charge did not have the intended effect on the public, and there were many murmurings of discontent that the trial was a sham. Secondly, George was one of the most prominent members of the court, and Cromwell was not naive enough to underestimate his wit and intelligence. George and Anne were known to be close, and George would have moved heaven and earth to try to save her. He seems to have been arrested doing just that - attempting to see the King at Whitehall. George was far too dangerous to be allowed his liberty. Although there was realistically nothing he could have done to save Anne, he had the verbal acumen to have protested her innocence persuasively and to have caused an uproar at court. By allowing him his freedom, there was a risk he would cause disruption to the Crown's case, and would be able to convince powerful people of her innocence. Ironically, he did this anyway due to his impressive display in court, but Cromwell was not to know that at the time. If Anne had to go then so did her brother. Thirdly, there is every possibility that, in a similar way to Wolsey's abuse of the reform of the Privy Council in 1526, Cromwell used Henry's desire to be rid of Anne as a means of also getting rid of one of the most powerful and influential members of Henry's court, and therefore one of Cromwell's greatest rivals.

There is another, even less palatable reason, why George may have been specifically chosen as a victim. Henry was infuriated by Anne's failure to give him a son, and this fury had turned his love for her into hatred. The incest charge may well have been an opportunity to cause Anne more pain by attacking her beloved brother. Her brother's fate may also have proved to be a bargaining chip in getting Anne to agree to an annulment of the marriage after her condemnation: agree and your brother will be saved the full horrors of a traitor's death. There is no way of knowing whether this was the way Henry's mind was working, but his capacity for almost childlike cruelty means it is not completely outside the realms of possibility.

The evangelical Anne and George could not have been charged with a crime that would have caused them more anguish, shame and dishonour than incest. Not only did they lose their lives, their reputations were completely destroyed and their names blackened for centuries to come. Even today, the Boleyn siblings are portrayed in film and fiction as committing incest in order to cement their meteoric rise at court. They were not wide-eyed innocents; they knew what the King was capable of, and they had used their influence over him to further their family and careers, but in May 1536, they were still sacrificial lambs to the King's ambition.

20 Arrests

The court had been due to travel to Calais on 2 May 1536 for the arranged meeting between Henry and Francis I. As we have seen, it was George Boleyn who had been instructed to organise the travel arrangements. This was the meeting that had been rescheduled because of Anne's pregnancy two years previously. At 11 o'clock on the evening of 30 April, however, the trip was suddenly cancelled and instructions given that the King would be travelling a week later. The cancellation could have come about due to an altercation that Anne had with Sir Henry Norris on 29 April, or because of Mark Smeaton's arrest.

On 30 April, two days before the arrests of Anne and George, a court musician, Mark Smeaton, was arrested.[1] He was taken to Cromwell's house in Stepney for interrogation. Within 24 hours, he had confessed to having committed adultery with the Queen on three separate occasions. He was then removed to the Tower of London, arriving at 6 p.m. on 1 May. Whether his confession was made under torture or purely through psychological pressure, will probably be never known. Similarly, whether he was encouraged, in his fear and confusion, into implicating Henry Norris and George Boleyn is unknown, but their arrests followed swiftly after his confession.

On 1 May, George Boleyn had been the principal challenger, and Sir Henry Norris the principal answerer, at the May Day joust.[2] The watching public noticed nothing untoward until the King left abruptly for Westminster, taking Norris with him. The King had read a piece of paper which had been handed to him, and which was probably Mark Smeaton's confession. His departure effectively brought the tournament to an end. It was rumoured that the King had offered Norris a pardon if he admitted to adultery with the Queen. Horrified, the honourable Norris had sworn that he was innocent, but was immediately arrested and charged with adultery and treason. He was taken to the Tower at dawn the following day.

George Boleyn was arrested on the afternoon of 2 May 1536 at Whitehall.[3] This did not become common knowledge until the following day, which must mean it was orchestrated to be carried out as privately as possible. Upon hearing that he was in the Tower, not even Chapuys could come up with an explanation as to why he had been arrested. It was initially believed that he was an accessory to the charges brought against his sister: "Her brother is imprisoned for not giving information of her crime."[4] When the charge of incest became public knowledge there was general shock and disbelief. George had been taken to the Tower from Whitehall, arriving at approximately 2 p.m.. His sister Anne arrived shortly afterwards at approximately 5 p.m.. She had been arrested earlier that day while attending a tennis match, and had initially been interrogated at Greenwich. It is not known whether George was aware of her earlier arrest, and had himself been arrested while making frantic attempts to see Henry in order to protest his sister's treatment – this would explain George being at Whitehall, rather than Greenwich when he was arrested.[5] He may, however, have been completely unaware of Anne's arrest and simply walked into a trap.

The general disbelief at the arrests was nothing compared to the shock and horror of the principal characters. On 1 May, Anne was Queen of England, enjoying a jousting competition in which her brother took a leading role. George was in his prime and one of the most envied men in England. Neither of them, on that warm May Day, could possibly have seen what was coming. The following day they were both in the Tower charged with high treason and facing certain death. The horror at their reversal of fortune, and their shock at the situation into which they were suddenly catapulted, initially had a debilitating effect on both of them.

Anne Boleyn appears to have undergone some sort of mental breakdown following her arrest and imprisonment. She vacillated between hysterical laughter at the absurdity of the charges, and floods of tears. In her fear and distress she also babbled incessantly, trying to make some sense of what had happened to her. Lady Kingston, wife of the Constable of the Tower, and three other unsympathetic women were placed with Anne, day and night, to spy on her and report back. Anne spoke of conversations she'd had with Norris, Weston and Smeaton as possible reasons for her arrest and imprisonment. She spoke of the altercation with Henry Norris, in which she had accused him of being in love with her, and, looking "for dead men's shoes, for if aught came to the king but good, you would look to have me". With regards to Weston, she reported that he had claimed that he loved one of her house better than his wife, and that he had stated that the person he referred to was Anne herself. Anne "defied" him for his comment. In relation to Smeaton, she had found him at the window one day in a sad pose. When asked by her why he was so sad, he said it was no matter. The Queen told him off saying, "You may not look to have me speak to you as a noble man." Smeaton replied, "No madam, a look will suffice me; so fare you well." Her comments were obviously far from confessions to adultery, but despite this they were used against her and her fellow prisoners as evidence. Anne was also unable to hide her affection for George.

Her initial reaction when entering the Tower was to ask where her "sweet brother" was. When she was eventually told that he too had been arrested she felt comforted by his closeness to her, telling the Constable of the Tower, William Kingston, "I am very glad we both be so nigh together." Later, when reality hit her, she was unable to hide her anxiety and concern for George, crying, "My lord, my brother will die..." She did not show the same level of distress for any of the other prisoners, but it was natural for her to be worried about her own flesh and blood.[6]

Initially, George also exhibited great distress following his arrest. On 4 May, Jane Boleyn sent a message to George via Kingston. In it, she asked after her husband and promised that she would "humbly [make] suit unto the king's highness" for him.[7] The message was delivered by Sir Nicholas Carew and Sir Francis Bryan with the express permission of the King, thereby maliciously giving false hope to a man who had been the King's companion for over ten years. No evidence exists that Jane ever made the petition she mentions in her message but, as Julia Fox points out, her chances of pleading for George with the King were slim because access to the King was "virtually impossible" at that time, and carefully controlled.[8]

And what of the two men who delivered the message? Sir Nicholas Carew had always been an enemy of the Boleyns. Indeed, Carew was housing Jane Seymour and, with the help of others, was coaching her on how to win the King's heart and take over from Anne. Likewise, although Sir Francis Bryan had previously been a staunch supporter of the Boleyns and Reform, he had recently changed sides. He obviously had a strong sense of self-preservation, and as we know, in December 1534 he had fortuitously argued with George. This had the long-term effect of enabling him to exhibit his change of commitment when such a change was most needed. Two obvious enemies of the Boleyns, both of whom enjoyed freedom while George was incarcerated in the Tower, delivered the message from his wife. The fact that these two in particular were chosen is an example of the depth of malicious cruelty of which the King was capable.

On receipt of Jane's letter, George appeared comforted and told Kingston that he wanted to "give her thanks", but after asking Kingston what time he was due to come before the council, he began weeping, commenting, "for I think I shall not come forth till I come to my judgement." George knew that any pleas for mercy before his trial would go unheard. It seems that George never did go before the council, and unsurprisingly was never made aware of the evidence the Crown intended to rely upon until he actually faced the court at his hearing. Cromwell was fully aware of George Boleyn's wit and intelligence, and would not have wanted to provide any prior knowledge that could have assisted him in his defence.

Despite the shock and distress of their arrests, neither George Boleyn nor Henry Norris would make any admission of wrongdoing. In a letter to Cromwell, Edward Baynton wrote:

> This shall be to advertise you that here is much communication that no man will confess anything against her, but only Mark of any actual thing. Wherefore (in my foolish conceit) it should much touch the king's honour if it should no farther appear. And I cannot believe but that the other two [Norris and Rochford] be as fully culpable as ever was he. And I think assuredly the one keepeth the other's counsel... I hear further that the queen standeth stiffly in her opinion... which I think is in the trust that she hath of the other two.[9]

Baynton was suggesting that if a conviction could only be obtained against Mark then this would humiliate the King. If his wife preferred the company of a lowly musician to that of the King of England, this would, "touch the king's honour". However, if it could be shown that she had committed adultery with a variety of different men, including her own natural brother, then she could be shown to be an evil, wanton woman. Therefore, once it was found that no confession could be obtained from Norris or George, a general trawl brought the further arrests of Francis Weston, William Brereton, Thomas Wyatt and Richard Page. Wyatt and Page were lucky to escape with their lives, but both Weston and Brereton went to the scaffold. They died simply to ensure that the King's "honour" was not impugned.

Even before the trials of the prisoners, inventories of their estates and belongings were being prepared. The inventory of George's lands and offices, and the account of their yearly value, show that the only lands held by him at the date of his death were Grimston Manor, worth £10 a year, and the honour and lordship of the manor of Rayleigh, in which George had sold his interest to his father. However, his offices were numerous, and included the stewardship of Beaulieu, the keepership of "Our Lady of Bethlem", the parks of Rayleigh and Thundersley, the manor and park of Penshurst, and the bailiwick of Rochford. His list of offices and the monies deriving from them is lengthy, but his total yearly income, exclusive of his salary as a courtier, diplomat and Warden of the Cinque Ports, amounted to £441 10s 9d, including the pensions granted to him by Wolsey (which made up 75% of this figure). Although this was a substantial amount, it was significantly smaller than the income which Henry Norris derived from his lands and offices, which came to a total of £1327 15s 7d, or William Brereton's yearly income of £1236 12s, 6 ½ d. Indeed, had it not been for Wolsey, George's income from lands and offices would have been tiny for a man of his status.[10]

The Queen's household was broken up and her servants discharged on 13 May, before she was even tried and condemned, so certain was the King that the jury would do its duty. There was also an undignified scrummage for the lands and offices of Norris, Rochford and Brereton upon their respective arrests. Lord Lisle wrote a begging letter on 8 May, four days before the trials of the four commoners, irrespective of the fact that Norris had been his personal friend. Lisle got nothing from the spoils, despite Cromwell's promise that he "shall have something", because others beat him to it.[11] The men's estates began to be distributed before they had even faced a judge and jury, and many of those who received a share were to sit on the juries that condemned them. The Earl of Sussex received the Chief Stewardship of Beaulieu, and two days before George's trial Sir Thomas Cheyney was formally named Lord Warden of the Cinque Ports in his place - although for decency's sake the official grant was not made until the day of George's execution.[12]

What of the four commoners implicated in the tragedy? Henry Norris was born in the 1490s, making him a similar age to the King, and at the time of his arrest was Groom of the Stool and Keeper of the Privy Purse. He was the closest to a personal friend that Henry VIII had; he had accompanied the royal party on their visit to Calais in 1532, and was most probably a witness at Henry's wedding to Anne in 1533. He was held in great esteem, and as we have seen, was one of the most influential members of the Privy Chamber. He was also a key member of the Boleyn allies at court, and Anne had arranged to have his son educated with her ward and nephew, Henry Carey, under the tutelage of the Reformer Nicholas Bourbon. Francis Weston was the only son of Sir Richard Weston, who along with Sir William Kingston was one of only four knights put into the Privy Chamber to counterbalance the King's younger favourites. Francis was Henry's favourite page and was described as being "daintily nourished under the King's wing".[13] Weston was also a Boleyn devotee, though without the weight and influence of either Norris or Rochford, and he was made a Knight of the Bath at Anne's coronation. He was only about 25 when he was arrested; his family, including his wife, made strenuous attempts to save the young man's life following his condemnation, as did the French ambassadors, Antoine de Castelnau (Bishop of Tarbes) and Jean, Sieur de Dinteville - but to no avail.[14] Despite his son's death, Richard Weston continued in the King's service as a trusted servant, only retiring in 1542 due to age and infirmity.

Quite why William Brereton was involved in the tragedy

is more difficult to establish. Thomas Wyatt describes him as "the one who I least knew". He was certainly a royal favourite, accompanying the King and Queen on a number of hunting expeditions and enjoying a host of royal grants and offices, but he was clearly not as important as Norris or Rochford. Brereton was "the dominant royal servant in Cheshire and north Wales," and it appears that his arrest and subsequent execution had more to do with his opposition to Cromwell's reforms there.[15]

The last of the four victims was Mark Smeaton, a young musician in his early twenties. The court's leading lights in fashion, poetry and culture had looked with favour on the young man due to his talent. He was said to be Henry's favourite musician, and he revelled in the attention he received from his betters. Thomas Watt describes him as "a rotten twig upon too high a tree"; although Smeaton was accepted for his talent, the likes of Wyatt, Rochford and the Queen would never have accepted him as an equal, and probably saw him more as a source of entertainment. It was a distinction the young man appeared unable to grasp. His lowly position meant that the proud Anne Boleyn would never have contemplated him as a lover, even if she had been inclined to do so (and had seen an opportunity to take a lover in the first place). His arrest, along with that of Brereton, may simply have been a matter of being in the wrong place at the wrong time.

21 Trial

There has been much debate over the last 470 years as to whether Anne and George Boleyn were guilty of any of the charges laid against them. The overwhelming weight of academic opinion is in favour of them being innocent on all counts and being framed for the crimes. George Wyatt, the grandson of Thomas Wyatt and Anne's first biographer, recognised that due to the constant attention under which the Queen was always kept, it would have been impossible for her to have acted in the way alleged.[1] For her to have committed the offences she was charged with, her ladies-in-waiting would have had to have been aware, and would either have had to assist in the deceit, or else to have chosen to overlook it. To do so would have been treason in itself, as Jane Boleyn, Lady Rochford, found to her cost less than six years later.

Yet none of Anne's ladies were arrested and no charges of aiding and abetting the Queen were ever brought. None of Anne's ladies provided direct evidence of wrongdoing, despite the Crown's claims to the contrary. Compare this with the wealth of evidence given in the case of Catherine Howard, in a desperate bid for self-preservation.

The Baga de Secretis contains the charges brought against Anne and George Boleyn, and the other four men implicated in the plot.[2] These papers were thought to have been destroyed, but were discovered in the late nineteenth century. The indictments include a schedule of alleged offences with specific dates and places. Many of these can be ruled out as it can be proved that Anne could not have been in the places alleged on the given dates. On other occasions, it can be proved that she was with the King. In 12 cases, either Anne was elsewhere or the man was. She was accused of having sexual relations with her brother on 2 and 5 November 1535 at Westminster, and again on 22 and 29 December at Eltham Palace. In November 1535, it can be proved that Anne was in fact with Henry at Windsor. Two other alleged offences with Henry Norris were impossible because Anne was recovering from childbirth and had not been churched (formally blessed after her recovery from childbirth). The only two cases where there is no alibi are November 1533 with Brereton, and December 1535 with her brother, for obviously George would have been with her and the court over the Christmas period. The catchall was the Crown's insertion of the words, "and on divers other days and places, before and after".[3] In other words, even if a specific date could be challenged, this would not be enough to prove innocence.

Those charged with treason in the sixteenth century were at a huge disadvantage. They were not entitled to legal representation, and were therefore reduced to desperately trying to defend themselves against the full weight of the law. It was also not a case of "innocent until proven guilty" in those days; "the burden of proof was on the accused to prove their innocence of the charges contained in the indictment".[4] The defendant was often unaware of the actual evidence being adduced against him until he attended court at his trial, and therefore had no hope of rebuttal. In the case of Anne and George Boleyn, it is likely that they were not even aware of the nature of the charges against them until they came to trial, and they would certainly have been unaware of the evidence upon which the Crown intended to rely. They had no hope of defending themselves, even if the jury had not been loaded.

The next question is whether Henry VIII actually believed they were guilty. He authorised Cromwell to investigate a selection of treasons on 24 April 1536. There is no explanation for this other than the investigation must have been with the intention of freeing him from his marriage with Anne. Shortly afterwards, Cromwell came up with the perfect plot. Did Henry conveniently forget that his own instructions had led to the conspiracy about to be unleashed on his wife and her brother? Did he delude himself that the allegations were true, irrespective of his instructions to Cromwell? All human beings are capable of self-deception and dissimulation, and Henry VIII was particularly shallow and self-absorbed. It is theoretically possible that in a matter of a few days he convinced himself of their guilt, but even for him this must be unlikely. He no doubt chose to believe their guilt to alleviate his own conscience, but in his more rational moments he must have appreciated the absurdity of the charges. Henry was many things, but he was far from stupid. Yet for us to accept he was totally blameless for the 1536 tragedy, we must also accept that Cromwell and Anne's enemies were able to completely deceive him. If Henry was as intelligent as his apologists give him credit for, then this was only because he let them.

Historians Derek Wilson and John Schofield see Henry VIII as the prime mover in the fall of the Boleyns. Schofield believes Henry's involvement is proven by the nonsensical case that was built against Anne, pointing to the lack of logic in Anne being condemned for adultery even though Henry's marriage to her was annulled. It was far from the "watertight case" that Cromwell, as a lawyer, would have wanted. It was overly complicated, it extended the treason law in a rather "unwarranted" manner, and it bore the stamp of a man who had grown to hate his wife, and who now wanted to completely annihilate her and blacken her name.[5][6] On 24 May, Cromwell admitted to Chapuys that he had set himself to arrange the plot, and that following the King's specific authority to do so he had "brought about the whole affair"[7] in order to assist an alliance with Charles V. However, in a letter to ambassadors Stephen Gardiner and John Wallop in Paris, Cromwell referred to the plot being "the King's proceeding".[8] The plot was ultimately down to Henry VIII; Cromwell was the King's servant who ran with the idea and put it into action.

The trial of Smeaton, Norris, Weston and Brereton took place at Westminster Hall on Friday 12 May 1536. By trying the four men first, Anne's frantic babbling upon her arrest was used as evidence against them before she had the opportunity to challenge the interpretation of her words. The men were faced with Anne's revelations with no possibility of refuting them. Only Smeaton pleaded guilty; the others maintained their innocence right to the very end. Irrespective of their defence, the jury was specially selected and hopelessly weighted, consisting of men who owed Cromwell or the King a favour, or who would benefit from the fall of the Boleyns. There was no possibility of an acquittal. All four men were found guilty and sentenced to be hanged, drawn and quartered.[9] [10] Anne and George's father, the Earl of Wiltshire, formed part of the jury and gave a guilty verdict, thereby condemning his own daughter, as it obviously takes two to commit adultery. Norris, Weston and Brereton were also prejudiced by the confession of Mark Smeaton. After all, it is easier to believe in the possibility of multiple adultery if one of the accused has confessed. It would be easy to be hard on Smeaton and call him a coward, but he was only a very young man of limited education and must have been terrified. Unlike the other prisoners, he was kept in chains during his whole incarceration in the Tower, and he had the threat of a brutal traitor's death hanging over him. He was under huge psychological, and perhaps physical, pressure, with which he was ill equipped to deal.

Wiltshire was spared the ordeal of sitting on the trials of his children and watching them desperately try to defend themselves against impossible odds. However, had he been ordered to do so, who is to say whether he could have refused? He had already effectively condemned his daughter by giving guilty verdicts on the other four men. His behaviour is difficult for us to understand, and he has been accused of turning his back on Anne and George, but in reality there was nothing Wiltshire could have done to save his children; the die was cast and he had to consider the future.

As peers, Anne and George were not tried with the four commoners. Their trial took place on Monday 15 May 1536 in front of a jury of 26 peers in the Great Hall of the Tower of London. Again, the majority of the jury had been pre-selected from those opposed to the Boleyns, including a cousin of Jane Seymour, and Lord Morley, George's father-in-law, who was a Catholic supporter of the Princess Mary. The jury selection ensured a hopelessly prejudicial trial. Whether they were Boleyn opponents or not, though, each jury member knew their duty was to find the defendants guilty or risk the King's wrath.

A scaffold had been specially erected to hold the estimated 2000 spectators. The trial was a very public affair, in an attempt to show the so-called fairness of the proceedings. However, due to the magnificent performance of the two principal characters in the charade, this backfired spectacularly.

The peers who were summoned to sit on the jury were the Duke of Suffolk, the Earls of Exeter, Arundel, Oxford, Northumberland, Westmoreland, Derby, Worcester, Rutland, Sussex and Huntingdon, and the Lords Audeley, LaWarr, Mountague, Morley, Dacres, Cobham, Maltravers, Powes, Mouneagle, Clinton, Sandys, Windsor, Wentworth, Burgh and Mordaunt.[11] Anne and George's uncle, Thomas Howard, Duke of Norfolk, represented the King as Lord High Steward, presiding over the trial. Norfolk was a hard-nosed survivor, and his relationship with Anne had never been an easy one; indeed, it had completely disintegrated in1534, with Norfolk complaining that she treated him worse than a dog. He was a man who made self-preservation into an art form, and whatever his personal feelings may have been, these did not prevent him from doing his duty to the King. Whether he found it difficult to pronounce sentences of death on his own nephew and niece cannot be known. When reading out the siblings' respective sentences, tears are supposed to have poured like water down his face.[12] It is possible that his tears were of relief that it was Anne and George on trial and not him. But whatever his feelings towards Anne, he was still her uncle, and likewise George was his nephew. He had been on two embassies to France with George, and had worked closely with him right up until at least July 1535. However hard and callous Norfolk was, it may be doing him a disservice to suggest that his tears were entirely fake.

The charges for which Anne stood trial were adultery, incest, and plotting with the other accused men to murder the King. The charges her brother faced were incest, and conspiring with Anne to kill the King. There was never an allegation in court that either George or any of the accused men was Elizabeth's father. This was a slander that came later, through rumour, gossip and innuendo. According to the Crown's own case, Anne's first offence was allegedly with Norris in October 1533, and George allegedly had sex for the first time with his sister on 2 November 1535. Likewise, although George appeared to have been given responsibility for Anne's last miscarried child, the available evidence disproves this inferred allegation. The alleged offences in November have already been shown to be impossible, and the assertion that he had sexual relations with Anne during late December 1535 does not support the inference that he was the father. Anne miscarried a foetus thought to be about three and a half months in gestation on 29 January 1536, meaning it was conceived around the end of October or early November.

The Crown's case was poorly prepared because it knew it would not have to prove guilt beyond doubt, and although the prosecution may have intimated that George was the father, it made little attempt to actually prove it. There has also grown a fiction that George and the other men who died as Anne's alleged lovers were charged with sodomy as well as the allegations of treason. None of the men were charged with sodomy, and at the time of their deaths there were no rumours of homosexual activity by any of them. This myth only dates back to the 1980s and the work of historian Retha Warnicke, who saw the men who surrounded Anne as "libertines [who] were expected to move in a progression from adultery and fornication to buggery and bestiality".[13] Likewise, there was no allegation of witchcraft ever levelled against Anne. The charges contained in the *Baga de Secretis* contain no indictment for witchcraft. This is a fiction that has grown over the intervening years and which stems from Catholic propaganda and novels. Similarly, neither Anne nor George faced charges of poisoning Catherine of Aragon or intending to poison Mary. This was not included in the original indictment, and was again a story which evolved later, as was the rumour that Anne and George murdered Henry Fitzroy, Duke of Richmond by administering to him a slow-acting poison which took his life two months after theirs.

Anne was tried first, because whereas she was already pre-judged due to the guilty verdicts of the four commoners, her brother was not. The evidence against her was little short of pathetic. One piece of supposed evidence was an alleged deathbed revelation from Lady Bridget Wingfield. Lady Wingfield was the daughter of Sir John Wiltshire of Stone Castle in Kent. She had been one of Catherine of Aragon's ladies-in-waiting, but she was also an old friend of Anne Boleyn. A note written by John Spelman, one of the judges reads, "Note that this matter was disclosed by a woman called the Lady Wingfield who was a servant of the said queen and shared the same tendencies. And suddenly the said Wingfield became ill and a little time before her death she showed the matter to one of her etc."[14] It is not known exactly when Lady Wingfield died, or precisely what she is supposed to have revealed on her deathbed. Whatever was or was not said, any revelation she may have made was not deemed necessary to bring to anyone's attention until Cromwell started asking questions immediately prior to the Boleyns' trial. Of course, at the time of the trial Lady Wingfield was conveniently dead; any evidence deriving from her could not be confirmed, and likewise could not be challenged by the defendants.

Although three other court ladies were supposed to have provided information, they did not give formal evidence, and certainly did not attend court. It is far more likely that these women were mentioned as providing information purely to lend credence to the prosecution's case, and to further blacken the defendants' names without foundation. There is no official record of the names of these women who supposedly provided Cromwell with what at best could only have been court gossip. It is probable that one of them was the Countess of Worcester, who was the sister of Sir Anthony Browne of the Privy Chamber. Her identification is via the poetry of Lancelot de Carles, secretary to the French ambassador, who described her as the sister of one of the King's councillors, and letters written by John Husee, Lord Lisle's servant in London where "the lady Worserter" is named as "the fyrst accuser".[15] [16]

It is not known precisely what Lady Worcester did or did not say, but it probably was not a great deal because Spelman makes no mention of her. De Carles says of her involvement that when her brother reprimanded her for loose behaviour, the countess responded by saying she was "no worse than the Queen who had offended with Mark Smeaton and her own brother."[17] Eric Ives suggests that this was exaggeration, and that she probably meant she was no more of a flirt than the Queen.[18] If Lady Worcester had actually said these words, and meant them as they were being interpreted, then why was she not called to court to give her supposedly damning evidence verbally? Probably because she was not giving any such evidence. Her words had either been manufactured by the Crown or taken completely out of context, and there was no chance the prosecution would have risked her being called to give evidence, firstly because she may well have admitted the truth and secondly because in cross examination George would have destroyed her supposed evidence. Whatever the nature of the so-called evidence, Spelman's assessment was that "all the evidence was of bawdry and lechery, so there was no such whore in the realm".[19] In other words it was gross exaggeration based solely on supposition and gossip. No formal transcript of the hearings exists, and whatever "evidence" was relied upon has long since been destroyed, presumably because it did not amount to evidence of guilt at all.

Cromwell's official version of events presents evidence that never actually existed. He told England's diplomats abroad that the evidence was so abominable that much of it had not been given in evidence at court. On 14 May he wrote to Gardiner and Wallop, the ambassadors at the French court, saying, "I write no particularities; the things be so abominable that I think the like was never heard." According to Cromwell, because "the Queen's abomination, both in incontinent living and other offences towards the King's Highness, was so rank and common", her ladies talked of it so much that it came to the attention of some of the Council.[20] When Gardiner asked for more information, in particular asking who had accused the Queen, Cromwell wrote back to him on 5 July, saying, "As to his great desire for news, had written as fully as he could, unless he could have sent the very confessions 'which were so abominable that a great part of them were never given in evidence, but clearly kept secret.'"[21] The tone of Cromwell's letter is clearly highly defensive, which speaks volumes as to the truth of the matter. To suggest evidence was kept back, particularly bearing in mind the public's scepticism of the charges, is totally ridiculous. If there had been any hard evidence, it would have been shouted out loudly in triumph. The reality was that there was no evidence of guilt arising out of anything Anne's ladies may or may not have said. There were also no confessions, save that of Mark Smeaton. Any information Cromwell and his cronies had attempted to extract had failed, and Cromwell's aggressive defensiveness was an obvious bluff to cover up the inadequacy of the case.

Anne is said by the chronicler, Charles Wriothesley, to have "made so wise and discreet answers to all things laid against her, excusing herself with her words so clearly, as though she had never been faulty of the same."[22] Irrespective of her performance in court, she was found guilty by all 26 peers, including her former love Henry Percy, now the Earl of Northumberland. Upon her condemnation, her uncle gave sentence that she be either burned or beheaded according to the King's pleasure.[23] Cromwell had cleverly orchestrated the order in which the trials took place in advance. Anne's condemnation was a forgone conclusion, as her trial followed that of the four men found guilty of adultery with her. The same could not be said of her brother, who was not necessarily prejudiced by the other men's earlier convictions. He was, however, hopelessly prejudiced by his sister's conviction, as he could hardly be innocent of incest when his sister had already been found guilty. He would have been aware upon entering the court that his trial was a mere formality.

Upon Anne's removal from the court, her brother was brought to the bar. The brother and sister did not see one another, and were not allowed the consolation of a final farewell. Ironically, during life it was Anne who was the more tempestuous and reckless of the two siblings, yet she faced her accusers with the quiet and restrained dignity of a true queen. It was her brother who approached the trial with all guns blazing. As anticipated, George put up an impressive, spirited, yet inevitably futile, defence. His performance in court was not to save his life, which he must have known was inevitably forfeit, but to retain some semblance of his shattered reputation and honour. According to Charles Wriothesley, "he made answers so prudently and wisely to all articles laid against him, that marvel it was to hear, and never would confess anything, but made himself as clear as though he had never offended." Lancelot de Carles speaks of his calm behaviour and good defence and suggests that Thomas More himself did not reply better.[24] Even Eustace Chapuys confirmed this opinion, saying, "To all he replied so well that several of those present wagered 10 to 1 that he would be acquitted, especially as no witnesses were produced against either him or her, as is usual to do, particularly when the accused denies the charge."[25] The odds being laid during the trial against George's condemnation were a clear indication that the vast number of those present believed him to be innocent. This must have caused great concern to the prosecutors. This was a public trial, and they must have deeply regretted not holding it in private. All members of the jury knew their duty was to find him guilty; he was going to die. The problem was, the vast majority of the crowd of spectators were on the side of the accused. He was answering too well. The crowd would know there was insufficient evidence to convict, which in turn would mean they would know the trial was rigged. Cromwell must have been sweating at the bad publicity this very public trial would cause.

Despite Chapuys' assessment, George was well aware that he would be found guilty. There had been a damning piece of evidence used against him. His wife Jane did not attend court, but she did provide evidence that Anne had confided in her that the King was experiencing erectile problems and that she had then spoken to George about it.[26] Whether Anne actually made such a sensitive comment to her sister-in-law will never be known, but if she did then she could only have been referring to occasional sexual dysfunction; clearly Henry was not impotent. If he had been, the prosecution would have had very little trouble providing evidence of adultery, bearing in mind Anne's last pregnancy. The allegation that Anne made this comment to her sister-in-law cannot have been used as a charge against George unless either he was being accused of spreading the rumour, or it was being used to suggest a motive for Anne taking lovers in the first place. If George was being accused of spreading the rumour, then it was treason, since this kind of talk impugned the King's issue. If on the other hand it was being suggested as a reason for Anne's behaviour, then it provided a motive for the incest. Either way, George was damned. According to Chapuys, this allegation was written on a piece of paper and handed to George Boleyn:

I must not omit that among other things charged
against him as a crime was, that his sister had
told his wife that the King was impotent. This he
was not openly charged with, but it was shown
him in writing, with a warning not to repeat it.
But he immediately declared the matter, in great
contempt of Cromwell and some others, saying
he would not in this point arouse any suspicion
which might prejudice the Kings issue.[27]

It has been suggested that by reading out what should have
been kept secret George sealed his fate. This is unlikely as a guilty
verdict was expected of the jury in any event, whatever the viewing
public may have thought. Irrespective of this, Cromwell must have
been mortified by George's reckless disregard of his instructions
not to read the allegation out loud. Not only had George been
allowed to make a fool out of the King, Cromwell had given him
the ammunition to do so. But George's recklessness was not mere
arrogance, as is so often suggested. It actually exemplified his
intelligence and linguistic skills. Chapuys says that George was
referring to any future issue the King may have produced from
any subsequent marriage, thereby effectively bringing out into the
open the likelihood of the King's imminent remarriage, and the
real reason for the trial. But George may also have spoken out in
an attempt to protect his niece, the future Queen Elizabeth, from
any subsequent rumours relating to her paternity. The fact that
the issue was raised at all shows that gossip regarding the King's
virility was circulating. Although George read the allegation out
loud, he did not admit it was true.

With regard to evidence relating to the incest charge, Chapuys
reported that "no proof of [George's] guilt was produced except
that of his having once passed many hours in her company, and
other little follies."[28] This was the only evidence of incest used
against George, meaning that if Chapuys is correct, he was
convicted on the sole basis that on one occasion he had been alone

with his sister for a long time. It was a very weak case.

A number of minor allegations were raised at George's trial that do not appear to have featured at his sister's. These consisted of evidence of "pastimes in the queen's chamber" and were raised with the specific purpose of making a case against him. These were perhaps thrown in by the prosecution as a last-ditch attempt to blacken George's name due to how well he had answered the incest allegation. Knowing how intelligent he was, and knowing that the only evidence brought against him was that he had once spent a long time alone with Anne, we can almost hear George's scathing derision of the Crown's case.

The prosecutors put to him that he and Anne had poked fun at the King's poetry and fashion sense, and George was accused of leading Anne in the dance and thereby handing her on to other men. Anne had written to George telling him she was pregnant, which was now interpreted as being highly suspicious. The fact that George greeted his sister with a kiss was now alleged to be "French kissing". Although Anne and George had always been affectionate to one another in public, including in front of the King, this was now objected to, despite the fact that their behaviour had never previously been cause for comment. It was also suggested that George had questioned Elizabeth's paternity. To this allegation, according to Chapuys, George made no reply.[29] Whether he answered the charge or not, it was never explained why George would question the legitimacy of his own niece, thereby insinuating his beloved sister was a whore. On the contrary, as suggested above, he had gone out of his way at the trial to defend Elizabeth against such a claim. He probably merely told his accusers contemptuously that such a question was not worthy of answering, which was interpreted by Chapuys as failing to answer.

The evidence was mere hearsay. There were no witnesses called to confirm that George had questioned Elizabeth's paternity, or to confirm that rumours regarding the King's sexual problems had been spread by George, rather than through natural court gossip. Likewise, no one had confirmed that they had witnessed George and Anne acting inappropriately towards one another. The reason for this was simple: nobody had. Likewise, no witnesses were called to confirm that Anne and her brother had laughed at the King behind his back about his clothes and his poetry. They were both highly intelligent people. Even if they had laughed at the King together, it is unlikely that they would have done this in the open and in front of their enemies. Any such laughter would surely have been good-natured, affectionate jesting that was deliberately taken completely out of context. The whole case was a substitution of accusations and allegations for evidence. Were these specific allegations raised simply to infuriate Henry to the extent that he was happy to sacrifice his impudent brother-in-law, irrespective of the eventual incest charge? Or were they suggested by a king who wanted revenge on the Boleyns for the humiliation he felt that their empty promises had brought him? It is impossible to be certain.

In reality, due to the calibre of George Boleyn's performance in court, the incest charge actually damaged the plausibility of the prosecution case rather than enhancing it. The general impression left on the public was that the trials were rigged and that they were a mockery of justice. When the charges first became public knowledge, it was believed that there must be some evidence to prove what was being alleged, but by having the trials played out in public, it became common knowledge that this was not actually the case. For the first time in her life, Anne began to win public sympathy.

A unanimous verdict of George's guilt was delivered by all 25 peers who sat on the jury. They must have known they were condemning an innocent man to a traitor's death. The Earl of Northumberland was not present at George's trial, having been taken ill immediately after Anne's trial. He died only a few months later. George was sentenced by his uncle: "That he should go again to prison in the Tower from whence he came, and to be drawn from the said Tower of London through the City of

London to the place of execution called Tyburne, and there to be hanged, being alive cut down, and then his members cut off and his bowels taken out of his body and brent [burned] before him, and then his head cut off and his body to be divided into 4 pieces, and his head and body to be set at such places as the King should assign."[30]

The proceedings were a sham, and Eric Ives puts it best when he states, "A case sufficient to quiet the general public and satisfy pliant consciences had been manufactured by innuendo and implication, but those in the know were aware how flimsy it was."[31] The trials were one of the worst travesties of justice ever to disgrace an English court. Defamation of character was the objective, not proof of guilt, and this was just as true for George as it was for Anne.

Following the brutal sentence handed down to him, George Boleyn, as with his sister before him, did not fall apart. He acknowledged his condemnation and sentence with calm stoicism. Following the conventions of the age, he accepted death, saying that, as sinners, did not all men deserve death every day? Although continuing to deny his guilt, he stated that he submitted to the law that had found him guilty and as such he would no longer maintain his innocence. His main concern was for those to whom he owed money. According to Chapuys, "He only begged the King that his debts, which he recounted, might be paid out of his goods."[32] Lancelot de Carles confirms that he "asked the judges that they would ask the king to pay his debts."

George Wyatt said a few years later, "The young nobleman the Lord Rochford, by the common opinion of men of best understanding in those days, was counted and then openly spoken, condemned only upon some point of a statute of words then in force."[33] Even Chapuys, an archenemy of the Boleyns, had no doubt of their innocence, as indeed did the majority of the spectators.

After the trial, Chapuys stated that the King carried a book of poems around with him, to which he would regularly refer.

Chapuys believed these were possibly those that Anne and George had allegedly laughed at, and which had been "put to them and objected to as a great crime". The sarcasm behind this comment marks the depth of Chapuys' scepticism as to the guilt of the defendants, and the acknowledgement of the harshness of the sentences.[34]

Following his condemnation, George was taken back to his rooms in the Martin Tower of the Tower of London to await death. The condemned were allowed to write farewell letters to their families, but unfortunately none have survived save for Francis Weston's poignant letter to his parents and wife:

> Father and mother and wife, I shall humbly desire you for the salvation of my soul to discharge me of this bill [a schedule of his debts is included in the letter], and for to forgive me of all my offences that I have done to you, and in especial my wife, which I desire for the love of God to forgive me and to pray for me, for I believe prayer will do me good. God's blessing have my children and mine. By me a great offender of God.[35]

As can be seen from the contents of the letter, all of the men were concerned that their debts be paid. George continued to be troubled that his death could cause financial ruin to those whom he owed money. In a letter to Cromwell dated 16 May, the day after George's trial, William Kingston wrote, "Sir, the said Lord [Rochford] much desires to speak with you, which touches his conscience much as he says, wherein I pray you I may know your pleasure, for by cause of my promise made unto my said Lord to do the same."[36] It is not known whether Cromwell ever did attend in person to speak with George, but it would seem unlikely, particularly as Kingston continued to be used as an intermediary.

There is a second letter written by Kingston to Cromwell regarding George's debts. In *Letters and Papers* it is dated 18 May, but must have been written before this, since George died on 17 May. George had acted as a go-between to assist in the appointment of a monk, and had charged a fee of £200. He had received £100, but a further £100 was to follow. As the abbey into which the monk had been appointed had been, as George puts it, "suppressed", George was begging the King through Cromwell not to pursue the further £100 against a man who would have no way of paying it. Kingston writes:

> I have been with my Lord of Rochford, and showed him the clause of your letter. He answered that he had sent to you word by Dr Alryge [the priest]. Notwithstanding, he says that he made suit to you for promotion of White Monk, of the Tower Hill, and with your help he was promoted to the Abbey of Vale Sante Crewsys, in Cheshire, and he had for the promotion £100, and at Whitsuntide next should receive £100 more, but for this the king has the obligations. He supposes the said abbey is suppressed and the abbot undone, and his sureties also.[37]

Kingston then goes on to discuss the arrangements for the executions, but also begs Cromwell to help George's conscience:

> For the gentlemen, the sheriffs of London must make provision. As yet I hear of no writ, but they are all ready, and, I trust clean to God. They shall have warning in the morning, and I shall send at once to Master Eretage for carpenters to make a scaffold of such height that all present may see it... You must help my Lord of Rochford's conscience for the Monk, if need be; and also he spake to me for the bishop of Develyn [Dublin], for he must have of the said bishop £250.

At the most terrifying moment of his life, when he had just been sentenced to a brutal traitor's death, the most pressing concern on George Boleyn's mind was not his imminent grisly execution. His main concern was only for those to whom he owed money, and for those who owed him money, and who would suffer if forced to repay the debt to the King. Kingston was a hardened jailer, but he had just witnessed George's performance in court. Although by then everybody had turned their backs on the Boleyns, at least George's jailer was prepared to show him a modicum of compassion by pleading with Cromwell to help his charge's conscience.

Whether George's debts were paid prior to confiscation of his assets is not recorded. Bearing in mind Henry VIII's mercenary nature it would seem unlikely that he was prepared to show compassion. However, by reading out his list of creditors in court, George Boleyn had brought to everybody's attention precisely to whom he owed money. If those debts were not paid, it would be very apparent. Failure to repay them would be a breach of the King's honour, and George was well aware of that. In the letter to Cromwell dated 16 May, Kingston informed him that he had been with the King that morning to present the petitions of Lord Rochford, and that he had been answered. Kingston then went on to say that George wished to speak to Cromwell regarding his outstanding debts. You can deduce from this that the petitions Kingston referred to were a request to the King that the debts be paid. The fact that upon hearing Henry's answer, George immediately requested an audience with Cromwell, suggests that his petitions had been met with a negative response.

Whether or not Henry intended to repay George's debts, it shows a singular cruelty not to provide consolation to a man in his final hours. George was right to be concerned about those who owed him money; Henry was quick to call in the monies owed to him. George had specifically referred to a debt owed to him of £250, and had asked that this be waived by the King. Despite George's entreaties, two years after George's execution George Brown, Archbishop of Dublin, was forced to write to Cromwell in order to obtain a release of the debt, saying "It may please your good

Lordship to be further advised, that where I was indebted to the late Lord of Rochford in the sum of £400 sterling." He explained that the sum of £250 had already been repaid to George and that a further £50 was paid for the redemption of a cup of gold of the said Lord Rochford. The balance should have been paid for the residue of a house, "which the said Lord Rochford had of me, even as it was agreed between us". Archbishop Brown argued that the £100 balance should be waived because Cromwell's nephew had the benefit of the property and that he himself had never used it.[38] This letter is clear evidence of the selfish greed of the King who cruelly pursued debts owed to George, despite the fact that it was the young man's dying wish for these to be remitted. It took until July 1542, over six years after George's death, for the Archbishop to be released of the debt of £250 by the King.[39]

When writing to Cromwell on 16 May, Kingston confirms that he has told the men, including George that they are to die the following day: "The time is short, for the King supposes the gentlemen to die tomorrow, and my Lord of Rochford with the residue of gentlemen, and as yet without confession which I look for, but I have told my Lord of Rochford that he be in readiness tomorrow to suffer execution, and so he accepts it very well, and will do his best to be ready, notwithstanding he would have reserved his rights, which has not been used in especially here."[40] Although George accepted the guilty verdict found against him, his insistence on his innocence remained the same right up to his execution. George specifically requested the sacrament to swear his innocence before God prior to his death. Despite Kingston looking for a confession, this was not forthcoming from either George or Anne. Anne also swore her innocence upon the sacrament twice prior to death. There was nothing else they could possibly have said or done to make their innocence clearer.

22 Lady Rochford and the Fall of the Boleyns

It has often been assumed that Jane Boleyn, Lady Rochford, was instrumental in bringing down her husband and sister-in-law. This assumption has arisen from various historical sources. Martyrologist John Foxe, in his *Acts and Monuments*, first published in 1563, states that "It is reported by some, that this lady Rochford forged a false letter against her husband and Queen Anne, his sister, by which they were both cast away."[1] Edward, Lord Herbert of Cherbury, in his *The Life and Raigne of King Henry VIII*, first published in 1649, declared that "the wife of the late Lord Rochford, was a particular instrument in the death of Queen Anne."[2] On a first-edition copy of Herbert's book, which is contained in the Bodleian library in Oxford, there are notes by Thomas Tourneur who, according to one historian,[3] was quoting from the lost journal of Antony Antony, a Surveyor of the Ordinance of the Tower, and Groom of the Chamber. This quote appeared to be reiterating Herbert's view, but, as John Guy points out, Turner was reading "a dozen or so works, among which were the now lost chronicle and Herbert's own book" and his notes about Jane actually came from Herbert's book; he even quotes the page number.[4][5][6]

According to Lancelot de Carles, George is supposed to have exclaimed bitterly, "On the evidence of this one woman you are willing to believe this great evil of me, and on the basis of her allegations you are deciding my judgement."[7] Although George may have been speaking of his wife, equally he may have been speaking of either Lady Wingfield or Lady Worcester; surely he would have said "on the evidence of my wife" if he was referring to Jane. Bishop Burnet, writing in 1679, is the only source for Jane's involvement regarding the incest allegation. He wrote that Jane "carried many stories to the King, or some about him, to persuade that there was a familiarity between the Queen and her brother, beyond what so near a relationship could justify." We do not know what he was using as a source, although he suggests that he read a contemporaneous account, "writ by one Antony Antony".[8] Jane's biographer, Julia Fox, notes that in later volumes of his work, Burnet actually contradicts himself by saying that "the confession of Smeaton was all that could be brought against her [Anne]."[9]

A Portuguese gentleman in London at the time described the executions of George and the rest of the men, which he witnessed, in a letter to a friend. He refers to "that person, who more out of envy and jealousy than out of love towards the King, did betray this accursed secret, and together with it, the names of those who had joined in the evil doings of the unchaste Queen."[10] Unfortunately he gave no indication of the identity of the person he was referring to or even their gender, so it could refer to anyone - even Mark Smeaton. Apart from Chapuys' report that Anne confided in Jane about the King's sexual problems, there is no surviving contemporaneous document that mentions Jane's involvement. The only other documents that identify the Queen's accusers are Spelman's reference to Lady Wingfield, Lancelot de Carles' vague reference to Lady Worcester, and John Husee's letter which refers to Lady Worcester, Nan Cobham and one other lady as the three ladies who accused the queen.

George Wyatt, grandson of poet Thomas Wyatt, states in his *Life of Queen Anne Boleyn*, written towards the end of the sixteenth century, "For this principal matter between the queen and her brother, there was brought forth, indeed, witness, his wicked wife accuser of her own husband, even to the seeking of his blood, which I believe is hardly to be showed of any honest woman ever done."[11] Wyatt does not give a source for this claim, but his biography of Anne was based on information given to him by two women, one of whom had served Anne and knew her well, and another who was a noblewoman and contemporary of Anne's. Samuel Weller Singer, the nineteenth century editor of Wyatt's work, identified the first lady as Anne Gainsford, Lady Zouche, but she died before Wyatt was even born. It is likely, therefore, that Wyatt's biography was based on family stories and, as Julia Fox points out, these are "notoriously unreliable". Wyatt's claim regarding Jane cannot be corroborated, particularly considering that he, like Burnet, goes on to contradict himself by saying that George Boleyn was only found guilty "upon some point of a statute".[12]

Another accuser of Jane is Cardinal Wolsey's gentleman usher, George Cavendish. In his poetry, *Metrical Visions*, he refers to Jane once "bearing the name on an honest wife, / Whereas now my slander for ever shall be rife". However, he also refers to her fall (her execution for treason after assisting Catherine Howard in arranging secret assignations with Thomas Culpeper), and her receiving the "due debt" of her "unjust desires", showing that he writes with the hindsight of knowing her involvement in Catherine's tangled and shocking love life. The "slander" could easily refer to her evidence regarding Henry VIII's sexual problems in 1536.[13]

Whatever the evidence for her involvement, the most Jane ever said regarding the incest allegation was that the siblings spent a long time alone together on one occasion. She may also have said that Anne and George's relationship was closer than that of a usual brother-sister relationship - but being close to your sister does not make you guilty of incest. If Jane did assist a prosecution case that was clutching at straws, to what at best did her evidence amount? To any rational, unbiased judge and jury the answer is obvious: nothing. None of it was evidence of incest. George Boleyn was completely innocent, and as Chapuys said, he was found guilty merely on a presumption. Nothing his wife may or may not have said made any difference to that general perception.

Jane's reputation has been dragged through the mud over the last five centuries, and her character has progressively become blacker and blacker with every book in which she appears. Yet George was married to her for 11 years, and during that time, despite his alleged womanising, there was no scandal surrounding them, or suggestion that the marriage was a particularly unhappy one. Her reputation over the intervening years must surely be a huge exaggeration, probably begun shortly after the trials and exacerbated by her later involvement in the fall of another of Henry's wives. She was known to have provided evidence that was used against her husband, and the exact nature of that evidence was confused and exaggerated over time.

There have been many theories as to why Jane told Cromwell anything at all, as surely she would have known that her information would be used against her husband and sister-in-law. It has been suggested that she provided evidence because of her husband's reputation as a womaniser, or because of jealousy of the closeness of George to his sister. However, unless Jane was seriously unstable, it is highly unlikely she would have deliberately assisted in the total destruction of her own husband - the breadwinner - for any of these reasons. It is more likely that Jane was simply telling the truth under extreme psychological pressure during an interrogation. Following her husband's arrest, Jane may also have been in the position of either providing the Crown with a useful statement, or potentially facing charges herself as an accomplice, seeing as she too had discussed the King's problems. It may even be that she provided the statement regarding Henry's impotence without appreciating that it would be specifically used against her husband; according to Chapuys, her statement made no mention of George. This seems unlikely bearing in mind that she knew of his arrest, and must have known that her evidence was being demanded with the sole purpose of making a case against him. Whatever her understanding may have been, would any of us have the courage to act any differently when it was clear that the Boleyns had no chance?

The ridiculous notion that she believed the allegations against her husband because she was aware that he was homosexual and that he also subjected her to "sexual practices that outraged her"[14] does not have a single scrap of evidence to support it. This idea relies on Cavendish's poetry, *Metrical Visions*, and George's own scaffold speech. *Metrical Visions* has George talk of his "unlawful lechery" and his "living bestial", and go on to say that "shame restrains me the plains to confess, / Least the abomination would all the world infect."[15] To suggest that George is talking about homosexuality here is to take these phrases totally out of context. When the whole verse is read, Cavendish is clearly speaking of the incest charge: "For which by the law, condemned am I doubtless". Cavendish's verses on Henry VIII talk of Henry's "unlawful lechery" and his verses on Thomas Culpeper, Catherine Howard's alleged lover, have Culpeper warning his fellow courtiers of their "bestiality". It is clear that Cavendish is talking not about homosexuality but about adultery. In his scaffold speech, George refers to himself as "a wretched sinner" and "a perverse sinner", but he is simply following the usual scaffold etiquette, accepting that he is a sinner deserving of death. It was considered honourable for the convicted man to accept death as he deserved.[16]

The statement Jane gave to the court did not in itself condemn her husband, or the Queen. Both were already prejudged. There was never a chance that either would be spared, regardless of the evidence laid before the court - or more accurately, the lack of evidence. When George was initially arrested, it is probable that there was a vague intention of charging him as an accessory to his sister's misdemeanours, as surmised by Chapuys. Anne was certainly unaware for at least a day after her arrest that George had also been arrested; therefore, Anne was initially not questioned as to a possible charge of incest. It is more likely that the charge was later concocted after George had been arrested. George had also been charged with planning with Anne to kill the King. The prosecution made no attempt to prove this at his hearing; if the incest charge had not been brought, no doubt this charge would have been pursued with vigour, irrespective of the fact Anne and George had the most to lose by Henry's death. Their power and influence came solely from the King, and both siblings would have been at great personal risk without Henry's protection. George's wife's allegation at best only amounted to a suggestion that brother and sister spent a suspiciously long time alone together. The evidence for Jane's involvement is vague and inconclusive, and she cannot be accused of betraying the siblings or of being the Crown's chief witness.

Jane was in dire straits, financially, after losing her husband and her mistress in May 1536. She was forced to write to Cromwell requesting financial support, and calling herself a, "poor desolate widow without comfort". She went on to tell Cromwell of his "gentle manner to all them that be in such lamentable case" and asked for "such power stuff and plate as my husband had, whom God pardon; that of his gracious and more liberality I may have it to help me to my power living". She then raised the issue of her dowry, to which the King contributed: "And further more, where that the King's Highness and my Lord my father paid great sum of money for my jointer to the Earl of Wiltshire to the sum of 2000 Marks, and I not assured of no more during the said Earl's natural life than 100 Marks; which is very hard for me to shift the world withal". She asked for Cromwell's specific help because there was no way that she could live on just 100 marks a year: "That you will so specially tender me in this behalf as to inform the Kings Highness of these premises, whereby I may the more tenderly be regarded of his gracious person, your word in this shall be to me a sure reward, which doth promise good to them that help power forsaken widows."[17] It was a humble letter from a woman in need, and Cromwell reacted by interceding for her with the King. Henry VIII then put pressure on Jane's father-in-law, who increased her allowance to £100. Cromwell also helped Jane by giving her a position in the household of the new queen, Jane Seymour, a position which brought Jane into regular contact with Henry VIII's eldest daughter Mary, who gave Jane gifts of fabric and money for her servants.[18] By the time of her own execution in February 1542, Jane, who had now served five of Henry VIII's wives, was an extremely wealthy woman. Her wealth and position, however, did not mean that she was being rewarded for her help in bringing down the Boleyns. Cromwell and the King may have felt obligated to help the widow.

It is easy to use Jane as a scapegoat, but just as the Boleyn siblings should be given the benefit of the doubt due to the lack of evidence for the charges against them, so the same courtesy should be extended to Jane.

23 Execution

George Boleyn and the other four men were publicly executed on the scaffold on Tower Hill on 17 May 1536. Royal "mercy" had commuted all five sentences to beheading, even the lowly Mark Smeaton. The five men were brought together within the confines of the Tower in the early morning. This would have been the first time George had seen a friendly face since his arrest, and it would have been a poignant meeting of old friends, joined together in the most extreme adversity. They were brought out of the Tower and, as the scaffold on Tower Hill was at some distance from the Tower, they would have been forced to walk through a potentially hostile crowd. Henry had been so convinced that the public spectators would be gratified by the deaths of these traitors that he had ordered the scaffold to be built especially high so as to give everyone in the crowd a good view. No doubt he had expected them to be booed, hissed and spat at, especially his brother-in-law the allegedly incestuous pervert. The potential for abuse, vilification and humiliation was great. But Henry had not banked on the English people's sense of fair play, and if he had expected the prisoners to be given a hard time, he was to be disappointed. For George's speech to have been recorded in as much detail as it was, the crowd must have been virtually silent during the men's speeches and their executions. There could have been little or no booing and jeering of the condemned men as with other state executions. These men, particularly George Boleyn and Henry Norris, were respected courtiers, and their deaths were largely viewed with sadness at their wasted lives. Many in the vast crowd believed them to be innocent, and their deaths caused general disgust, particularly following the marriage of Henry VIII to Jane Seymour less than two weeks later. In fact, pamphlets regarding the new royal romance had already been published and circulated, and had caused "great derision" against Henry and Jane; the people's sympathy must surely have been with these men.[1]

The first execution was that of George, Lord Rochford, the highest in rank. This meant that those who died after him had the horror of witnessing the deaths of their friends and fellow prisoners, knowing that they would be next. When George died, the other men knew there could be no hope of a late pardon. Sir Henry Norris was the second to be executed and said virtually nothing on the scaffold: perhaps out of shock; perhaps because he felt there was no longer anything to say; or simply because he felt George Boleyn had said it all for him. Lancelot de Carles confirms that the other four also said very little, "as if they had commissioned Rochford to speak for them". Francis Weston was next, and is reported to have said, "I thought to have lived in abomination yet this twenty or thirty years and then to have made amends. I had little thought it would come to this." William Brereton came the closest to denying his guilt when he said, "I have deserved to die if it were a thousand deaths. But the cause whereof I die, judge not. But if ye judge, judge the best." Mark Smeaton did not withdraw his confession, simply saying, "Masters I pray you all pray for me for I have deserved the death." By the time Smeaton was put to death, the scaffold must have been awash with blood, and the poor boy apparently stumbled as he approached the block before pulling himself together.

George had gone from palace to prison to execution within 15 days, and it is a testament to his courage and strength of character that he was able to defend himself so well at his trial and give such an impassioned speech on the scaffold, when lesser men would still have been in shock. He made a long penitent speech, which found admiration with the vast crowd gathered to witness the executions. There are a number of different versions of George's speech, but they all agree on the basic content. Only Chapuys has George confessing that he deserved death for "having so contaminated and so contaminating others with the new sects", and praying everyone to abandon such heresies. That is clearly not what he said, and is more a matter of wishful thinking by Chapuys.[2] After stepping on to the scaffold, George addressed the crowd:

> I was born under the law, and I die under the law,
> for as much as it is the law which has condemned
> me.

According to two eyewitnesses, he said this three times, almost as if he were collecting his thoughts before continuing. But there was another reason. To say he died "under the law", rather than admitting his guilt, was the closest he dared go to declaring his innocence. Therefore, he ensured the point was reiterated to the vast crowd of spectators, many of whom knew him personally. He went on to say that he was not there to preach a sermon but to die. He told the vast crowd that he deserved death because he was a wretched sinner who had grievously and often offended. He did not relate his sins, telling the crowd that they would derive no pleasure from hearing them, and that he would derive no pleasure from stating them. He merely said that God knew them all. He warned everyone present to use him as an example, especially his fellow courtiers. He warned them "not to trust in the vanity of the world, and especially in the flatterings of the Court, and the favour and treacheries of Fortune", which he said raised men up only to "dash them again upon the ground". He blamed fortune for his current pitiful condition - or rather, he blamed himself, saying he had leaned too heavily on fortune, "who hath proved herself fickle and false unto me". He said he prayed for the mercy of God, and that he forgave all men. He begged forgiveness of God and of anyone he might have offended. He begged those present to ask anyone not there to forgive him if he had offended them, and he told them that "having lived the life of a sinner, I would fain die a Christian man."[3]

There has been much speculation in the latter part of the twentieth and the early years of the twenty-first century about what it was to which George Boleyn was referring to when he said he was a wretched sinner who deserved death, but refused to name his sins. The condemned had their families to protect, and no protestations of innocence would have been acceptable to the Crown. Besides, it was the honourable thing to accept that death was deserved. The Christian doctrine was that we are all sinners deserving of death because of original sin. The shame and dishonour George says he dies for is clearly the incest conviction ("with worse shame and dishonour than hath ever been heard of before"), but at no point in the speech does he make an admission of the offence of which he had been found guilty.

Though one of the sins he refers to, but does not mention, is suggested to be sodomy, there is no evidence for this. George Cavendish suggests that George was referring to promiscuity. This may have been partly true, but the behaviour for which he apologises could refer to an amalgamation of supposed sins. Although George did not ask for the King's forgiveness, he did ask forgiveness of anyone whom he might have offended. Indeed, he went further than this and virtually begged for forgiveness. As a Christian man about to face death, he would have been acutely aware of his flaws and faults. He was proud, and totally lacked humility. He was typically ruthless and self-seeking for a man of the age. He sat at the trial of Thomas More and was present at the appalling executions of the Carthusian monks, despite his protestations of being a "Christian man". He showed no sympathy or compassion towards Catherine of Aragon or her daughter Mary. We do not know how he treated his wife, but his reputation as a high-living womaniser would support the notion that he was not ideal husband material. He had even turned his back on his sister Mary in her hour of need. When facing death, George Boleyn, a highly intelligent and religious man, would have been painfully aware of these failings. Hence his speech went above and beyond that which was expected of him.

He admitted he had relied too heavily on fortune and trusted too much in the vanity of the world and the flattery of the court. His positions of favour and power had resulted in sycophantic flattery by friends and enemies alike, and he had swallowed it whole. He had waltzed around the court with an air of arrogance in the certainty of his position, and because of his confidence in himself and the respect in which he was held. Yet those same people who had fawned over him were here now, watching him die. It was all false, and only at the very end did he realise this.

In his speech he went on to highlight his religious convictions, as previously quoted in the chapter on religion, before finishing by praying "God save the King". Knowing the sort of irreverence to which George Boleyn was prone, this last sentence could be read with a great deal of irony; but whatever was happening to him, his upbringing would never have allowed him to think ill of the King. As far as George was concerned, this was his own fault.

Following his speech, he calmly and courageously knelt down, placed his head on the block, and submitted his neck to the axe. His head was removed with a single stroke, and his severed head was held up to the crowd as the executioner intoned the words, "So ends the lives of all the King's enemies." George Boleyn had many faults, but treason had never been one of them, and Henry must have known that. None of the men's heads were put on display on spikes, as was usual with convicted traitors; this would surely have been the case if Henry seriously thought they were guilty, just as Thomas Culpeper's would be five years later. It was the only small consideration that Henry showed his innocent friends. George's body and head were taken to the Chapel of St Peter ad Vincula within the Tower, where his sister would join him two days later. The other men were buried in two graves, two men in each, in the chapel graveyard.

It is unlikely, as Chapuys alleges, that Anne was forced to watch the executions of her brother and friends, but she may have seen the men congregated together before they were marched out of the Tower - perhaps allowing her one last look at her beloved brother. One man who did witness the executions was Thomas Wyatt, who was imprisoned in the Tower still and who wrote about them in verse, illustrating the danger of being too close to the throne:

> These bloody days have broken my heart.
> My lust, my youth did them depart,
> And blind desire of estate.
> Who hastes to climb seeks to revert.
> Of truth, circa Regna tonat.
>
> The Bell Tower showed me such a sight
> That in my head sticks day and night.
> There did I learn out of a grate,
> For all favour, glory, or might,
> That yet, circa Regna tonat.

In a way this verse reiterates the words of George Boleyn on the scaffold, when he warned his listeners not to trust the vanities of the world and the flattery of the court. His "blind desire of estate" and his "haste to climb" had led him to this end. This was certainly the passage of his speech that was specifically remembered by most of those present, particularly courtiers. On 18 September 1536, John Husee had cause to write to Lady Lisle, "but now I remember my Lord of Rochford's words, who exhorted every man to beware of the flattering of the court."[4] There was many a young courtier who heard those words with trepidation.

Although open mourning for the victims of the May executions would have been a dangerous pastime, there were those who were prepared to pour out their sadness in writing. Wyatt's later poem, "In Mourning Wise since Daily I Increase", was written to honour the five men, and implied that he considered them to be innocent. He suggests that only Smeaton deserved to die - "Since that thy death thou hast deserved best" - presumably due to his false confession.[5]

Anne Boleyn was executed two days after her brother. On the day after her trial, after a visit from Archbishop Cranmer, she had been in hope of life and had spoken of being sent to a nunnery.[6] This suggests that Anne may have been offered some kind of deal by Cranmer in exchange for her agreement to the annulment of her marriage to Henry VIII. By 18 May, the day after her brothers execution, her mood had changed, however. Kingston wrote to Cromwell, "I have seen many men and women executed and at they have been in great sorrow, and to my knowledge this lady has much joy and pleasure in death."[7] Anne knew that she was going to die and she was ready.

Before she was executed, Anne was put through one final humiliation. Her marriage to Henry VIII was pronounced void, just as Catherine's had been, and again it was Thomas Cranmer who made the pronouncement. It was made void, "because of certain just, true and lawful impediments unknown at the making". The Earl of Northumberland had already been contacted regarding a possible consummated marriage contract between him and Anne in order to use this as the basis for divorce. If Anne was pre-contracted to Henry Percy, and if it had been consummated, then she would not have been free to marry the King, and the marriage could reasonably be held void. The Earl denied that there had been any consummated pre-contract between him and Anne, and reiterated that he had made the same denials in 1532, prior to Anne's marriage with the King.

The grounds for the annulment are not made clear, but were probably because of Henry's earlier affair with Anne's sister Mary.

In other words, Henry's marriage to Anne was null and void because he had previously had intercourse with her sister, thus causing an impediment of affinity. Once again, by having the marriage declared void, Henry was again condemning a daughter (this time Elizabeth) to illegitimacy. By doing so, Henry no longer had any legitimate children. It does not appear to have been considered that if he had never been married to Anne, she could hardly have been guilty of adultery.[8]

Anne was executed within the confines of the Tower and, unlike her brother, had the dignity of a private execution. On the scaffold, Anne showed the courage and composure of a true queen. According to an eyewitness she looked "much amazed and exhausted", but she managed to address the crowd, echoing George's comments from two days earlier:

> Good Christian people, I have not come here to preach a sermon; I have come here to die. For according to the law I am judged to die, and therefore I will speak nothing against it. I am come hither to accuse no man, nor to speak of that whereof I am accused and condemned to die, but I pray God save the King and send him long to reign over you, for a gentler nor a more merciful prince was there never, and to me he was ever a good, a gentle, and sovereign lord. And if any person will meddle of my cause, I require them to judge the best. And I take my leave of the world and of you all, and I heartily desire you all to pray for me.[9]

She was executed by a single stroke of a sword wielded by the "Sword of Calais", the executioner who had been summoned from Calais prior to her trial and conviction. Her body and head were put in an old elm chest, which had once contained bow staves, and she was buried in the Chapel of St Peter ad Vincula, close to the resting place of her brother.

The beginning of her speech, and the general undercurrent of her words, was so similar to that of George's that she must have been told what he had said. The manner of the address, and the overall meaning behind the words, are too similar for this to be purely coincidental, even taking into account the conventions of the sixteenth century. The fact that she chose to reiterate his comments emphasises as nothing else the bond between brother and sister, even at the very end.

It is difficult for us today to understand why people who are so obviously innocent do not reaffirm their innocence on the scaffold. Sixteenth century values and conventions are poles apart from our own. George's speech reiterated what he had said at his trial: that the verdict proved he deserved death. He explained that he died under the law, because it was the law that had condemned him. The law was the word of God, and God had decided he must die. He must, therefore, be a wicked and perverse sinner deserving of death, even though he happened to be innocent of the crimes alleged against him. To question your conviction would be to say the law had got it wrong and that God had got it wrong, and that of course was impossible. Furthermore, it was not the honourable thing to do, and therefore certainly something George Boleyn would never do. Some years later, even the pure and virtuous Lady Jane Grey went to her death on the scaffold saying she deserved to die.

The death of the Boleyns was a sordid affair from which no one involved emerged with a modicum of credit or integrity. The tragedy of 1536 will forever haunt the reign of Henry VIII. It is not for his great kingship that he is remembered. Most people today remember him as a tyrant who executed two of his wives and many of his associates and friends. His reputation will always be tarnished by his cruel and brutal actions, and his memorial will remain that of a tyrant and bully, despite the fact that he achieved so much. During the trial of Anne and George, and at their subsequent executions, they were the only people involved who showed courage and dignity. Even Cromwell, in a conversation with Chapuys on 24 May, "greatly praised the sense, wit and courage of the Concubine and of her brother."[10] In the world of men like Cromwell and Henry VIII, sense, wit and courage were not enough to save the siblings. In fact, they were the very attributes that ensured George Boleyn's death.

24 Aftermath

On 20 May 1536, the day after Anne Boleyn's execution, Henry VIII was betrothed to Jane Seymour, marrying her on 30 May. The image of Jane as a sweet, gentle young woman is rather tarnished by the thought of her preparing for her marriage in the knowledge that her predecessor and five innocent men were in the Tower awaiting death. The King had told her on the morning of Anne's trial that he would send news to her later "of the condemnation of the putain."[1] Without a doubt, she knew they were not guilty. Having been one of Anne's ladies-in-waiting she would have known the accusations could not possibly be true.

Queen Jane gave birth to the long-awaited son, the future Edward VI, on 12 October 1537, but died on 24 October after contracting puerperal, or childbed, fever. Henry VIII was not at her bedside, but he was devastated by news of her death and hid himself away at Windsor, refusing to see anyone. He wallowed in his grief for three weeks and wore full mourning for three months after Jane's death.

Henry's illegitimate son, Henry Fitzroy, Duke of Richmond,

died on 23 July 1536, probably of consumption. He was just 17 years old. Of Henry's four children, not one of them had children of their own to carry on the Tudor dynasty. So much brutality had been carried out, and so many innocent people had died, to ensure that the King had a legitimate son, and in the end it was all for nothing. Henry's only success as a father was Elizabeth, who, had she been a boy, would have saved the lives of her mother and uncle.

Elizabeth Boleyn, George and Anne's mother, died in April 1538, two years after the deaths of her youngest children. Thomas Boleyn was forced to relinquish the Privy Seal to Cromwell and retire to the obscurity of the country following the disgrace of his children, but quickly set about working his way back into royal favour. He helped suppress the rebels in autumn 1536 at the Pilgrimage of Grace, was present at Edward VI's christening in October 1537, and even lent Cromwell his chain and Garter badge at one point. By January 1538 he was back in court, but ill health overtook him, and he died in March 1539. The Boleyns' world completely crumbled in 1536, but at least Thomas had been spared his life. It is difficult to claim that Thomas was not proud of his son's accomplishments. George had met, and exceeded, all expectations; Thomas must have been grief-stricken at his death.

As we have seen, following William Carey's death in 1528, Mary Boleyn secretly married William Stafford in 1534. Stafford was a commoner with a small income and no rank. For marrying below her station, Mary and her husband were banished from court by her sister. Although Anne later helped her sister financially, it is possible that the sisters never met again, and Mary made no known attempt to contact either Anne or George following their arrests. It is not known where Mary was in 1536, but she and Stafford were in England from January 1540, when Stafford became an Esquire of the Body. After her parents' deaths, Mary inherited some of the Boleyn properties in Essex, but she died on 19 July 1543.

The appalling experiences of the Boleyn family did not prevent Mary Boleyn's children from forging court careers of their own.

Mary's daughter Catherine became Maid of Honour to Anne of Cleves and Catherine Howard. She married Francis Knollys, a favourite at Henry VIII's court, in 1540; Francis was knighted by Edward VI in 1547. The Knollys' Protestant beliefs led to them leaving England in 1553 when the Catholic Mary I came to the throne, to live in exile in Germany. In 1558, Catherine and Francis returned to England; Francis became a member of Elizabeth I's Privy Council, and later Vice-Chamberlain of the Household and Captain of the Halberdiers. Catherine became one of Elizabeth's Ladies of the Privy Chamber, serving her cousin as the Chief Lady of the Bedchamber. Catherine was taken ill in late 1568 and died on 15 January 1569 at Hampton Court Palace, having served her queen up until her death. Elizabeth I gave her good friend a lavish funeral and Catherine was buried in St Edmund's Chapel, Westminster Abbey.

Mary's son, Henry Carey, was knighted by Elizabeth I in 1558 and then made 1st Baron Hunsdon in January 1559. He was one of the Queen's favourites, holding many prestigious offices, including Privy Councillor and Lord Chamberlain of the Household, and was made a Knight of the Garter in 1561. He died on the 23 July 1596 at Somerset House; it is said that on his deathbed, Elizabeth I offered him the title Earl of Wiltshire, a title once held by his grandfather Thomas Boleyn, but Hunsdon refused Elizabeth's offer, saying, "Madam, as you did not count me worthy of this honour in life, then I shall account myself not worthy of it in death." He was buried at Westminster Abbey on the 12 August 1596 in St John the Baptist's Chapel, in a tomb which is the tallest in the Abbey, measuring 36 feet in height.

Henry VIII married Anne of Cleves in January 1540. Thomas Cromwell had orchestrated the marriage in an attempt to form an alliance with Germany. Henry hated his bride on sight, which resulted in Cromwell's position becoming untenable. Cromwell was beheaded for treason in 1540, shortly after Henry's marriage to Anne was annulled, and on the same day that the King married his fifth wife, Catherine Howard. This choice of date was obviously intentional. By involving George Boleyn in Anne's downfall, Cromwell had destroyed his principal noble supporter on the council. The irony is not lost on historian Rory McEntegart, who suggests that George was "the man best placed to offset the anti-Cromwellian feelings of conservative noblemen such as the Duke of Norfolk."[2] In the long term, the deaths of Anne and George had considerably weakened Cromwell's position.

Cromwell had been created 1st Earl of Essex in April 1540. This honour no doubt lulled him into a false sense of security; he was put to death on 28 July that same year. As Henry married his fifth wife, it is unlikely that he spared a compassionate thought for the man who had served him so diligently for so many years. Cromwell had a particularly gruesome death. The executioner was an inexperienced, nervous young boy who took three strokes of the axe to remove his head. The chronicler Edward Hall said of Cromwell's death, "Many lamented, but more rejoiced", and went on to say, "For in deed he was a man that in all his doings seemed not to favour any kind of Popery."[3] Whatever Cromwell's personal religious persuasions may have been, he had played a major part in the English Reformation. On the scaffold, Cromwell stated that he died "in the Catholicke faithe, not doubtyng in any article of my faith, no nor doubtyng in any Sacrament of the Churche", and although this has been used by some to argue that he was a closet Catholic and had used Reformist beliefs for political gain, John Schofield believes that Cromwell was using the word "catholic" to refer to the "Holy Catholic and Apostolic Church", rather than the Church of Rome, and that it was effectively gallows humour and irony.[4] He finished by declaring, "I waver nothyng in my faithe."

Prior to his death, Cromwell wrote to Henry from the Tower begging the King for mercy, "with the heavy heart and trembling hand of your highness's most heavy and most miserable prisoner and poor slave. Most gracious prince. I cry for mercy, mercy, mercy."[5] Following the Boleyns' deaths Cromwell had praised their sense, wit and courage. Unfortunately, he was not able to emulate their courage or their dignity when faced with his own misfortunes.

Jane Seymour's brothers came to an equally sticky end. Thomas Seymour was executed for treason on 20 March 1549 and Edward Seymour on 22 January 1552. A number of Jane's other supporters also suffered unpleasant deaths, including Nicholas Carew, who had coached Jane on how to capture the King's heart. He was beheaded for treason in 1539, just three years after the executions of Anne and George.

Shortly after her husband's death, Jane Boleyn, Lady Rochford, returned to court and became one of Jane Seymour's ladies. This was despite the fact that she had been married to a man who was not only a convicted traitor, but had also been found guilty of the unnatural and perverted crime of incest. For her to have retained her position she would, at the very least, have had to renounce her husband for his alleged crimes. Unless she had been prepared to acquiesce in his death, and confirm that her allegiance and loyalty lay with Henry, and not the Boleyns, it is inconceivable that she would have been brought back to court in such a prominent and privileged position. Jane Seymour would surely have baulked at the notion of the widow of the man she had partly helped destroy becoming her lady-in-waiting. Lady Rochford would have had to have hidden her grief, and any hatred of those who had a hand in her husband's death.

When Jane Seymour died, Jane Boleyn was prominent at her funeral, travelling in the "second chair" at the funeral procession with other ladies of superior rank, whilst Elizabeth Boleyn was entirely absent. Indeed, at the funeral Jane was second only to the Princess Mary, whose train she had the honour of holding.[6]

Following the deaths of the Boleyns, Jane developed a good relationship with the Princess Mary. Jane gave the Princess the gift of a clock for New Year 1537, and she regularly featured in Mary's Privy Purse expenses. As early as January 1537, only eight months after her husband's death, she received a gift of ten shillings from the Princess, and in February Mary gave Jane four pounds ten shillings to purchase 12 yards of black satin. There are a further five entries between April 1537 and January 1540, concerning Mary's gifts of money to Jane's servants.[7] For her to have gained the Princess's trust and friendship, Jane would have had to make her own loyalty to Mary and her late mother obvious. No sorrow for her deceased husband could have been shown or even hinted at. Jane obviously had no difficulty in appearing completely uncaring as to her husband's fate, judging by the regard in which she was held by Mary, Jane Seymour and the King. However, there is an interesting line in George Cavendish's verses, which refers to Jane:

I aspied a wydowe in blake full woo begon...[8]

This could be taken simply as Cavendish emphasising that Jane was George's widow, rather than literally meaning that she wore mourning clothes and was woebegone at her husband's death. However, the phrase is more meaningful when considering the inventories taken of Jane's possessions. An inventory taken in 1536, at the time of her husband's execution, shows a multitude of different coloured clothing (crimson satin sleeves and placards, yellow satin sleeves, white placards and sleeves, russet placards etc.), but the inventory taken at the time of her own death in 1542 shows that, without exception, all of her clothes were black.[9] Although it could be argued that black was a sign of status and wealth, this would seem a little excessive, and Jane was of just a high status in 1536. Was she mourning her husband nearly six years after his death? Was she brave enough to exhibit mourning for him by constantly wearing black? There is no way of knowing for sure, but Cavendish's words and the difference in her preferred manner of dress between 1536 and 1541 could point in that direction.

Under the terms of her jointure on her marriage, Jane had a life interest in manors at Aylesbury and Bierton in Buckinghamshire. In 1538, Thomas Boleyn wished to sell the properties, but needed Jane's signature to do so. Just as he had done previously, Cromwell acted as intermediary for Jane in her negotiations with her former father-in-law. Jane eventually agreed to sign the necessary documentation to enable Thomas to sell the manors in return for a life interest in the manors of Swavesey in Cambridge, Calthorpe, Filby, Stiffkey, Postwick and Blickling. These were in addition to two manors in Warwickshire, which had been granted to Jane by the King. The manors alone provided Jane with an annual income of £200. Although the Boleyn properties would revert back to the Boleyn family upon Jane's death, during her lifetime she had become an extremely wealthy woman.

After Jane Seymour died, there was no longer a role for Jane Boleyn at court, and as soon as she acquired Blickling, she immediately moved in. The inventory of her belongings taken at her death shows that Jane had significant personal possessions and jewellery, much of which she had been allowed to retain following her husband's death. Her wealth meant that she did not have to return to the dangerous world of the court; she now had a choice. When Henry remarried, Jane was recalled to court and chose to accept the position of lady-in-waiting to his fourth wife, Anne of Cleves, returning to the violent, brutal court that had taken her husband's life. Jane was more than capable of surviving in such an environment. When required to do so, Jane, together with two of Anne of Cleves' other ladies, later provided evidence confirming Anne's relationship with Henry remained unconsummated after six months of marriage. This provided the grounds for an annulment, and could have resulted in Anne of Cleves' execution if she had refused to agree to it. The court was a dangerous place.

Following Henry's parting from Anne of Cleves, he married his fifth wife, the young Catherine Howard, a cousin of George and Anne, and once again Jane became lady-in-waiting to a queen. This time, Jane did not survive court intrigue. She was beheaded along with Catherine Howard on 13 February 1542 for aiding the Queen in her illicit, albeit probably platonic, relationship with Thomas Culpeper. When approached to give evidence regarding Catherine's relationship with Culpeper, it was Jane who revealed that following Catherine's confinement to her apartments, the

Queen had asked three or four times every day what had become of Culpeper. Jane also gave evidence that although she was not privy to a sexual encounter between the two, she believed they knew each other carnally, "considering all things that she had heard and seen". After such evidence, neither Catherine nor her erstwhile young lover had a chance of survival, although they attempted to blame everything on Jane and paint her as some kind of bawd.

When faced with a decision as to whether to help the Crown and save herself, or refuse to give evidence and face ruin and possible death, Jane chose the former. In this she was no worse than Thomas Boleyn, who actively participated in the trials of the four commoners in 1536. Thomas Boleyn and Jane Rochford saved themselves by their actions in 1536. Anne and George Boleyn are unlikely to have expected them to have acted in any other way. With our twenty-first century sentimentality, we are probably harder on Thomas and Jane than either Anne or George would have been.

On the scaffold, Jane is alleged to have said:

> God has permitted me to suffer this shameful doom as punishment for having contributed to my husband's death. I falsely accused him of loving, in an incestuous manner, his sister, Queen Anne Boleyn. For this I deserve to die. But I am guilty of no other crime.[10]

However, as historian John Guy pointed out, this speech is a forgery - "the much later work of Gregorio Leti who (says historian Patrick Collinson after investigating many such stories) 'invented some of his sources and made things up'."[11]

The one known eyewitness, Ottwell Johnson, makes no mention of this speech. He wrote to his brother two days after the executions saying, "They made the most Godly and Christian's end, that ever was heard tell of (I think) since the world's creation; uttering their lively faith in the blood of Christ only, and with goodly words and steadfast countenances they desired all Christian people to take regard unto their worthy and just punishment with death for their offences."[12]

It is likely that Jane's words were embellished in the years following her death, just as stories regarding the nature of the evidence she gave were embellished. Jane's body was buried in the Chapel of St Peter ad Vincula, along with her mistress Catherine Howard and near to where her husband and sister-in-law were buried.

Henry VIII's grief upon discovering Catherine Howard's nocturnal escapades illustrates, as nothing else does, the lack of belief he actually had in Anne Boleyn's guilt. While Anne, George and the other men were in the Tower, Henry continued enjoying life to the full, showing no distress or humiliation at his supposed cuckolding. Yet for Catherine Howard he wept copious tears in front of his Privy Council. Of course, that did not stop him executing the young girl he was supposed to have adored.

Henry married his sixth and final wife, the widow Catherine Parr, on 12 July 1543. She was lucky enough to still be his wife when Henry died four and a half years later, narrowly escaping a plot against her.

Edward, Henry's son by Jane Seymour, ascended to the throne at the age of 9 when his father died in January 1547. He died in 1553, at the age of 15, probably from consumption. Edward had been a staunch Protestant and did not want his country to return to Catholicism. Henry had eventually re-established Mary and Elizabeth to the line of succession. This meant that Mary would be Queen on Edward's death if Edward died without issue, which would mean a return to Catholicism. To stop this from happening, prior to his own death, Edward once again altered the line of succession, appointing his cousin Lady Jane Grey as his successor. Upon Edward's death in July 1553, Lady Jane Grey became queen, but ruled for only 13 days. Following an uprising in favour of Mary, Lady Jane was removed from power and Mary took the throne, having the 16 year-old girl beheaded in February

1554. Mary burned hundreds of Protestants during her reign, including Thomas Cranmer, the man who had annulled her parents' marriage and caused her to be made illegitimate. She died childless and largely unlamented in 1558. Only Henry himself put to death more people than his eldest daughter. In his 38-year reign it is alleged that he executed an estimated 72,000 people, although this is probably exaggerated.[13] Even so, Charles Dickens described Henry as a "disgrace to human nature, and a blot of blood and grease upon the history of England".

Unfortunately, despite his long reign and many achievements, Henry did not gain the fame he craved because of his great kingship; he gained it by breaking with Rome and by becoming a man seen by the general public as an obese, egotistical tyrant who took six wives and murdered two of those unfortunate women.

As for the Duke of Norfolk and his son Henry Howard, Earl of Surrey, they were arrested by Henry VIII in December 1546 and interrogated. Accusations had been made regarding Surrey's incorporation of the royal arms into his coat of arms, showing that he had "monarchic ambitions", and allegedly telling his sister Mary, widow of the Duke of Richmond, to try and become the King's mistress so that her family would be favoured. They were both found guilty of treason and sentenced to death. Surrey was executed on 19 January 1547 but Norfolk was saved by the death of Henry VIII, which preceded the date set for his execution. He was eventually released from the Tower on the accession of Mary I and died on 25th August 1554 at the age of 82.

George and Anne Boleyn died as traitors, their honour and reputations stripped from them. Following their deaths, nobody had the courage to speak up for them in public for fear of retribution from the King. Their names were not spoken, unless it was to abuse and vilify them. George had been a gifted courtier, diplomat and politician, respected and admired. He had been a proud man to whom honour and respectability were of paramount importance. In later years Thomas Wyatt warned his son, "Men punish with shame as the greatest punishment on earth, yea! greater than death." In George's own words, the incest charge meant that he died "with more shame and dishonour than hath ever been heard of before". Now he was, in the words of Cavendish, a vile wretch:

> Alas! Quote the first, with full heavy care,
> And countenance sad, piteous, and lamentable,
> George Boleyn I am, that now doth appear;
> Some time of Rochford Viscount honourable,
> And now a vile wretch, most miserable.[14]

This vilification continued for many years, during which, George and Anne Boleyn each came to be seen as persona non grata. But on Mary I's death, Anne's daughter Elizabeth came to the throne, and to a certain extent her mother came back into favour. This did not completely prevent Anne's continued vilification, or that of her brother, and although Elizabeth's ascension prevented her mother from being written out of history, George's immortality remained uncertain. Even today, despite all the evidence to the contrary, there are those who insist on George and Anne's guilt. This view is not helped by fictional works, some of which demonise the Boleyns, or play on the incest allegation for dramatic effect.

Love or hate them, George and Anne Boleyn, whether together or individually, were hard to ignore in a way with which plain, quiet Jane Seymour could never compete. No wonder, then, that Anne remains the most famous of Henry's queens. This book opened by noting that George and Anne were an immensely attractive pair, and that the court was a much less glamorous place without them. When they and the other four men died, Henry lost his six main sources of entertainment. The court must have seemed very dull in their absence. It is not surprising that following the Boleyns' fall, Henry aged rapidly. Within three years he became a flaccid, bloated, petulant old man who was never again able to fully capture the lively, intellectual, witty atmosphere of the Boleyn court. If he ever regretted his actions of 1536, this would no doubt have been because his gifted friends were no longer alive to entertain him. Their brightness had been snuffed out way too soon.

The court only regained its Boleyn charisma under Anne's daughter. Elizabeth's reign was one of the most glorious of any English monarch, and England prospered as never before. Under Elizabeth, England remained a Protestant country, and to this extent Anne and George Boleyn were eventually vindicated. The fear, which George expressed on the scaffold, of a return to the orthodox Catholic faith was only temporary. For this at least, George Boleyn would have felt that he did not die entirely in vain.

Part 4 - Additional Information

Chronology

28 June 1491	Birth of Henry VIII
21 April 1509	Death of Henry VII and accession of Henry VIII
11 June 1509	Marriage of Henry VIII and Catherine of Aragon
24 June 1509	Coronation of Henry VIII and Catherine of Aragon
c. 1499/1500	Birth of Mary Boleyn
c. 1501	Birth of Anne Boleyn
c. 1502-1504	Births of Thomas and Henry Boleyn
c. 1504/1505	Birth of George Boleyn
c. 1505-06	The Boleyn family move from Blickling Hall in Norfolk to Hever Castle in Kent

1513	Anne Boleyn travels to the Low Countries to serve Margaret of Austria
1514	Mary Boleyn travels to France as lady-in-waiting to Mary Tudor, where she is joined by Anne
Christmas 1514	George Boleyn appears in a Christmas Melee at the court of Henry VIII
c. 1515-16	George is appointed page to the King
18 February 1516	Catherine of Aragon gives birth to the Princess Mary
15 June 1519	Birth of Henry VIII's illegitimate son, Henry Fitzroy
c. 1519	Mary Boleyn returns from France and has an adulterous relationship with the King, which may have begun as early as 1519 and finished as late as 1525.
4 February 1520	Mary Boleyn marries William Carey
June 1520	Field of the Cloth of Gold meeting between the Kings of France and England
Late 1521	Anne Boleyn returns from France
1 March 1522	The The Château Pageant featuring Anne and Mary Boleyn, and Jane Parker
April 1522	Thomas and George Boleyn receive grants of various properties previously belonging to the executed Duke of Buckingham, including Tunbridge
c. 1524	Mary Boleyn gives birth to Catherine Carey
June 1524	George receives the grant of Grimston Manor, the first royal grant in his sole name

Late 1524/early 1525   George marries Jane Parker

c. 1525/1526   Anne first attracts the attention of the king

June 1525   Thomas Boleyn becomes Lord Rochford

January 1526   George loses his position in the Privy Chamber following the Eltham Ordinances. The same month he is appointed cupbearer to the King

March 1526   Mary Boleyn gives birth to Henry Carey

June 1528   George Boleyn travels with the court to Waltham Abbey where he contracts the disease known as sweating sickness. Anne and Thomas Boleyn also contract the disease at Hever Castle. All three survive.

22 June 1528   William Carey dies of sweating sickness

1528   George is appointed Master of the Buckhounds

26 September 1528   George is appointed Esquire to the Body

15 November 1528   George is appointed keeper of the Palace of Beaulieu

1 February 1529   George is appointed chief steward of Beaulieu

27 July 1529   George is appointed governor of St Bethlehem Hospital

October 1529   George is knighted

October 1529   George escorts the new imperial ambassador, Eustace Chapuys, to court

October 1529   George is appointed Ambassador to France and attends his first embassy to France at the end of the month

c. November 1529	George is restored to the Privy Chamber as a gentleman of the Privy Chamber

\\\

8 December 1529	Thomas, Lord Rochford becomes the Earl of Wiltshire, and George is granted the courtesy title of Lord Rochford. This ceases to become a courtesy title the following year

\\\

December 1529	George receives annuities from Cardinal Wolsey's estates of £200 and 200 marks

\\\

End February 1530	George returns from a four month embassy to France

\\\

10 February 1531	George delivers various tracts to Convocation to persuade them to agree to recognising Henry as head of the Church of England

\\\

March 1532	George and a group of leading courtiers attend a meeting with the clergy demanding their submission

\\\

16 May 1532	Formal submission of the clergy.

\\\

1 September 1532	Anne Boleyn is created Marchioness of Pembroke

\\\

11 October 1532	The King, the Boleyns and leading courtiers set sail for Calais where Anne is introduced to the King of France as Queen-in-waiting

\\\

25 January 1533	Anne Boleyn marries King Henry VIII in a secret ceremony at Whitehall

\\\

5 February 1533	George is called to Parliament for the first time

\\\

11 March 1533	George receives a warrant to travel to France to advice King Francis of the marriage, and to raise with him the differences between England and Scotland
	\\
8 April 1533	George returns from France with a wedding gift for his sister from Francis
	\\
April 1533	George is appointed the wardship of Edmund Sheffield
	\\
29 May 1533	George attends his third embassy to France (with his uncle, the Duke of Norfolk) to be present at a meeting scheduled between the Pope and the King of France
	\\
1 June 1533	The Coronation of Queen Anne Boleyn
	\\
28 July 1533	George arrives back in England with news that the Pope has excommunicated Henry
	\\
8 August 1533	George returns to France with instructions to try and prevent the meeting between the Pope and Francis until the threat of excommunication is lifted
	\\
End August 1533	George and Norfolk return to England
	\\
7 September 1533	Anne gives birth to the Princess Elizabeth
	\\
10 September 1533	Princess Elizabeth's christening at the Church of Observant Friars in Greenwich
	\\
October 1533	George is granted the Palace of Beaulieu, and immediately moves in
	\\
April 1534	The Act of Succession, enacted the previous month, comes into force
	\\

16 April 1534	George travels to France for his fourth diplomatic mission to urge Francis to adopt similar legislation against the Pope as that taken in England, and to arrange a meeting between the two kings, Anne, and Francis' sister
May 1534	George returns to England
16 June 1534	George is appointed Lord Warden of the Cinque Ports and Constable of Dover Castle
7 July 1534	George receives instructions to travel to France to reschedule the meeting between the Kings due to Anne's pregnancy
27 July 1534	George returns to England with confirmation that Francis had agreed to defer the meeting
Summer 1534	Anne has her first miscarriage/stillbirth
Autumn 1534	Lady Rochford is banished from court for allegedly conspiring with Anne to have a rival removed
Autumn 1534	Mary Boleyn is banished from court for falling pregnant and marrying William Stafford without permission
11 November 1534	The Admiral of France arrives in England, where he is escorted and entertained by George on the way to London
December 1534	George allegedly has a quarrel with his cousin, Francis Bryan, in which the King sides against his brother-in-law
February 1535	The Act of Supremacy, enacted in November 1534, comes into force

10 April 1535	George receives a grant of one of Thomas More's Kent Manors and sells it immediately afterwards
4 May 1535	George and his father are present at the executions of the Carthusian monks
20 May 1535	George arrives in France on his sixth, and final, diplomatic mission to negotiate a marriage between the Princess Elizabeth and the King of France's third son
22 May 1535	George and Norfolk meet the Admiral of France, but no agreement can be reached
24 May 1535	George returns to England for further instructions, arriving in London the following day. He sought a lengthy meeting with Anne before reporting to the King
Beginning of June 1535	George returns to France with instructions not to compromise, which results in the meeting breaking up in acrimony on 17th June
22 June 1535	Execution of John Fisher
1 July 1535	Trial of Thomas More, at which George and Thomas Boleyn form part of the special commission of oyer and terminer to hear the case
6 July 1535	Execution of Thomas More
Summer 1535	Demonstration in favour of the Princess Mary, at which Lady Rochford is alleged to have taken an active role
1535	Jane Seymour becomes one of Anne's ladies-in-waiting

7 January 1536	Death of Catherine of Aragon
29 January 1536	Anne has her second miscarriage
4 February 1536	Lord La Warr's proxy vote goes to George
March 1536	Further grants to George and his father, but an inventory of all grants made to them is prepared
18 April 1536	Eustace Chapuys is summoned to court to discuss an imperial alliance, where he is met and entertained by George. Chapuys is manoeuvred into recognising Anne as queen for the first time
23 April 1536	George fails to receive the Order of the Garter
24 April 1536	The King authorises the setting up of two special commissions of oyer and terminer
30 April 1536	Mark Smeaton is arrested
1 May 1536	May day joust at which George and Henry Norris are the principal jousters. The same day Henry Norris is arrested
2 May 1536	George and Anne Boleyn are arrested
Around 4 May 1536	Francis Weston and William Brereton are arrested
Around 5 May 1536	Thomas Wyatt and Richard Page are arrested, and Francis Bryan is ordered to London for questioning.
12 May 1536	Trials of the four commoners. All four are found guilty and sentenced to be hanged, drawn and quartered. Thomas Boleyn was on the jury, and found the men guilty

15 May 1536	Anne stands trial in the morning and is sentenced to be burned or beheaded, according to the King's wishes. George stands trial in the afternoon and is sentenced to be hanged, drawn and quartered
17 May 1536	George and the four commoners have their sentences commuted, and all five are beheaded on Tower Hill
19 May 1536	Anne is beheaded by sword on Tower Green
20 May 1536	Henry VIII and Jane Seymour become betrothed
29 May 1536	Henry VIII marries Jane Seymour
18 June 1536	Death of Henry Fitzroy, Duke of Richmond
12 October 1537	Birth of Edward VI
24 October 1537	Death of Queen Jane Seymour
6 January 1540	Henry VIII marries Anne of Cleves
9 July 1540	Henry divorces Anne of Cleves
28 July 1540	Henry marries Catherine Howard, and Cromwell is beheaded
13 February 1542	Catherine Howard and Lady Jane Rochford are executed on Tower Green
12 July 1543	Henry marries Catherine Parr
28 January 1547	Death of Henry VIII
6 July 1553	Death of Edward VI
10 July 1553	Lady Jane Grey is proclaimed Queen
19 July 1553	Lady Jane is overthrown and Mary I takes the throne
12 February 1554	Lady Jane Grey is beheaded on Tower Green

17 November 1558   Death of Mary I and accession of
                   Elizabeth I

15 January 1559   Elizabeth I's Coronation

24 March 1603   Death of Elizabeth I

George Boleyn's Poetry

See Chapter 3 for a discussion of these poems.

The Lover Complaineth the Unkindness of His Love

My lewt, awake! Performe the laste!
Labour that thow and I shall waste;
And ende that I have nowe begunne:
For when this song is sunge and past,
My lewt be still, for I have done.

As to be heard where eare is none,
As lead to grave in marble stone,
My song may pearce her heart as sone:
Shuld we then sighe, or singe, or mone?
No, no, my lewte, for I have done.

The rockes do not so cruellye
Repulsse the waves contynually,
As she my sute and affection;
So that I am past remedie,
Whearby my lute and I have done.

Vengeance shall fall on thie disdaine
That makest but game on earnest payne:
Thinck not alone under the sonne,
Unquyte to cause thie lovers playne,
Althoughe my lute and I have done.

Perchaunce they lye withered and olde,
The winter nightes that are so colde,
Playninge in vayne unto the moone:
Thie wishes then dare not be tolde,
Care then whoe liste, for I have done.

And then may chaunce thee to repent
The tyme that thow hast lost and spent,
To cawse thie lovers sighe and swone;
Then shalt thou know bewtie but lent,
And wishe and want as I have done.

Now cease my lewte! This is the last
Labour that thow and I shall waste,
And endid is that we begunne;
Now is this songe both sunge and past,
My lewte be still, for I have done![1]

O death rock me asleep

Oh, death rock me on sleepe,
Bring on my quiet reste;
Let passe my verye guiltless goste,
Out of my careful brest:
Toll on the passinge bell,
Ringe out the dolefull knell,
Let the sounde my dethe tell,
For I must dye,
There is no remedy,
For now I dye.

My paynes who can expres?
Alas! They are so stronge,
My dolor will not suffer strength
My lyfe for to prolonge;
Toll on the passinge bell, etc.

Alone in prison stronge,
I wayle my destenye;
Wo worth this cruel hap that I
Should taste this miserye.
Toll on the passinge bell, etc.

Farewell my pleasures past,
Welcum, my present payne;
I fele my torments so increse,
That lyfe cannot remayne.
Cease now the passing bell,
Rong is my dolefull knell,
For the sound my deth doth tell,
Death doth draw nye,
Sound my end dolefully,
For now I dye.[2]

Appendix B

George Cavendish's Metrical Visions (Relating to Lord Rochford)

Set out below are George Cavendish's verses relating to George Boleyn, Lord Rochford. These verses were written almost solely on the basis of Cavendish's interpretation of George's scaffold speech. As can be seen, when they are read in context, Cavendish was suggesting that on the scaffold George admitted he deserved death due to his promiscuity. It was not until the late twentieth century that Cavendish's verses were re-interpreted to suggest that he was covertly referring to homosexual activity. These verses, however, cannot be seen as intimating that George was homosexual, they are actually saying the complete opposite.

Cavendish hated the Boleyns and everything they stood for. In his verses, he seeks to criticise and vilify them as much as possible.

By the time of George's death, "buggery" had been made illegal by the Buggery Act of 1533. As a member of Parliament, George would have voted for the introduction of the act. If Cavendish had believed George Boleyn was guilty of not only a crime, but what in the sixteenth century would have been a perversion against God, then he had no incentive to hide the fact. Indeed, he, and every other Boleyn enemy, would have declared it to the rafters. See Chapter 22 on Jane Boleyn for more on this.

Cavendish's later verses relating to Henry VIII, upon the King's own death, accept that not all of the people executed during his reign were actually guilty of the crimes for which they were condemned. The verses confirm Cavendish's own belief that a number of the condemned traitors died merely because of Henry's love of change. *Metrical Visions*, in which the victims of the May 1536 plot are viciously demonised and insulted, appear to say far more about Cavendish's own pious hypocrisy than about the innocent people he slanders.

Viscount Rocheford

> ALAS! Quod the first, with a full hevy chere,
> And countenance sad, piteous, and lamentable,
> George Bulleyn I am, that now doth appere;
> Some tyme of Rocheford Viscount honorable,
> And now a vile wretch, most myserable,
> That ame constrayned with dole in my visage,
> Even to resemble a very deadly image.

God gave me grace, dame Nature did hir part,
Endewed me with gyfts of natural qualities:
Dame Eloquence also taughte me the arte
In meter and verse to make pleasant dities,
And fortune preferred me to high dignyties
In such abondance, that combred was my witt,
To render God thanks that gave me eche whitt.

It hath not been knowen nor seldome seen,
That any of my yeres byfore this day
Into the privy councell preferred hath been:
My soverayn lord in his chamber did me assay,
Or yeres thryes nine my life had past away;
A rare thing suer seldom or never hard,
So yong a man so highly to be preferrd.

In this my welthe I had God clean forgot,
And my sensuall apetyte I did always ensewe,
Esteming in my self the thyng that I had not,
Sufficient grace this chaunce for to eschewe,
The contrary, I perceyve, causithe me now to rewe;
My folly was such that vertue I set asyde,
And forsoke God that should have been my gwyde.

My lyfe not chaste, my lyvyng bestyall;
I forced wydowes, maydens I did deflower.
All was oon to me. I spared none at all,
My appetite was all women to devoure,
My study was both day and hower,
My onleafull lechery how I might it fulfill,
Sparyng no woman to have on hyr my wyll.

Allthoughe I before hathe both seene and rede
The word of God and scriptures of auctoritie,
Yet could not I resist this onlefull deede,
Nor dreade the domes of God in my prosperitie;
Let myn estatte, therefore, a myrror to you be,
And in your mynd my dolors comprehend
For myne offences how God hath made me dissend.

See how fortune can alter and change hir tyde,
That to me but late could be so good and favorable,
And at this present to frowne and set me thus aside,
Which thoughte hyr whele to stand both firme and stable,
Now have I found hyr very froward and mutable;
Where she was frendly now she is at discord.
As by experience of me Viscount Rocheford.

For where God list to punysh man of right,
By mortal sword, farewell all resistence;
When grace faylyth, honor hath no force or myght,
Of nobilitie also it defacyth the high preeminence,
And changythe their power to feeble impotence;
Then tornyth fortune hyr whele most spedely
Example take of me for my lewde avoultrie.

All noblemen, therefore, with stedfast hart entyer,
Lyft up your corages, and think this is no fable;
Thoughe ye sit high, conceive yt in your chere,
That no worldly prynce in yerthe is perdurable;
And since that ye be of nature reasonable,
Remember in your welthe, as thing most necessary,
That all standythe on fortune when she listeth to vary.

Alas! To declare my life in every effect,
Shame restraynyth me the playnes to confess,
Least the abhomynation would all the world enfect:
Yt is so vile, so detestable in words to expresse,
For which by the lawe, condempned I am doughtlesse,
And for my desert, justly juged to be deade;
Behold here my body, but I have lost my hed.[1]

Appendix C

George Boleyn's Scaffold Speech

George Boleyn's scaffold speech was the most famous of its day. Its contents became widespread throughout England and Europe, and it was renowned and admired for its eloquence and piety, and for the bravery of the condemned man who gave the speech immediately before his death. For that reason, it is only right that it is set out below in its entirety. One paragraph is in parentheses and this is because it is only reported by one source; it does not form part of any of the main sources. If this section did form part of the speech, then its exact position in the speech is unknown.

> I was born under the law, and I die under the law, for as much as it is the law which has condemned me. Masters all, I am come before you not to preach and make a sermon but to die. And I beseech you all , in his holy name, to pray unto

God for me, for I have deserved to die if I had twenty (or a thousand) lives, yea even to die with more shame and dishonour than hath ever been heard of before. For I am a wretched sinner, who has grievously and often times offended; nay in truth, I know not of any more perverse sinner than I have been up till now. Nevertheless, I mean not openly now to relate what my many sins may have been, since it were no pleasure to you to hear them, nor yet for me to rehearse them, for God knoweth them all. Therefore masters all, I pray you take heed from me, and especially ye gentlemen of the court, the which I have been among you, take heed by me, and beware such a fall, and I pray to the Father, Son and Holy Ghost, three persons in one God, that my death may be an example to you all, and beware, trust not in the vanity of the world, and especially in the flatterings of the court, and the favour and treacheries of Fortune, which only raises men aloft that with so much the greater force she may dash them again upon the ground. She in truth it is who is the cause that, as ye all witness, my miserable head is now to be severed from my neck; or rather, in greater truth, the fault is mine, and it is I who ought to be blamed for having adventured to lean on fortune, who hath proved herself fickle and false unto me, and who now makes me a sad example to you all and to the whole world. And do you all, Sirs, take notice, that in this my sorrowful condition, I pray for the mercy of God Almighty, and that I do moreover forgive all men, with all my heart and mind, even as truly as I hope that the Lord God will forgive me. And if I have offended any man that is not here present, either in thought, word or deed, and if ye hear of any such, I entreat you heartily on my behalf, pray that he may in his charity forgive me; for, having lived the life of a sinner, I would fain die a Christian man.

Nor must I fail, while there is still time, to tell you who now hearken to me, that men do common and say that I have been a setter forth of the word of God. I was a great reader and a mighty debater of the Word of God, and one of those who most favoured the Gospel of Jesus Christ.

[Truly so that the Word should be among the people of the realm I took upon myself great labour to urge the king to permit the printing of the Scriptures to go unimpeded among the commons of the realm in their own language. And truly to God I was one of those who did most to procure the matter to place the Word of God among the people because of the love and affection which I bear for the Gospel and the truth in Christ's words.]

Wherefore, least the Word of God should be slandered on my account, I now tell you all Sirs, that if I had, in very deed, kept his holy Word, even as I read and reasoned about it with all the strength of my wit, certain am I that I should not be in the piteous condition wherein I now stand. Truly and diligently did I read the Gospel of Jesus Christ, but turned not to profit that which I did read; the which had I done, of a surety I had not fallen into such great errors. Wherefore I do beseech you all, for the love of God, that ye do at all seasons, hold by the truth, and speak it, and embrace it; for beyond all peradventure, better

profiteth he who readeth not and yet doeth well,
than he who readeth much and yet liveth in sin.
God save the King.

In the sixteenth century, it was not considered appropriate for a convicted traitor to rail against injustice, or to proclaim their innocence on the scaffold. An honourable death was one where the accused accepted his death as deserved. Whatever other aspect there may have been to his character, George Boleyn seems always have at least tried to be honourable, and he certainly tried to die so. Yet despite the conventions of the day, which he always followed with committed zeal, and which partly guided his final words, the subtle nuance of the entire speech is that of innocence. The beginning of the speech confirms that he is dying only because the law has condemned him, not because he was guilty of the crimes alleged against him. He goes on to say that his death is actually due to the fact that he relied too heavily on fortune, the vanities of the world and flatteries of the court. In other words, he is dying because fortune was against him, not because he was guilty. Again, he could not have expressed his innocence any clearer.

The fact that some felt that it was an admission of guilt merely confirms that George was far more intelligent than some of those who heard his speech, and his verbal gymnastics were above them, or perhaps it was merely that some of those listening simply heard what they wanted to hear.

The Execution Poetry of Sir Thomas Wyatt

In Mourning Wise Since Daily I Increase

Sir Thomas Wyatt the Elder wrote this poem to honour the five men who were executed for adultery with Anne Boleyn. It implies that Wyatt thought that these men were innocent.

In Mourning wise since daily I increase,
Thus should I cloak the cause of all my grief;
So pensive mind with tongue to hold his peace'
My reason sayeth there can be no relief:
Wherefore give ear, I humbly you require,
The affect to know that thus doth make me moan.
The cause is great of all my doleful cheer
For those that were, and now be dead and gone.
What thought to death desert be now their call.
As by their faults it doth appear right plain?
Of force I must lament that such a fall should
light on those so
wealthily did reign,
Though some perchance will say, of cruel heart,
A traitor's death why should we thus bemoan?
But I alas, set this offence apart,
Must needs bewail the death of some be gone.

As for them all I do not thus lament,
But as of right my reason doth me bind;
But as the most doth all their deaths repent,
Even so do I by force of mourning mind.
Some say, "Rochford, haddest thou been not so proud,
For thy great wit each man would thee bemoan,
Since as it is so, many cry aloud
It is great loss that thou art dead and gone."

Ah! Norris, Norris, my tears begin to run
To think what hap did thee so lead or guide
Whereby thou hast both thee and thine undone
That is bewailed in court of every side;
In place also where thou hast never been
Both man and child doth piteously thee moan.
They say, "Alas, thou art far overseen
By thine offences to be thus dead and gone."

Ah! Weston, Weston, that pleasant was and young,
In active things who might with thee compare?
All words accept that thou diddest speak with tongue,
So well esteemed with each where thou diddest fare.
And we that now in court doth lead our life
Most part in mind doth thee lament and moan;
But that thy faults we daily hear so rife,
All we should weep that thou are dead and gone.

Brereton farewell, as one that least I knew.
Great was thy love with divers as I hear,
But common voice doth not so sore thee rue
As other twain that doth before appear;
But yet no doubt but they friends thee lament
And other hear their piteous cry and moan.
So doth eah heart for thee likewise relent
That thou givest cause thus to be dead and gone.

Ah! Mark, what moan should I for thee make more,
Since that thy death thou hast deserved best,
Save only that mine eye is forced sore
With piteous plaint to moan thee with the rest?
A time thou haddest above thy poor degree,
The fall whereof thy friends may well bemoan:
A rotten twig upon so high a tree
Hath slipped thy hold, and thou art dead and gone.

And thus farewell each one in hearty wise!
The axe is home, your heads be in the street;
The trickling tears doth fall so from my eyes
I scarce may write, my paper is so wet.
But what can hope when death hath played his part,
Though nature's course will thus lament and moan?
Leave sobs therefore, and every Christian heart
Pray for the souls of those be dead and gone.

V. Innocentia Veritas Viat Fides Circumdederunt me inimici mei

by Sir Thomas Wyatt, the Elder

The final verse of this poem shows that Wyatt knew only too well that pleading innocence was no help at all when it came to justice in Henry VIII's court.

Who list his wealth and ease retain,
Himself let him unknown contain.
Press not too fast in at that gate
Where the return stands by disdain,
For sure, *circa Regna tonat**.

The high mountains are blasted oft
When the low valley is mild and soft.
Fortune with Health stands at debate.
The fall is grievous from aloft.
And sure, *circa Regna tonat.*

These bloody days have broken my heart.
My lust, my youth did them depart,
And blind desire of estate.
Who hastes to climb seeks to revert.
Of truth, *circa Regna tonat.*

The bell tower showed me such sight
That in my head sticks day and night.
There did I learn out of a grate,
For all favour, glory, or might,
That yet *circa Regna tonat.*

By proof, I say, there did I learn:
Wit helpeth not defence too yerne,
Of innocency to plead or prate.
Bear low, therefore, give God the stern,
For sure, *circa Regna tonat*.

circa regna tonat means "about the throne the thunder rolls".

Appendix E

The Clonony Boleyn Girls and George Boleyn, Dean of Lichfield

At the 1868 annual general meeting of the Historical and Archaeological Society of Ireland in Kilkenny, a rubbing from the inscription on a tomb slab from Clonony Castle was examined. This slab was known locally as the monument of "Queen Elizabeth's cousins" and reads:

HERE UNDER LEYS ELIZABETH AND MARY BULLYN DAUGHTERS OF THOMAS BULLYN SON OF GEORGE BULLYN THE SON OF GEORGE BULLYN VISCOUNT ROCHFORD SON OF SIR THOMAS BULLYN EARLE OF ORMONDE AND WILTSHIRE

The slab was recorded as measuring 7 feet by 4 feet, and being 16 inches in thickness. It was stated that it had been removed from a nearby quarry to the castle in the first quarter of the nineteenth century.[1] Reference was then given to an article in *The Irish Penny Magazine* (September 1833), which told the story of the discovery of the tomb slab.[2] According to the magazine article, labourers busy gathering stone for building work near Clonony Castle, in 1803, found a cave about a hundred yards from the castle. In the cave in the limestone rock, "about twelve feet under the surface" and beneath a pile of stones, they found a "large limestone flag" and "a coffin cut in the rock", which contained the remains of two bodies.

From the inscription on the limestone flag, these remains were identified as second cousins of Queen Elizabeth I, being great-granddaughters of George Boleyn, Lord Rochford. The writer of the magazine article went on to ponder how these Boleyn girls ended up "interred in this obscure corner of the King's county", wondering if their father was employed in Ireland during the troubles in Elizabeth I's reign or whether members of the Boleyn family fled from England to Ireland "to escape the fury of King Henry VIII" when Anne Boleyn and her brother fell in 1536.

When the writer of the article shared the discovery of the tombstone with the Earl of Rosse, who was descended through his mother from Alice, daughter of Sir William Boleyn of Blickling, the Earl showed him portraits of two young women at Birr Castle. Nobody knew who they were, but the paintings were marked "*Anno aetatis* 18" and "*Anno aetatis* 19" and "*Anno Dni* 1567, meaning that the girls were in their 18th and 19th years when they were painted in 1567, and the Earl suggested that these were portraits of Elizabeth and Mary Boleyn. The portrait of the girl thought to be Mary pictured her with a marigold, for "Mary", stuck behind an ear while the other girl was pictured wearing a jewel in the form of an "E" for Elizabeth. Both the Earl and the writer of the article became convinced that these girls were the Boleyn girls of the tomb.

Birthdates of 1548 and 1547, however, make no sense if these girls are meant to be granddaughters of George Boleyn. Lady Rosse, the present owner of Birr Castle, believes the girls depicted in the portrait to be Margaret and Elizabeth Clere, daughters of John Clere of Ormesby St Margaret, Norfolk, who was the son of Robert Clere and Alice Boleyn, Anne Boleyn's paternal aunt.[3] The present Earl of Rosse descends from the Cleres through his great-great-great-great-grandmother, Mary Clere. When I researched the Cleres, I found that Margaret Clere married Walter Haddon (1514/1515-1571) and gave him four children. Haddon remarried in December 1567 so Margaret must have been dead by this time and it appears unlikely that she would have been 18 at her death in 1567, the year she was said to have been painted. However, there appears to be a Boleyn link as the paintings came into the Parsons family (the Earl of Rosse's family) at the same time as a head and shoulder portrait of Anne Boleyn.[3]

Lady Rosse believes, and I agree with her, that the girls from the portraits are not the girls of the Clonony tomb. Both pairs of girls are linked to the Boleyns, with regards to the Clere family and the tombstone inscription, but they cannot be the same sisters.

In *Burke's Peerage*, there is a mention of an "Anne Boleyn", wife of Sir Robert Newcomen, baronet, and a "great-niece of Queen Elizabeth", in the seventeenth century in Ireland. This suggests that she too descended from George Boleyn and may have been the sister of Elizabeth and Mary.[4]

The story told locally is that Clonony Castle was given to Thomas Boleyn, Earl of Ormond and Wiltshire, father of Anne Boleyn, by Henry VIII after it was ceded to the King by John Óg MacCoghlan. When George and Anne Boleyn were executed in 1536, George's illegitimate son was moved to Clonony to keep him safe. Mary and Elizabeth Boleyn were descended from this man. When Elizabeth died young, Mary was devastated and committed suicide, throwing herself from Clonony Castle tower. The sisters were buried behind the castle and their grave eventually forgotten, until it was found by labourers digging stone for the canal which they were building by the castle. The girls' remains were reinterred in a local graveyard and the tombstone moved to the castle, where it still lies beneath a hawthorn tree. It is difficult to decipher the inscription today, due to weather damage, but rubbings have been made.[5]

There has often been talk that George Boleyn, Dean of Lichfield from 1576-1603, was George Boleyn's son, either with Jane or illegitimately. However, although he referred to himself as a kinsman of the Carey and Knollys families (Mary Boleyn's children's families) and named Lord Hunsdon (Mary's son) as an executor in his will, he does not seem to have ever claimed to have been George Boleyn's son, and there is no record of Jane Boleyn ever giving birth. In 1597, George Carey, 2nd Baron Hunsdon and Mary Boleyn's grandson, sent a letter to Lord Burghley asking for advice regarding petitioning Elizabeth I concerning the earldom of Ormond. This earldom had once been held by his great-grandfather, Thomas Boleyn, and Hunsdon's claim to it was based on the belief that the title "should have passed to his father and then on to himself by virtue of their descent from Sir Thomas Boleyn's eldest daughter, Mary." If George Boleyn, Dean of Lichfield, was George Boleyn's son surely he, not George Carey, would have had claim to it, but no objection was raised at the time.

Julia Fox writes of how Sir Thomas Boleyn had been forced to pass on the Ormond ancestral horn, which he had inherited from his grandfather, to the St Leger branch of the family due to the fact that his son George Boleyn had died without issue. If the Dean had been George's legitimate son then he would have inherited it. Even if he had missed out on the horn due to illegitimacy, the Dean would surely have been recognised or helped in some way by the surviving Boleyn family after his father's death. There would also have been no reason for George Boleyn, Lord Rochford, not to recognise an illegitimate son, particularly as he had no legitimate heirs.[6] The Dean appears to have been a rather colourful character, being described as having a "chollerick" nature and having a tendency to swear, and getting into trouble for threatening to nail a Dean to a wall and attacking a preacher with a dagger. He would also take his dog to church with him.[7] An interesting character, but his parentage remains a mystery.

There is no evidence at all that the Boleyn girls of Clonony or George Boleyn, Dean of Lichfield, were descended from George Boleyn, Lord Rochford. There is no mention of Jane having a child when she was executed in 1542, and no mention in any records of George having an illegitimate son. It is not impossible, however, for him to have had an illegitimate son who grew up in Ireland away from the English court. It would be nice to think that George left something behind.

Figure 19 - Clonony Castle

Figure 20 - Hawthorn tree and tomb slab at Clonony Castle

Notes

Introduction

1 Warnicke, *The Rise and Fall of Anne Boleyn: Family Politics at the Court of Henry VIII*, 4.
2 Carley, *The Books of King Henry VIII and His Wives*, 133.

PART 1 - THE BEGINNINGS

1) Family Background

1 W. L. E. Parsons, Rev. Canon, "Some Notes on the Boleyn Family."
2 Bindoff, *The History of Parliament: The House of Commons 1509-1558*.
3 Cockayne, *The Complete Peerage of England, Scotland, Ireland, Great Britain, and the United Kingdom Extant, Extinct, or Dormant*, vol. X.
4 Nicolas, *Testamenta Vetusta: Being Illustrations from Wills, of Manners, Customs Etc.*, II:465.

5 Ridgway, *The Anne Boleyn Collection II*, 236–237. Sources include: Friar William Peto; Princess Mary's confessor; Elizabeth Amadas, a woman said to have been a past mistress of Henry VIII; and the Catholic writers Nicholas Harpsfield, William Rastell and Nicholas Sander. When Sir George Throckmorton spoke to the King of rumours that he had "meddled both with the mother and the sister", Henry VIII replied, "Never with the mother". LP xii. 952.

2) Birth and Childhood

1 "Letters and Papers, Foreign and Domestic, Henry VIII, Volume 11: July-December 1536," n. 17.

2 "Letter Written by Anne Boleyn."

3 Gairdner, "New Lights on the Divorce of Henry VIII," 685. Gairdner's source is State Papers, VII, p3, Knighte to Henry VIII, 13 September 1527.

4 "Letters and Papers, Foreign and Domestic, Henry VIII, Volume 4: 1524-1530," n. 546, grant of Grimstone Manor.

5 Scheurer, *Correspondance du Cardinal Jean du Bellay*, 1 1529–1535:104–106. Du Bellay does not comment on George's age,; he mentions Thomas Boleyn counting on the ambassadors to treat his son as du Bellay is treated in England and that George's household will be honoured and well-kept.

6 Cavendish, *The Life of Cardinal Wolsey, Volume 2*, 2:21.

7 Starkey, "The King's Privy Chamber 1485-1547," 139–140. Starkey writes that the original Privy Chamber, before the Eltham Ordinances, consisted of "two noblemen (Dorset and Exeter), two Knights of the Body (Weston and Kingston), the Groom of the Stool (Compton), the Treasurer of the Chamber (Wyatt), seven Gentlemen (Tyler, Carew, Bryan, Cheyney, Norris, and Cary), the King's Physician (Chamber), two Gentlemen Ushers (Ratcliff and Palmer), four Grooms (West, Wellisburn, Brereton, and Parker), the King's Barber (Villiard), and the King's Page (Boleyn), or twenty-two persons in all."

8 Ives, *The Life and Death of Anne Boleyn*, 15.

9 Bapst, *Deux Gentilshommes-Poetes de La Cour de Henry VIII*, 13.

10 "Letters and Papers, Foreign and Domestic, Henry VIII, Volume 4: 1524-1530," n. 6539.

11 Wood, *Athenae Oxonienses: An Exact History of All the Writers and Bishops Who Have Had Their Education in the University of Oxford*, 1:98.

12 Starkey, *The Reign Of Henry VIII: The Personalities and Politics*, 79 – This is often misquoted as him having "some of Anne's talent and all of her pride." Starkey meant the comment as a compliment, not as a snide remark.

13 "Calendar of State Papers, Spain, Volume 5 Part 1: 1534-1535," 198, also LP vii. 871.

14 "Letters and Papers, Foreign and Domestic, Henry VIII, Volume 10 - January-June 1536," n. 450 – "per una grandissima ribalda et infame sopre tutte".

15 Ives, *The Life and Death of Anne Boleyn*, 13.

16 Starkey, "The King's Privy Chamber 1485-1547," 133–181.

17 "Letters and Papers, Foreign and Domestic, Henry VIII, Volume 2: 1515-1518," 1500–1502.

18 Bapst, *Deux Gentilshommes-Poetes de La Cour de Henry VIII*, 10.

19 ed. Gough Nichols, *The Chronicle of Calais In the Reigns of Henry VII and Henry VIII to the Year 1540*, 24–25. "The lady Boleyne" and "mistres Carie" are listed.

20 Ives, *The Life and Death of Anne Boleyn*, 31.

3) Court Poet

1 Holinshed, *Holinshed's Chronicles of England, Scotland, and Ireland*, 4:1613.

2 Wood, *Athenae Oxonienses: An Exact History of All the Writers and Bishops Who Have Had Their Education in the University of Oxford*, 1:98.

3 Cavendish, *The Life of Cardinal Wolsey, Volume 2*, 2:20.

4 Bale, *Scriptorum Illustrium Majoris Britanniae Catalogus*.

5 Ellis, *Original Letters, Illustrative of English History*, 2:58.

6 Wharton, *History of English Poetry from the Twelfth to the Close of the Sixteenth Century*, 4:58.

7 Arber, *Tottel's Miscellany: Songs and Sonettes (1557-1587)*, 64. Here, the poem is attributed to Thomas Wyatt.

8 Walpole, *The Works of Horatio Walpole, Earl of Orford*, 1:528.

9 Harington, *Nugæ Antiquæ: Being a Miscellaneous Collection of Original Papers, in Prose and Verse Written During the Reigns of Henry VIII, Edward VI, Queen Mary, Elizabeth, and King James*, 400.

10 *Private Correspondence of Horace sWalpole, Earl of Orford*, 4:10–11.

11 Bapst, *Deux Gentilshommes-Poetes de La Cour de Henry VIII*, 139.

12 Ibid., 1–6.

4) Personal Attributes

1   Cavendish, *The Life of Cardinal Wolsey, Volume 2*, 2:20.
2   Bapst, *Deux Gentilshommes-Poetes de La Cour de Henry VIII*, 10–12.
3   Ives, *The Life and Death of Anne Boleyn*, 70.

5) Social Pursuits

1   Nicholas, *The Privy Purse Expenses of King Henry the Eighth, from November 1529, to December 1532*, 72, 76, 144, 145, 195, 209, 210 and 226.
2   St Clare Byrne, *The Lisle Letters*, 1981, 1:671.
3   Ibid., 1:672.
4   St Clare Byrne, *The Lisle Letters*, 1981, 2:175–176.
5   Nicholas, *The Privy Purse Expenses of King Henry the Eighth, from November 1529, to December 1532*, 34.
6   Ibid., 37.
7   Ibid., 34, 37, 68, 72, 128, 144, 156, 189, 195, 209, 210, 226, 232, 263.
8   Wegemer and Smith, *A Thomas More Source Book*, 231.
9   "Royal MS 20 B Xxi, Fo. 2v and Fos. 99v-100."
10   Burke, *The Book of Gladness/Le Livre de Leesce: A 14th Century Defense of Women, in English and French, by Jehan Le Fèvre*, 1–23.
11   Pratt, "The Strains of Defense: The Many Voices in Jean LeFèvre's Livre de Leesce," 113–114.
12   Ibid., 127–128.
13   Brigden, *Thomas Wyatt: The Heart's Forest*, 100.
14   Warnicke, *The Rise and Fall of Anne Boleyn: Family Politics at the Court of Henry VIII*, 218–219.
15   Ibid.
16   Carley, The Books of King Henry VIII and His Wives, p133.
17   Brigden, *Thomas Wyatt: The Heart's Forest*, 44–45. Also note 30 on p578.
18   Fox, *Jane Boleyn: The Infamous Lady Rochford*, 121 and notes on p345. The National Archives record for this manuscript, SP 9/31/2, says "MS. volume, bound in sheepskin. 'The Ordre of Knyghthod, translated out of frenche by T.W. Wyndesore H (Thomas Wall, Windsor Herald) anno 1532'. Undertaken at the instigation of Lord George Rochefort and dedicated to the King. Begun on 9th, finished on16th January. On the leather binding is a fragment of a Percy family tree."

6) Religion

1   Loades, *The Boleyns: The Rise and Fall of a Tudor Family*, 111.

2   Rosin, "The Reformation Response to Skepticism: Ecclesiastes Commentaries of Luther, Brenz, and Melanchthon," 260.

3   Ibid., 287.

4   Ives, *The Reformation Experience*, 80.

5   Hughes, *Lefèvre: Pioneer of Ecclesiastical Renewal in France*, ix,97, 155–156.

6   Bedouelle and Giacone, *Jacques Lefèvre d'Étaples et Ses Disciples: Epistres et Evangiles Pour Les Cinquante et Deux Dimanches de L'an*, 2, 285.

7   Hughes, *Lefèvre: Pioneer of Ecclesiastical Renewal in France*, 99.

8   Lindberg, "Jacques Lefèvre d'Étaples by Guy Bedouelle." Bedouelle sees him as someone who adopted "a middle position" who viewed "a renewed and unified reading of the Bible" as "enough for the needed reformation of the Church."

9   "Harley MS 6561," f. 1v.

10   "Harley MS 6561."

11   Brown and McKendrick, *Illuminating the Book*, sec. Her moost lovyng and fryndely brother sendeth gretyng – Anne Boleyn's Manuscripts and Their Sources by James P. Carley.

12   Ibid., 268.

13   Ibid., 267.

14   "Letters and Papers, Foreign and Domestic, Henry VIII, Volume 6 - 1533," n. 299, vii, also mentioned in LP vii. 923.

15   Brown and McKendrick, *Illuminating the Book*, 272.

16   Lefèvre d'Etaples, "Les Epistres et Evangiles." - The copy of The Epistles used by George for his translation.

17   Gruffudd, "Gruffudd's Chronicle." - The speculation as to where the account originates from is from Carley, Illuminating the Book, p. 277 n. 43.

18   Foxe, *The Acts and Monuments of John Foxe*, IV:657.

19   Hook, *An Ecclesiastical Biography Containing the Lives of Ancient Fathers and Modern Divines, Interspersed with Notices of Heretics and Schismatics, Forming a Brief History of the Church in Every Age*, V:561.

20   Eastman, *Historic Hever: The Church*.

21   "Calendar of State Papers, Spain, Volume 5 Part 2: 1536-1538," 91.

22   "Letters and Papers, Foreign and Domestic, Henry VIII, Volume 10 - January-June 1536," n. 699.

23   Bentley, *Excerpta Historica Or, Illustrations of English History*, 263. This is just a small part of the speech laid out in Bentley's book.

7) Court Life

1   "Letters and Papers, Foreign and Domestic, Henry VIII, Volume 3: 1519-1523," n. 1559.

2   Cavendish, *The Life of Cardinal Wolsey, Volume 2*, 2:71. Cavendish has Lady Rochford say, "Brought up in the court all my young age".

3   "Letters and Papers, Foreign and Domestic, Henry VIII, Volume 3: 1519-1523," n. 2214 (29).

4   Williams, *Katharine of Aragon*, 261.

5   Ibid., 139.

6   Scarisbrick, *Henry VIII*, 247–250.

7   "Letters and Papers, Foreign and Domestic, Henry VIII, Volume 4: 1524-1530," n. 1939 (14).

8) Marriage

1   "Letters and Papers, Foreign and Domestic, Henry VIII, Volume 4: 1524-1530," n. 546 (2).

2   Ibid., n. 1939 (12).

3   Fox, Jane Boleyn: The Infamous Lady Rochford, 39. Fox points out that £80 payment mentioned by Wolsey can only be deciphered by using ultraviolet light on the document.

4   "Letters and Papers, Foreign and Domestic, Henry VIII, Volume 4: 1524-1530," n. 1939 (4).

5   Carley, "Parker, Henry, Tenth Baron Morley (1480/81–1556)."

6   Cavendish, The Life of Cardinal Wolsey, Volume 2, 2:72. We know that Jane was attractive because Cavendish has her say, "And when my beauty began to be shent [spent]", which suggests she had been beautiful in her youth.

7   "Letters and Papers, Foreign and Domestic, Henry VIII, Volume 10 - January-June 1536," n. 1010.

8   Fox, Jane Boleyn: The Infamous Lady Rochford, 36–38.

9   Cressy, Birth, Marriage, and Death: Ritual, Religion, and the Life-Cycle in Tudor and Stuart England, 298.

10   Powell, The Victoria History of the County of Essex, 8:113–124.

11   Nicholas, The Privy Purse Expenses of King Henry the Eighth, from November 1529, to December 1532, 128.

12   "Letters and Papers, Foreign and Domestic, Henry VIII, Volume 4: 1524-1530," n. 4779.

13   "Letters and Papers, Foreign and Domestic, Henry VIII, Volume 5: 1531-1532," n. 751.

14   Nicholas, The Privy Purse Expenses of King Henry the Eighth, from November 1529, to December 1532, 100.

9) Sweating Sickness

1   "Letters and Papers, Foreign and Domestic, Henry VIII, Volume 2: 1515-1518," n. 3358. The Venetian ambassador reported, "This disease makes very quick progress, proving fatal in twenty-four hours at the furthest, and many are carried off in four or five hours."

2   "Letters and Papers, Foreign and Domestic, Henry VIII, Volume 4: 1524-1530," n. 4430.

3   Creighton, A History of Epidemics In Britain, 1: From AD 664 to the Extinction of Plague:253.

4   Love Letters of Henry VIII to Anne Boleyn, xxv.

5   Ibid., xxii.

6   It is possible that the Boleyns had built up some immunity to the disease from its outbreak in 1507 and that the disease had been responsible for the deaths of George's brothers Thomas and Henry.

7   Ibid., xxviii.

8   Ibid., 29.

9   "Letters and Papers, Foreign and Domestic, Henry VIII, Volume 5: 1531-1532," 306.

PART 2 - Career and Influence

10) The Waiting Game (1527-29)

1   Kelly, The Matrimonial Trials of Henry VIII, chap. 1. This chapter goes into detail on Wolsey's trial in May 1527.

2   Guy, Cardinal Wolsey: A Student's Guide.

3   Ives, The Life and Death of Anne Boleyn, 88–91.

4   Love Letters of Henry VIII to Anne Boleyn, vi.

5   Ibid., xiii – xv.

6   Ibid., xxxvii.

7   "Letters and Papers, Foreign and Domestic, Henry VIII, Volume 4: 1524-1530," n. 6513, 6514.

8   Cavendish, The Life of Cardinal Wolsey, 214–217.

9   Guy, Cardinal Wolsey: A Student's Guide.

10   "Letters and Papers, Foreign and Domestic, Henry VIII, Volume 4: 1524-1530," n. 6075.

11   Ibid., n. 4993 (15), 5248.

12   Ibid., n. 5815 (27).

13   The hospital was moved to new premises on several occasions, but merged with Maudsley Hospital in 1948 under the National Health Service. It remains the oldest psychiatric hospital in the world, but Liverpool Street station now occupies the grounds of the original thirteenth century building.

14   Ibid., n. 6073. Instructions to George Boleyn to travel on embassy to France confirm that he had been restored to the Privy Chamber by November 1529.

15   Ibid., n. 6114.

16   Ibid., n. 6115.

17   Apart from these large annuities, which formed 75 per cent of his income, by the time of his death George was only receiving just over £100 a year in royal offices, farms and grants, not including his income as Lord Warden of the Cinque Ports or his income derived from diplomatic missions abroad.

18   Ibid., n. 6026.

19   "Calendar of State Papers, Spain, Volume 4: Part 1, Henry VIII, 1529-1530," n. 265.

11) Reformation Parliament (1529-36)

1   Lehmberg, *The Reformation Parliament 1529-1536*, vii., quoting Kenneth Pickthorn in "Early Tudor Government: Henry VIII, 133

2   "Birth of the English Parliament: Reformation Parliament."

3   "Letters and Papers, Foreign and Domestic, Henry VIII, Volume 6 - 1533," n. 119, 123. Rochford was summoned to parliament on 5th February 1533, along with Lords Maltravers and Talbot.

4   "Folio 94 Rochford MS, a Treatise Delivered to the Convocation of the Clergy on 10 February 1531, by George Boleyn, Lord Rochford."

5   Lehmberg, *The Reformation Parliament 1529-1536*, 114.

6   "Letters and Papers, Foreign and Domestic, Henry VIII, Volume 5: 1531-1532," n. 1023.

7   "Letters and Papers, Foreign and Domestic, Henry VIII, Volume 6 - 1533," n. 529.

8   Lehmberg, *The Reformation Parliament 1529-1536*, 258.

9   "The Act of Supremacy 1534."

10   *Journal of the House of Lords*, Volume 1: 1509–1577:58. "MEMORANDUM, quod quinto decimo die mensis Januarii, recepte sunt Litere Procuratorie, in quibus Dominus La Ware, sub Regia gratia absens, (attestante Thoma Cromewell, Armigero,) Dominum Rochford suum constituit esse Procuratorem."

11 Lehmberg, *The Reformation Parliament 1529-1536*, 57. Lehmberg concludes that Cromwell arranged it.
12 Ibid., 218.

12) The League of Schmalkalden

1 McEntegart, *Henry VIII, the League of Schmalkalden, and the English Reformation*, 6.
2 Ibid., 18.
3 Ibid., 20–21. McEntegart has translated the original German from PA 409, f0. 23-v, Hessisches Saatsarchiv, Marburg.
4 Ibid., 21.
5 Gruffudd, "Gruffudd's Chronicle."
6 Loades, *Thomas Cromwell: Servant to Henry VIII*, 24.
7 Schofield, *The Rise and Fall of Thomas Cromwell: Henry VIII's Most Faithful Servant*, 34–42.
8 McEntegart, *Henry VIII, the League of Schmalkalden, and the English Reformation*, 27.
9 "Letters and Papers, Foreign and Domestic, Henry VIII, Volume 8," n. 475.
10 Ibid., n. 1062.
11 McEntegart, *Henry VIII, the League of Schmalkalden, and the English Reformation*, 73–76.
12 Ibid., 74.

13) The King's Great Matter

1 "Letters and Papers, Foreign and Domestic, Henry VIII, Volume 4: 1524-1530," n. 5983.
2 Scheurer, *Correspondance du Cardinal Jean du Bellay*, 1 1529–1535:96.
3 Elton, *Policy and Police: The Enforcement of the Reformation in the Age of Thomas Cromwell*, 161.
4 "Letters and Papers, Foreign and Domestic, Henry VIII, Volume 5: 1531-1532," 315.
5 *State Papers, Henry VIII*, VII, Part V:219–224. Also LP iv. 6073
6 "Jean du Bellay to Grand Master Montmorency, 29th December 1529."
7 *State Papers, Henry VIII*, VII, Part V:227.
8 "Letters and Papers, Foreign and Domestic, Henry VIII, Volume 4: 1524-1530," n. 6459.

9 Bapst, *Two Gentleman Poets at the Court of Henry VIII: George Boleyn & Henry Howard*, 33, note 23: This emerges from a letter written three years later, on 27 January 1533, by the Duke of Norfolk to Grand Master Montmorency (Bibliothèque National, Fonds français, 3040, folio 4): "I am even further astounded how Beda, a deliberate calumniator in the matter of my master the King – and seeing that the King your master promised to my Lord of Rochford that, even were there no other cause than that the said Beda is an enemy of the just matter, not only would he banish him from Paris but from all his kingdom – has been so suddenly recalled; which is far from the expectation of my said master and his council."

10 "Volumes Consacrés À L'histoire de l'Ordre Du Saint-Esprit. I-CXX « Minutes Du Recueil Pour Servir À L'histoire de l'Ordre et Des Commandeurs, Chevaliers et Officiers de l'Ordre Du Saint-Esprit, Par Clairambault," f. 69. Also mentioned in "Collection des ordonnances des rois de France: Catalogue des actes de François Ier", Tome Premier, p687, 3594. It is dated 1529 but the French New Year started in March. George also received a payment of 2,250 livres in April 1533 (Clairambault f. 72). See MacMahon, Luke, *The Ambassadors of Henry VIII, The Personnel of English Diplomacy, c.1500 – c.1550* for more on gifts to ambassadors.

11 Scheurer, *Correspondance du Cardinal Jean du Bellay*, 1 1529–1535:p122–123.

12 "Letters and Papers, Foreign and Domestic, Henry VIII, Volume 4: 1524-1530," n. 6245.

13 Cox, *Miscellaneous Writings and Letters of Thomas Cranmer*, 259.

14 Russell, *The Works of the English Reformers: William Tyndale and John Frith*, 272–273.

15 "Letters and Papers, Foreign and Domestic, Henry VIII, Volume 4: 1524-1530," n. 6539. In LP this letter is incorrectly attributed to July 1530.

16 Friedmann, *Anne Boleyn, A Chapter of English History, 1527-1536*, 118.

17 "Calendar of State Papers, Spain, Volume 5 Part 1: 1534-1535," n. 641.

18 MacCulloch, *Thomas Cranmer: A Life*, 54–59.

19 "Letters and Papers, Foreign and Domestic, Henry VIII, Volume 5: 1531-1532," 552, 563, 585.

20 Ibid., n. 1274.

21 Hall, *Hall's Chronicle*, 789–94. The festivities in Calais are set out in detail in Hall'sChronicle, pp. 789-94. It confirms that Lord Rochford travelled in the king's train. Also see, LP, v. 1484 and 1485

22 Ibid., 794.

14) Foreign Diplomat

1   Cox, *Miscellaneous Writings and Letters of Thomas Cranmer*, 246.
2   "Letters and Papers, Foreign and Domestic, Henry VIII, Volume 6 - 1533," n. 180.
3   Harpsfield, *A Treatise on the Pretended Divorce Between Henry VIII and Catharine of Aragon*, 234–235.
4   Cox, *Miscellaneous Writings and Letters of Thomas Cranmer*, 246.
5   "Letters and Papers, Foreign and Domestic, Henry VIII, Volume 6 - 1533," n. 1427.
6   Ibid., n. 229, 230.
7   Ibid., n. 229.
8   Ibid., n. 235.
9   "Calendar of State Papers, Spain, Volume 4: Part 2," n. 619.
10   "Letters and Papers, Foreign and Domestic, Henry VIII, Volume 6 - 1533," n. 230, Instructions for Lord Rochford, sent to the French court.
11   Bapst, *Two Gentleman Poets at the Court of Henry VIII: George Boleyn & Henry Howard*, 50.
12   "Letters and Papers, Foreign and Domestic, Henry VIII, Volume 6 - 1533," n. 254.
13   Ibid., n. 255.
14   "Jean du Bellay to Jean de Dinteville, 20th March 1533."
15   "Letters and Papers, Foreign and Domestic, Henry VIII, Volume 6 - 1533," n. 351.
16   The French records corroborate Chapuys' mention of a gift from France. George received a payment of 2,250 livres in April 1533 (Clairambault f. 72)
17   Ibid., n. 561, 562, 563, 583, 584, 585, 601. Anne's Coronation is also described in Wriothesley, Chronicle, pp. 17-22, Hall, Chronicle, vol ii, pp. 798-802
18   Ibid., n. 556.
19   Bapst, *Two Gentleman Poets at the Court of Henry VIII: George Boleyn & Henry Howard*, 53–54.
20   "Letters and Papers, Foreign and Domestic, Henry VIII, Volume 6 - 1533," n. 613.
21   Hall, *Hall's Chronicle*, 175.
22   Head, *The Ebbs and Flows of Fortune: The Life of Thomas Howard, Third Duke of Norfolk*, 2.
23   Hutchinson, *Thomas Cromwell: The Rise and Fall of Henry VIII's Most Notorious Minister*, 147.
24   "Calendar of State Papers, Spain, Volume 5 Part 1: 1534-1535," 484.

25   "Letters and Papers, Foreign and Domestic, Henry VIII, Volume 6 - 1533," n. 692.

26   Bapst, *Two Gentleman Poets at the Court of Henry VIII: George Boleyn & Henry Howard*, 57.

27   "Letters and Papers, Foreign and Domestic, Henry VIII, Volume 6 - 1533," n. 891.

28   Ibid., n. 918.

29   Ibid., n. 954.

30   Ibid., n. 973. In a letter from Francis to Bailly of Troyes dated 12 August 1533, Francis writes that he has heard that Lord Rochford has returned from England to the Duke of Norfolk, who has now left Lyon to come to Francis.

31   Bapst, *Two Gentleman Poets at the Court of Henry VIII: George Boleyn & Henry Howard*, 61.

15) Uncle to a Future Queen

1   "Calendar of State Papers, Spain, Volume 4: Part 2," n. 1123.

2   Hall, *Hall's Chronicle*, 805.

3   "Letters and Papers, Foreign and Domestic, Henry VIII, Volume 6 - 1533," n. 1111.

4   Ibid., n. 1125.

5   "Calendar of State Papers, Spain, Volume 4: Part 2," n. 1137.

6   Thurley, *The Royal Palaces of Tudor England*, 186.

7   "Letters and Papers, Foreign and Domestic, Henry VIII, Volume 7," n. 214.

16) French Alliance Put to the Test

1   "Letters and Papers, Foreign and Domestic, Henry VIII, Volume 6 - 1533," n. 1373.

2   "Letters and Papers, Foreign and Domestic, Henry VIII, Volume 7," n. 363,364.

3   Ibid., n. 470.

4   St Clare Byrne, *The Lisle Letters*, 2:123–124, document 167.

5   "Letters and Papers, Foreign and Domestic, Henry VIII, Volume 7," n. 546. In a letter of Martin Valles dated 26 April 1534 he confirms Rochford and Fitzwilliam had arrived at the French court on 21 April and that "they spoke with Francis and he made them great cheer".

6   Friedmann, *Anne Boleyn: A Chapter of English History, 1527-1536*, 2:4–7.

7   St Clare Byrne, *The Lisle Letters*, 2:145, letter 182.

8   "Letters and Papers, Foreign and Domestic, Henry VIII, Volume 7," n. 662.
9   Ibid., n. 661.
10 Ibid., n. 922 (16).
11 Ibid., n. 958.
12 Ibid., n. 980. Chapuys refers to George leaving for France in a dispatch dated 15 July, "Six days ago Lord Rochford set out for France in great haste. I do not know the reason, unless the king thinks that Francis wishes to be excused from the interview, in consequence of what he has said about the Papal authority."
13 St Clare Byrne, *The Lisle Letters*, 2:204, letter 227a.
14 "Letters and Papers, Foreign and Domestic, Henry VIII, Volume 7," n. 958.
15 Ibid.
16 Ibid., n. 1013.

17) Lord Warden of the Cinque Ports

1   St Clare Byrne, *The Lisle Letters*, 2:100, letter 155a.
2   Ibid., 2:107, letter 159.
3   "Letters and Papers, Foreign and Domestic, Henry VIII, Volume 7," n. 922 (16).
4   Ibid., 180, letter 212.
5   Peter Fleming, Anthony Gross, and J. R. Lander, Regionalism and Revision: The Crown and Its Provinces in England, 1200-1650 (Bloomsbury Academic, 1998), 124.
6   St Clare Byrne, *The Lisle Letters*, 2:480–481.
7   "Letters and Papers, Foreign and Domestic, Henry VIII, Volume 8," n. 911.
8   "Letters and Papers, Foreign and Domestic, Henry VIII, Volume 9 : August-December 1535," n. 22.
9   Ibid., n. 371 (4).
10 St Clare Byrne, *The Lisle Letters*, 2:516-517, letter 411.
11 "Letters and Papers, Foreign and Domestic, Henry VIII, Volume 7," n. 1478.

PART 3 - The End of an Era

18) Crisis at Home and Abroad

1   "Calendar of State Papers, Spain, Volume 5 Part 1: 1534-1535," 20. Lady Rochford's banishment is mentioned in Chapuys dispatches dated 13 October and 19 December 1534, Calendar of State Papers (Spanish), 1534-35, p.280, LP, vii. 1257, 1554

2   "Letters and Papers, Foreign and Domestic, Henry VIII, Volume 9 : August-December 1535," n. 566.

3   "Letters and Papers, Foreign and Domestic, Henry VIII, Volume 7," n. 1554.

4   Wood, *Letters of Royal and Illustrious Ladies of Great Britain, from the Commencement of the Twelfth Century to the Close of the Reign of Queen Mary*, 2:196.

5   "Letters and Papers, Foreign and Domestic, Henry VIII, Volume 7," n. 1263.

6   St Clare Byrne, *The Lisle Letters*, 1981, 2:304.

7   "Letters and Papers, Foreign and Domestic, Henry VIII, Volume 7," n. 1416.

8   Ibid., n. 1427. Cotton MS. Vesp. F. xiii

9   See "The King's Great Matter."

10   "Letters and Papers, Foreign and Domestic, Henry VIII, Volume 7," n. 1554.

11   St Clare Byrne, *The Lisle Letters*, 1981, 3:115.

12   "Letters and Papers, Foreign and Domestic, Henry VIII, Volume 7," n. 1554. L&P has "this favour" but Edmond Bapst, quoting from the original letter in the Vienna Archives, writes "disfavour" (Two Gentleman Poets, p78, note 9).

13   "Letters and Papers, Foreign and Domestic, Henry VIII, Volume 6 - 1533," n. 324.

14   "Letters and Papers, Foreign and Domestic, Henry VIII, Volume 8," n. 974.

15   Ibid., n. 632 (13).

16   Ibid., n. 662.

17   Ibid., n. 663, 666, 726, 909.

18   "Calendar of State Papers, Spain, Volume 5 Part 1: 1534-1535," 476. Also LP, viii. 826

19   "Letters and Papers, Foreign and Domestic, Henry VIII, Volume 8," n. 760.

20 Ibid., n. 826. Chapuys reported to the Emperor, "Before speaking to the King he went to the Lady, his sister, and conversed with her a long time."
21 Ibid.
22 Ibid., n. 792, 793.
23 Ibid., n. 776.
24 Ibid., n. 985.
25 "Letters and Papers, Foreign and Domestic, Henry VIII, Volume 9 : August-December 1535," n. 566.

19) Oncoming Storm

1 "Letters and Papers, Foreign and Domestic, Henry VIII, Volume 10 - January-June 1536," n. 282.
2 Ibid., n. 141.
3 Ibid.
4 Ibid., n. 282.
5 Ibid. Also Hall's Chronicle, p818, and A chronicle of England during the reigns of the Tudors, from A.D. 1485 to 1559, Charles Wriothesley, p 33.
6 Lehmberg, *The Reformation Parliament 1529-1536*, 57, 218.
7 "Letters and Papers, Foreign and Domestic, Henry VIII, Volume 10 - January-June 1536," n. 597.
8 Ibid., n. 409.
9 Ibid., n. 54.
10 St Clare Byrne, *The Lisle Letters*, 3:328, letter 677.
11 "Letters and Papers, Foreign and Domestic, Henry VIII, Volume 10 - January-June 1536," n. 699.
12 Ibid., n. 615.
13 *The Register of the Most Noble Order of the Garter (The Black Book)*, 394-395.
14 "Letters and Papers, Foreign and Domestic, Henry VIII, Volume 10 - January-June 1536," n. 715, 752.
15 *The Register of the Most Noble Order of the Garter (The Black Book)*, 399-401.
16 "Letters and Papers, Foreign and Domestic, Henry VIII, Volume 6 - 1533," n. 555 and LP viii. 174: "Presented the letter in favor of the 'Grand Escuyer' of England, to which he replied that the said place of the Chancellor of the Order was filled by the king of Scotland, and the number of 24 could not be exceeded. On the first vacancy he would remember the said Grand Escuyer." (Palamedes Gontier to Admiral Chabot).

17   Wriothesley, *A Chronicle of England During the Reigns of the Tudors, from A.D. 1485 to 1559*, 189–191. Baga de Secretis, Pouch VIII.

18   "Letters and Papers, Foreign and Domestic, Henry VIII, Volume 10 - January-June 1536," n. 736.

20) Arrests

1   George Constantine, *Archaeologia, Or, Miscellaneous Tracts Relating to Antiquity*, 23:64.

2   Wriothesley, *A Chronicle of England During the Reigns of the Tudors, from A.D. 1485 to 1559*, 35.

3   Ibid., 36.

4   "Letters and Papers, Foreign and Domestic, Henry VIII, Volume 10 - January-June 1536," n. 784.

5   This theory is put forward by Eric Ives (The Life and Death of Anne Boleyn, 328).

6   Cavendish, *The Life of Cardinal Wolsey*, 451–457.

7   Cavendish, *The Life of Cardinal Wolsey, Volume 2*, 2:220.

8   Fox, *Jane Boleyn: The Infamous Lady Rochford*, 192.

9   Cavendish, *The Life of Cardinal Wolsey*, 458.

10   "Letters and Papers, Foreign and Domestic, Henry VIII, Volume 10 - January-June 1536," n. 878.

11   St Clare Byrne, *The Lisle Letters*, 3:356–7.

12   "Letters and Papers, Foreign and Domestic, Henry VIII, Volume 10 - January-June 1536," n. 898.

13   Cavendish, *The Life of Cardinal Wolsey, Volume 2*, 2:31.

14   "Calendar of State Papers, Spain, Volume 5 Part 2: 1536-1538," 128.

15   Ives, "Court and County Palatine in the Reign of Henry VIII: The Career of William Brereton of Malpas."

21) Trial

1   Cavendish, *The Life of Cardinal Wolsey*, 445–446.

2   Wriothesley, *A Chronicle of England During the Reigns of the Tudors, from A.D. 1485 to 1559*, 189–226, Baga de Secretis.

3   "Letters and Papers, Foreign and Domestic, Henry VIII, Volume 10 - January-June 1536," n. 876.

4   Schauer and Schauer, "Law as the Engine of State: The Trial of Anne Boleyn."

5   Schofield, *The Rise and Fall of Thomas Cromwell: Henry VIII's Most Faithful Servant*, 127.

6   Wilson, *A Brief History of Henry VIII: Reformer and Tyrant*.

7   "Calendar of State Papers, Spain, Volume 5 Part 2: 1536-1538," n. 61.

8   "Letters and Papers, Foreign and Domestic, Henry VIII, Volume 10 - January-June 1536," n. 873.

9   Wriothesley, *A Chronicle of England During the Reigns of the Tudors, from A.D. 1485 to 1559*, 36.

10   "Letters and Papers, Foreign and Domestic, Henry VIII, Volume 10 - January-June 1536," n. 848.

11   Ibid., n. 876.

12   George Constantine, *Archaeologia, Or, Miscellaneous Tracts Relating to Antiquity*, 23:66.

13   Warnicke, *The Rise and Fall of Anne Boleyn: Family Politics at the Court of Henry VIII*, 4.

14   ed. Baker, *The Reports of Sir John Spelman*, 71.

15   Ascoli, *La Grande-Bretagne Devant L'opinion Française Depuis La Guerre de Cent Ans Jusqu'à La Fin Du XVIe Siècle*.

16   St Clare Byrne, *The Lisle Letters*, 3:378.

17   "Letters and Papers, Foreign and Domestic, Henry VIII, Volume 10 - January-June 1536," n. 1036, A précis of De Carles poem relating to the trials of the Boleyns.

18   Ives, *The Life and Death of Anne Boleyn*, 331–334.

19   ed. Baker, *The Reports of Sir John Spelman*, 71.

20   "Letters and Papers, Foreign and Domestic, Henry VIII, Volume 10 - January-June 1536," n. 873.

21   "Letters and Papers, Foreign and Domestic, Henry VIII, Volume 11: July-December 1536," n. 29.

22   Wriothesley, *A Chronicle of England During the Reigns of the Tudors, from A.D. 1485 to 1559*, 37–38.

23   Ibid., 38.

24   Ibid., 39, LP x. 1036.

25   "Calendar of State Papers, Spain, Volume 5 Part 2: 1536-1538," 126–8.

26   "Letters and Papers, Foreign and Domestic, Henry VIII, Volume 10 - January-June 1536," n. 908, "nestoit habile en cas de soy copuler avec femme et qu'il navoit ne vertu ne puissance ."

27   "Calendar of State Papers, Spain, Volume 5 Part 2: 1536-1538," 126–8.

28   Ibid., 126–128.

29   Ibid., 126–8.

30   Wriothesley, *A Chronicle of England During the Reigns of the Tudors, from A.D. 1485 to 1559*, 39.

31   Ives, *The Life and Death of Anne Boleyn*, 350.

32   "Calendar of State Papers, Spain, Volume 5 Part 2: 1536-1538," 126–8.

33   Cavendish, *The Life of Cardinal Wolsey*, 447.

34   "Calendar of State Papers, Spain, Volume 5 Part 2: 1536-1538," 126–8.

35   "Letters and Papers, Foreign and Domestic, Henry VIII, Volume 10 - January-June 1536," n. 869.

36   Cavendish, *The Life of Cardinal Wolsey*, 459.

37   "Letters and Papers, Foreign and Domestic, Henry VIII, Volume 10 - January-June 1536," n. 902.

38   *State_Papers, King Henry VIII, Part III: Correspondence between the Governments of England and Ireland 1538-1546*, 9–11.

39   Ibid., 396. "We be pleased, at your humble sutes, to forgeve to the Archebishop of Dublin the £250, which he ought to the late Lorde Rocheford..."

40   Cavendish, *The Life of Cardinal Wolsey*, 460.

22) Lady Rochford and the Fall of the Boleyns

1   Cattley, *The Acts and Monuments of John Foxe*, 5:462, notes.

2   Herbert, *The Life and Raigne of King Henry the Eighth.*, 384.

3   Weir, *The Lady in the Tower: The Fall of Anne Boleyn*.

4   n. Copy of Herbert containing Turner's notes, Oxford, Bodl. Fol 624.

5   Guy, "The Lady in the Tower: The Fall of Anne Boleyn by Alison Weir - Sunday Times Review."

6   Fox, *Jane Boleyn: The Infamous Lady Rochford*, 322.

7   Ives, *The Life and Death of Anne Boleyn*, 331.

8   Burnet, *The History of the Reformation of the Church of England*, 316.

9   Fox, *Jane Boleyn: The Infamous Lady Rochford*, 320.

10   Bentley, *Excerpta Historica Or, Illustrations of English History*, 261–2, LP x. 1107.

11   Cavendish, *The Life of Cardinal Wolsey*, 446.

12   Fox, "Jane Boleyn: The Infamous Lady Rochford - A Guest Post."

13   Cavendish, *The Life of Cardinal Wolsey, Volume 2*, 2:71–74.

14   Weir, *The Lady in the Tower: The Fall of Anne Boleyn*, 114.

15   Cavendish, *The Life of Cardinal Wolsey, Volume 2*, 2:24.

16   Gruffudd, "Gruffudd's Chronicle."

17   Ellis, *Original Letters, Illustrative of English History*, 2:67–8.

18   Madden, *Privy Purse Expenses of the Princess Mary, Daughter of King Henry the Eighth, Afterwards Queen Mary*, 7, 13, 17, 25, 51, 64, 65, 82.

23) Execution

1   Halliwell-Phillipps, *Letters of the Kings of England*, 1:353.

2   "Letters and Papers, Foreign and Domestic, Henry VIII, Volume 10 - January-June 1536," n. 908.

3   Bentley, *Excerpta Historica Or, Illustrations of English History*, 261–5. Details of the executions of the five men and their scaffold speeches can be found in Wriothesley's *Chronicles*, pp. 39-40; Bentley, *Excerpta Historica*, pp. 261-5; William Thomas' *The Pilgrim*, pp.116-17; *Chronicle of Calais*, pp.46-7, and in Constantine, in *Archaeologia* 23, pp. 64-6. Of them all, *Excerpta Historica* provides the most details and certainly the fullest version of George Boleyn's scaffold speech.

4   St Clare Byrne, *The Lisle Letters*, 3:491.

5   See Appendices for full poem.

6   "Letters and Papers, Foreign and Domestic, Henry VIII, Volume 10 - January-June 1536," n. 890.

7   Cavendish, *The Life of Cardinal Wolsey*, 461.

8   "Letters and Papers, Foreign and Domestic, Henry VIII, Volume 10 - January-June 1536," n. 896, LP, xiii. 1225, Kelly, *Matrimonial Trials*, pp. 250–9.

9   Cavendish, *The Life of Cardinal Wolsey*, 448, Anne Boleyn's scaffold speech can also be found in Foxe's *Acts and Monuments*, v. 134 and in Hall, *Chronicle*, p. 819.

10   "Calendar of State Papers, Spain, Volume 5 Part 2: 1536-1538," 137–8, LP x. 1069.

24) Aftermath

1   "Letters and Papers, Foreign and Domestic, Henry VIII, Volume 10 - January-June 1536," n. 908.

2   McEntegart, *Henry VIII, the League of Schmalkalden, and the English Reformation*, 103.

3   Hall, *Hall's Chronicle*, 838.

4   Schofield, *The Rise and Fall of Thomas Cromwell: Henry VIII's Most Faithful Servant*, 268.

5   "Letters and Papers, Foreign and Domestic, Henry VIII, Volume 15: 1540," n. 823.

6   Wriothesley, *A Chronicle of England During the Reigns of the Tudors, from A.D. 1485 to 1559*, 70–72, LP xii. 1060.

7   Madden, *Privy Purse Expenses of the Princess Mary, Daughter of King Henry the Eighth, Afterwards Queen Mary*, 7, 13, 17, 25, 51, 64, 65, 82.

8   George Cavendish, *The Life of Cardinal Wolsey*, vol. 2, Samuel Weller Singer, 1825, 71.

9   Jennifer Ann Rowley-Williams, "Image and Reality: The Lives of Aristocratic Women in Early Tudor England" (University of Wales, Bangor, 1998), 298, 299. Rowley-Williams quotes from P.R.O. S.P. 1/104/82 and P.R.O. S.P. 1/167/163-163v.

10   Alison Weir quotes this in her book *The Lady in the Tower: The Fall of Anne Boleyn* and refers to *Original Letters Illustrative of English History*, edited by Henry Ellis, but Ellis actually quotes Ottwell Johnson's account, not this fictional one (p128 of Volume II).

11   Guy, "The Lady in the Tower: The Fall of Anne Boleyn by Alison Weir - Sunday Times Review."

12   Ellis, *Original Letters, Illustrative of English History*, 2:128.

13   The figure of 72,000 comes from William Harrison's (1534-1593) "The Description of England" which was published as part of Raphael Holinshed's Chronicles: "It appeareth by Cardan (who writeth it upon the report of the bishop of Lexovia), in the geniture of King Edward the Sixth, how Henry the Eighth, executing his laws very severely against such idle persons, I mean great thieves, petty thieves, and rogues, did hang up threescore and twelve thousand of them in his time."

14   Cavendish, *The Life of Cardinal Wolsey, Volume 2*, 2:20.

Appendix A - George Boleyn's Poetry

1   Harington, *Nugæ Antiquæ: Being a Miscellaneous Collection of Original Papers, in Prose and Verse Written During the Reigns of Henry VIII, Edward VI, Queen Mary, Elizabeth, and King James*, 2:400–402.

2   Walpole, *Catalogue of Royal and Noble Authors of England, Scotland and Ireland,*, 1:44–45.

Appendix B - George Cavendish's Metrical Visions

1   Cavendish, *The Life of Cardinal Wolsey, Volume 2*, 2:20–24.

Appendix E - The Clonony Boleyn Girls and George Boleyn, Dean of Lichfield

1   *The Journal of The Historical and Archaeological Association of Ireland, Originally Founded as the Kilkenny Archaeological Society*, I Part I:85–86.

2   "Tomb of the Bullens - Cousins-German of Queen Elizabeth."

3   Correspondence between Claire Ridgway and Alison, Lady Rosse.

4   Burke, *A General and Heraldic Dictionary of the Peerage and Baronetage of the British Empire*, 2:484.

5   Told to me by Paudie Kennelly after he had visited Clonony Castle and spoken to Rebecca Black, the owner.

6   Fox, *Jane Boleyn: The Infamous Lady Rochford*, 214.

7   Lehmberg, "George Boleyn (d. 1603)."

Illustrations

Bibliography

Arber, Edward, ed. *Tottel's Miscellany: Songs and Sonettes (1557-1587)*. London, 1870.

Ascoli, Georges. *La Grande-Bretagne Devant L'opinion Française Depuis La Guerre de Cent Ans Jusqu'à La Fin Du XVIe Siècle*. Paris, 1927.

Bagley, J. J. *Henry VIII and his Times*. B. T. Batsford Ltd, 1962.

ed. Baker, J A. *The Reports of Sir John Spelman*. Selden Society, 1977.

Bale, John. *Scriptorum Illustrium Majoris Britanniae Catalogus*, 1557.

Bapst, Edmond. *Deux Gentilshommes-Poetes de La Cour de Henry VIII*. Paris, 1891.

Bapst, Edmond. *Two Gentleman Poets at the Court of Henry VIII: George Boleyn & Henry Howard*. Translated by J.A Macfarlane. MadeGlobal Publishing, 2013.

Bedouelle, Guy, and Franco Giacone, eds. *Jacques Lefèvre d'Étaples et Ses Disciples: Epistres et Evangiles Pour Les Cinquante et Deux Dimanches de L'an*. Leiden, E. J. Brill, 1976.

Bentley, Samuel, ed. *Excerpta Historica Or, Illustrations of English History*. London, 1831.

Bindoff, S. T., ed. *The History of Parliament: The House of Commons 1509-1558*. Vol. 1. Haynes Publishing, 1982.

Bostick, Theodore. *English Foreign Policy, 1528-1534: The Diplomacy of the Divorce*. University of Illinois, 1967.

Brigden, Susan. *Thomas Wyatt: The Heart's Forest*. Faber and Faber, 2012.

Brown, Michelle P., and Scot McKendrick, eds. *Illuminating the Book*. The British Library and University of Toronto Press, 1998.

Burke, John. *A General and Heraldic Dictionary of the Peerage and Baronetage of the British Empire*. Vol. 2. H. Colburn and R. Bentley, 1832.

Burke, Linda. *The Book of Gladness/Le Livre de Leesce: A 14th Century Defense of Women, in English and French, by Jehan Le Fèvre*. McFarland & Company, 2013.

Burnet, Gilbert. *The History of the Reformation of the Church of England*. 7 vols. Clarendon Press, Oxford, 1865.

"Calendar of Letters, Despatches and State Papers relating to the Negotiations between England and Spain preserved in the Archives of Simancas and Elsewhere" (Calendar of State Papers, Spain), edited by Pascual de Gayangos, TannerRitchie Publishing.

Carley, James P. "Parker, Henry, Tenth Baron Morley (1480/81–1556)." *Oxford Dictionary of National Biography*. Oxford University Press, 2004.

Carley, James P. *The Books of King Henry VIII and His Wives*. British Library, 2005.

Cattley, Rev. Stephen Reed, ed. *The Acts and Monuments of John Foxe*. Vol. 5. R.B. Seeley and W. Burnside, 1838.

Cavendish, George. *The Life of Cardinal Wolsey*. 2nd ed. London: Samuel Weller Singer, 1827.

Cavendish, George. *The Life of Cardinal Wolsey, Volume 2*. Vol. 2. Samuel Weller Singer., 1825.

Creighton, Charles. *A History of Epidemics In Britain*. Vol. 1: From AD 664 to the Extinction of Plague. Cambridge University Press, 2013.

Cockayne, G. E. *The Complete Peerage of England, Scotland, Ireland, Great Britain, and the United Kingdom Extant, Extinct, or Dormant*. Edited by Vicary Gibbs. London, 1910.

Constantine, George. *Archaeologia, Or, Miscellaneous Tracts Relating to Antiquity*. Vol. 23. ed. T Amyot, The Society, 1831.

Cox, Rev. John Edmund, ed. *Miscellaneous Writings and Letters of Thomas Cranmer*. The Parker Society, Cambridge University Press, 1846.

Cressy, David. *Birth, Marriage, and Death: Ritual, Religion, and the Life-Cycle in Tudor and Stuart England.* Oxford University Press, 1999.

Eastman, John. *Historic Hever: The Church.* John Eastman, 1905.

Ellis, Sir Henry. *Original Letters, Illustrative of English History.* Vol. 2. 1. London: Harding, Triphook and Lepard, 1825.

Elton, G.R. *Policy and Police: The Enforcement of the Reformation in the Age of Thomas Cromwell.* Cambridge University Press, 1985.

Fletcher, Catherine. *The Divorce of Henry VIII.* PalgraveMacmillan, 2012.

Fleming, Peter, Anthony Gross, and J. R. Lander. *Regionalism and Revision: The Crown and Its Provinces in England, 1200-1650.* Bloomsbury Academic, 1998.

"Folio 94 Rochford MS, a Treatise Delivered to the Convocation of the Clergy on 10 February 1531, by George Boleyn, Lord Rochford." SP 6/2. National Archives.

Foxe, John. *The Acts and Monuments of John Foxe.* Edited by Rev. Stephen Reed Cattley. Vol. IV. R.B. Seeley and W. Burnside, 1837.

Fox, Julia. *Jane Boleyn: The Infamous Lady Rochford.* Phoenix, 2007.

Fox, Julia. "Jane Boleyn: The Infamous Lady Rochford - A Guest Post." *The Anne Boleyn Files*, June 3, 2011.

Friedmann, Paul. *Anne Boleyn, A Chapter of English History, 1527-1536.* London: Macmillan, 1884.

Friedmann, Paul. *Anne Boleyn: A Chapter of English History, 1527-1536.* Vol. 2. Macmillan, 1884.

Gairdner, James. "New Lights on the Divorce of Henry VIII." *English Historical Review* XI (1896): 673–802.

ed. Gough Nichols, John. *The Chronicle of Calais In the Reigns of Henry VII and Henry VIII to the Year 1540.*

Gruffudd, Elis. "Gruffudd's Chronicle". The National Library of Wales.

Guy, John. *Cardinal Wolsey: A Student's Guide*, 2013.

Guy, John. "The Lady in the Tower: The Fall of Anne Boleyn by Alison Weir - Sunday Times Review." *The Sunday Times*, November 1, 2009.

Hall, Edward. *Hall's Chronicle.* London: J Johnson, 1809.

Halliwell-Phillipps, James Orchard. *Letters of the Kings of England.* Vol. 1. London: H. Colburn, 1848.

Harington, Sir John. *Nugæ Antiquæ: Being a Miscellaneous Collection of Original Papers, in Prose and Verse Written during the Reigns of Henry VIII, Edward VI, Queen Mary, Elizabeth, and King James.* Vol. 2. London, 1804.

"Harley MS 6561". British Library.

Harpsfield, Nicholas. *A Treatise on the Pretended Divorce between Henry VIII and Catharine of Aragon.* Camden Society, 1878.

Head, David M. *The Ebbs and Flows of Fortune: The Life of Thomas Howard, Third Duke of Norfolk.* University of Georgia Press, 1995.

Herbert, Edward. *The Life and Raigne of King Henry the Eighth.* London, 1649.

Holinshed, Raphael. *Holinshed's Chronicles of England, Scotland, and Ireland.* Vol. 4, 1577.

Hook, Walter Farquhar. *An Ecclesiastical Biography Containing the Lives of Ancient Fathers and Modern Divines, Interspersed with Notices of Heretics and Schismatics, Forming a Brief History of the Church in Every Age.* Vol. V. London: F and J Rivington, 1845.

Hughes, Philip Edgcumbe. *Lefèvre: Pioneer of Ecclesiastical Renewal in France.* Eerdmans, 1984.

Hutchinson, Robert. *Thomas Cromwell: The Rise and Fall of Henry VIII's Most Notorious Minister.* Weidenfeld & Nicolson, 2007.

Ives, Eric. *The Life and Death of Anne Boleyn.* New edition. Wiley-Blackwell, 2004.

Ives, Eric. *The Reformation Experience.* Lion, 2012.

Ives, E W. "Court and County Palatine in the Reign of Henry VIII: The Career of William Brereton of Malpas." *Transactions of the Historic Society of Lancashire and Cheshire* 123 (1971): 1–38.

"Jean Du Bellay to Grand Master Montmorency, 29th December 1529". Fonds francais, folio 29. Bibliotheque Nationale, Paris.

"Jean Du Bellay to Jean de Dinteville, 20th March 1533". Fonds Dupuy, folio 218. Bibliotheque Nationale, Paris.

Journal of the House of Lords. Vol. Volume 1: 1509–1577, 1767.

Kelly, Henry Ansgar. *The Matrimonial Trials of Henry VIII.* Wipf & Stock, 2004.

Knecht, R. J. *Francis I.* Cambridge University Press, 1982

Lefèvre d'Etaples, Jacques. "Les Épistres et Evangiles".

Lehmberg, Stanford. "George Boleyn (d. 1603)." *Oxford Dictionary of National Biography.* Oxford University Press, 2004.

355

Lehmberg, Stanford. *The Reformation Parliament 1529-1536.* Cambridge University Press, 1970.

"Letters and Papers, Foreign and Domestic, Henry VIII." (LP) Arranged and catalogued by J.S. Brewer, TannerRitchie Publishing.

"Letter Written by Anne Boleyn". MS. 119 fo. 21. Corpus Christi College, Cambridge.

Lindberg, Carter, ed. "Jacques Lefèvre d'Étaples by Guy Bedouelle." In *The Reformation Theologians: An Introduction to Theology in the Early Modern Period.* Wiley-Blackwell, 2001.

Loades, David. *The Boleyns: The Rise and Fall of a Tudor Family.* Amberley, 2011.

Loades, David. *Thomas Cromwell: Servant to Henry VIII.* Amberley, 2013.

Love Letters of Henry VIII to Anne Boleyn. Fredonia Books, 2006.

MacCulloch, Diarmaid. *Thomas Cranmer: A Life.* Yale University Press, 1998.

MacMahon, Luke. *The Ambassadors of Henry VIII: The Personnel of English Diplomacy, c.1500-c.1550.* University of Kent, Canterbury, 1999.

Madden, Frederick, ed. *Privy Purse Expenses of the Princess Mary, Daughter of King Henry the Eighth, Afterwards Queen Mary.* London: William Pickering, 1831.

McEntegart, Rory. *Henry VIII, the League of Schmalkalden, and the English Reformation.* The Royal Historical Society, 2002.

Nicholas, Nicholas Harris. *The Privy Purse Expenses of King Henry the Eighth, from November 1529, to December 1532.* London: W Pickering, 1827.

Nicolas, Nicholas Harris. *Testamenta Vetusta: Being Illustrations from Wills, of Manners, Customs Etc.* Vol. II. London: Nichols & Son, 1826.

Norton, Elizabeth. *The Boleyn Women.* Amberley, 2013.

Parliament UK. "Birth of the English Parliament: Reformation Parliament." *Parliament UK.* http://www.parliament.uk/about/living-heritage/evolutionofparliament/originsofparliament/birthofparliament/overview/reformation/

Parmiter, Geoffrey. *The King's Great Matter: A Study of Anglo-papal relations 1527-1534.* Barnes and Noble, 1967.

Parsons, Rev. Canon. W. L. E."Some Notes on the Boleyn Family." *Norfolk Archaeology or Miscellaneous Tracts Relating to the Antiquities of the County of Norfolk, Norfolk and Norwich Archaeological Society* XXV (1935): 386–407.

Pocock, Nicholas. *Records of the Reformation: The Divorce 1527-1533*. Clarendon Press, 1870.

Powell, W.R., ed. *The Victoria History of the County of Essex*. Vol. 8, 1983.

Pratt, Karen. "The Strains of Defense: The Many Voices in Jean LeFèvre's Livre de Leesce." In *Gender in Debate from the Early Middle Ages to the Renaissance*, 113–133. Palgrave, 2002.

ed. Richardson, Glenn. *The Contending Kingdoms: France and England 1420-1700*. Ashgate, 2008.

Ridgway, Claire. *The Anne Boleyn Collection II*. MadeGlobal Publishing, 2013.

Rosin, Robert L. "The Reformation Response to Skepticism: Ecclesiastes Commentaries of Luther, Brenz, and Melanchthon." Stanford University, 1986.

Rowley- Williams, Jennifer Ann. *Image and Reality: the Lives of Aristocratic Women in Early Tudor England*. University of Wales, Bangor, 1998

"Royal MS 20 B Xxi, Fo. 2v and Fos. 99v-100". British Library.

Russell, Thomas, ed. *The Works of the English Reformers: William Tyndale and John Frith*. Ebenezer Palmer, 1831.

Scarisbrick, J.J. *Henry VIII*. Methuen, 1968.

Schauer, Margery S., and Frederick Schauer. "Law as the Engine of State: The Trial of Anne Boleyn." *William and Mary Law Review* 22, no. 1 (1980): 49–84.

Scheurer, Remy. *Correspondance Du Cardinal Jean du Bellay*. Vol. 1 1529–1535. Paris: Librarie C. Klincksieck, 1969.

Schofield, John. *The Rise and Fall of Thomas Cromwell: Henry VIII's Most Faithful Servant*. The History Press, 2008.

Starkey, David. *Six Wives: The Queens of Henry VIII*. HarperCollins, 2003.

Starkey, David. "The King's Privy Chamber 1485-1547." University of Cambridge, 1973.

Starkey, David. *The Reign Of Henry VIII: The Personalities and Politics*. Littlehampton Book Services Ltd, 1985.

St Clare Byrne, Muriel, ed. *The Lisle Letters*. Vol. 1. University of Chicago Press, 1981.

St Clare Byrne, Muriel, ed. *The Lisle Letters*. Vol. 2. University of Chicago Press, 1981.

357

St Clare Byrne, Muriel, ed. *The Lisle Letters*. Vol. 3. University of Chicago Press, 1981.

State Papers, Henry VIII. Vol. VII, Part V, 1849.

State Papers, King Henry VIII, Part III: Correspondence between the Governments of England and Ireland 1538-1546.

"The Act of Supremacy 1534". National Archives.

"The Lord Warden of the Cinque Ports", article at http://cinqueports.org/lord-warden-officials/

The Journal of The Historical and Archaeological Association of Ireland, Originally Founded as the Kilkenny Archaeological Society. Vol. I Part I. Dublin: Dublin University Press, 1868.

The Register of the Most Noble Order of the Garter (The Black Book). London: John Barber, 1724.

Thurley, Simon. *The Royal Palaces of Tudor England*. Yale University, 1993.

"Tomb of the Bullens - Cousins-German of Queen Elizabeth." *Irish Penny Magazine*, September 21, 1833.

"Volumes Consacrés À L'histoire de l'Ordre Du Saint-Esprit. I-CXX "Minutes Du Recueil Pour Servir À L'histoire de l'Ordre et Des Commandeurs, Chevaliers et Officiers de l'Ordre Du Saint-Esprit, Par Clairambault," n.d. Bibliothèque nationale de France, Département des manuscrits, Clairambault 1215.

Walpole, Horace. *Catalogue of Royal and Noble Authors of England, Scotland and Ireland,*. Vol. 1. London: John Scott, 1806.

Walpole. Horace. *Private Correspondence of Horace Walpole, Earl of Orford*. Vol. 4. London: Rodwell and Martin, 1820.

Walpole, Horace. *The Works of Horatio Walpole, Earl of Orford*. Vol. 1. London: G.G. and J. Robinson, 1798.

Warnicke, Retha M. *The Rise and Fall of Anne Boleyn: Family Politics at the Court of Henry VIII*. Cambridge University Press, 1989.

Wegemer, Gerard B., and Stephen W. Smith, eds. *A Thomas More Source Book*. Catholic University of America Press, 2004.

Weir, Alison. *The Lady in the Tower: The Fall of Anne Boleyn*. Jonathan Cape, 2009.

Williams, Patrick. *Katharine of Aragon*. Amberley, 2013.

Wilson, Derek. *A Brief History of Henry VIII: Reformer and Tyrant*. Robinson, 2009.

Wharton, Thomas. *History of English Poetry from the Twelfth to the Close of the Sixteenth Century*. Vol. 4. London: Reeves and Turner, 1871.

Wood, Anthony A. *Athenae Oxonienses: An Exact History of All the Writers and Bishops Who Have Had Their Education in the University of Oxford.* Vol. 1. London, 1813

Wood, Mary Anne Everett. *Letters of Royal and Illustrious Ladies of Great Britain, from the Commencement of the Twelfth Century to the Close of the Reign of Queen Mary.* Vol. 2. London: Henry Colburn, 1846.

Wriothesley, Charles. *A Chronicle of England During the Reigns of the Tudors, from A.D. 1485 to 1559.* Camden Society, 1875.

Index

Acknowledgements

The authors would like to extend their thanks to Olga Hughes, Sharon Conrad, Dawn Hatswell, Teri Fitzgerald, and followers of The Anne Boleyn Files for their ongoing support and encouragement. Many thanks are also due to James Carley, for his feedback on Clare's initial draft manuscript and for his earlier work on Anne Boleyn's books; Julia Fox for her work on Jane Boleyn, and for answering our questions; the British Library, the National Archives and the Bibliothèque Nationale de France for their help with primary source documents for their help with primary source documents; Fran Middleton for her help locating a thesis; Pablo García Ibáñez for the wonderful author photographs; Rachael Beale for her copy-editing expertise; Paudie Kennelly for his photographs of Clonony Castle and for the information he gained on his visit there; Rebecca Black from Clonony Castle; Alison, Lady Rosse for her information on the Birr Castle portraits and her family's links to the Boleyns; and Edmond Bapst for the thorough notes and references in his biography of George Boleyn and Henry Howard.

Clare Cherry

Clare lives in Hampshire with her partner David. She works as a solicitor in Dorset, but has a passion for Tudor history and began researching the life of George Boleyn in 2006. She started corresponding with Claire Ridgway in late 2009, after meeting through The Anne Boleyn Files website, and the two Tudor enthusiasts became firm friends. Clare divides her time between the legal profession and researching Tudor history. Clare has written guest articles on George Boleyn for The Anne Boleyn Files, Nerdalicious.com.au, and author Susan Bordo's The Creation of Anne Boleyn website.

Photo © Pablo Garcia Ibañez 2014

Claire Ridgway

Claire is the author of the best-selling books ON THIS DAY IN TUDOR HISTORY, THE FALL OF ANNE BOLEYN: A COUNTDOWN, THE ANNE BOLEYN COLLECTION, and THE ANNE BOLEYN COLLECTION II, as well as INTERVIEWS WITH INDIE AUTHORS: TOP TIPS FROM SUCCESSFUL SELF-PUBLISHED AUTHORS. Claire was also involved in the English translation and editing of Edmond Bapst's 19th century French biography of George Boleyn and Henry Howard, now available as TWO GENTLEMAN POETS AT THE COURT OF HENRY VIII.

Claire worked in education and freelance writing before creating The Anne Boleyn Files history website and becoming a full-time history researcher, blogger and author. The Anne Boleyn Files is known for its historical accuracy and Claire's mission to get to the truth behind Anne Boleyn's story. Her writing is easy-to-read and conversational, and readers often comment on how reading Claire's books is like having a coffee with her and chatting about history.

Photo © Pablo Garcia Ibañez 2014

George Boleyn:
Tudor Poet,
Courtier & Diplomat

Clare Cherry and Claire Ridgway

Made in the USA
San Bernardino, CA
24 May 2020